Our Flag

The Flag of the United States

Fifty white stars
On a field of blue;
Seven red stripes,
And six white ones, too.

Name ______________________________

© Frank Schaffer Publications, Inc.

Name ____________________ Skill: Following directions

The Star-Spangled Banner

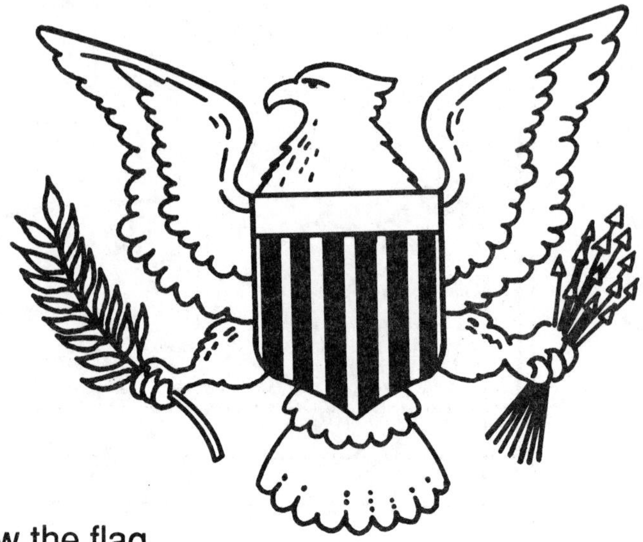

- ☐ Trace the dashed lines in red.
- ☐ Color stripes **1**, **3**, **5**, **7**, **9**, **11**, and **13** red.
- ☐ Leave the other stripes white.
- ☐ Leave the stars white.
- ☐ Color the spaces between the stars blue.
- ☐ Write the title of this page on the line below the flag.

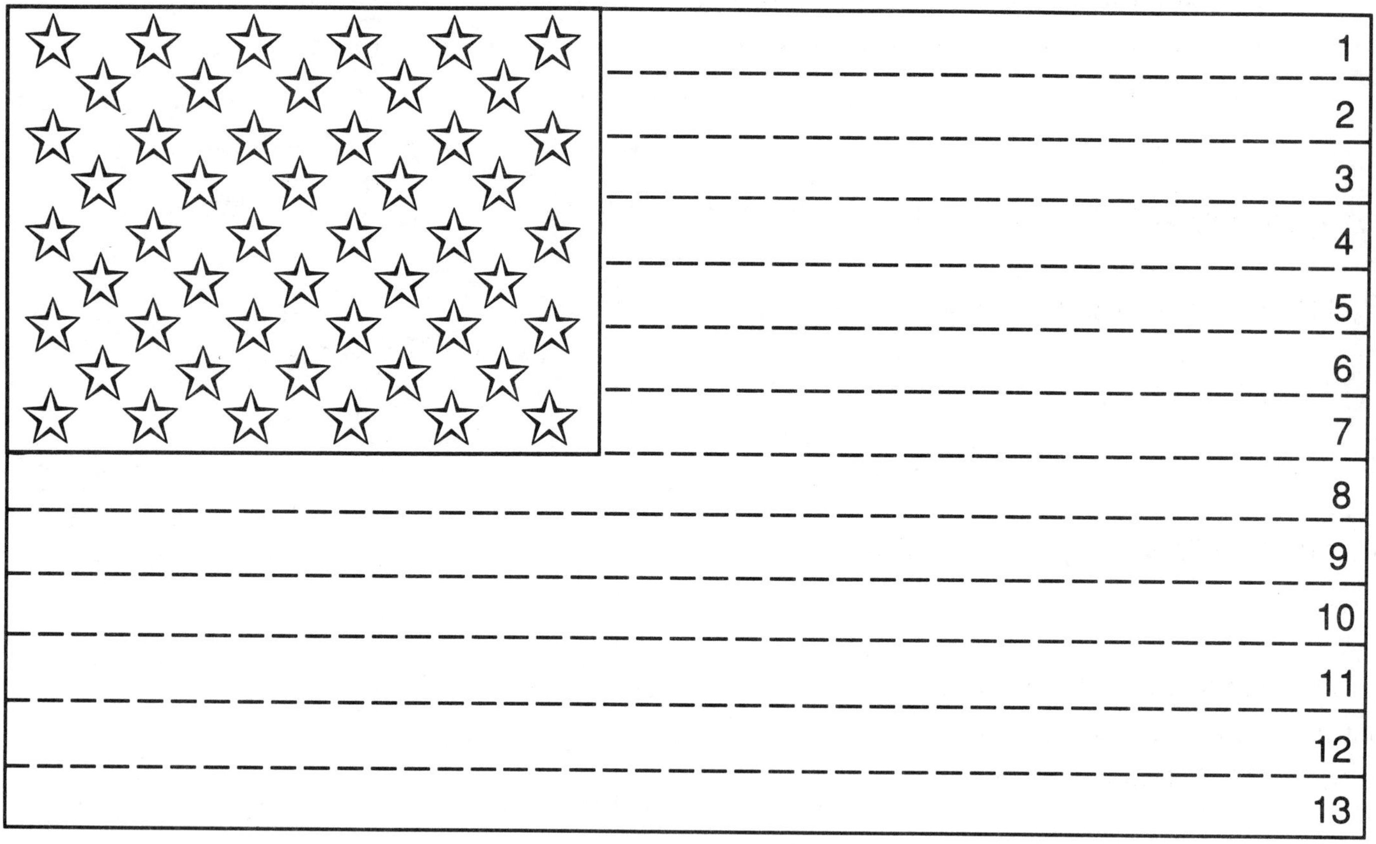
1
2
3
4
5
6
7
8
9
10
11
12
13

____

Brainwork! Create new words by using the letters in **Star-Spangled Banner**.

© Frank Schaffer Publications, Inc.

Name ______________________________ Skill: Interpreting an illustration

The American Flag

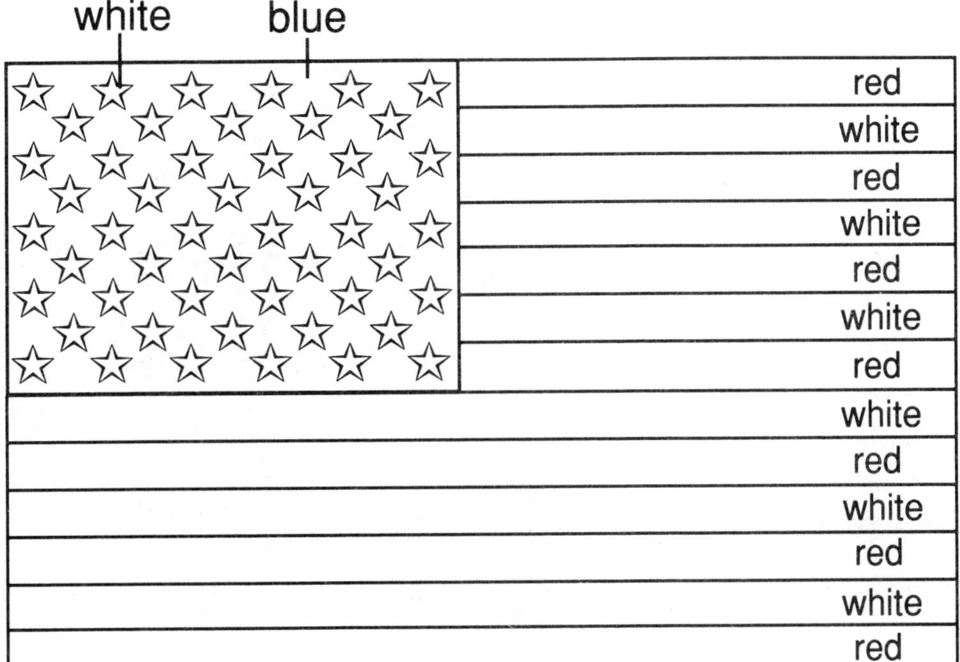

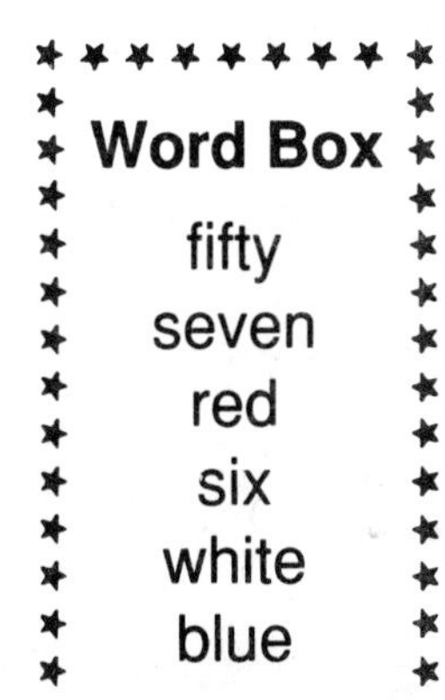

Use the flag and the words in the Word Box to help you finish the sentences.

1. The colors of the flag are __________ , __________ , and __________.
2. It has __________ red stripes.
3. It has __________ white stripes.
4. The flag has __________ stars.

Find a nickname for the flag. Write the letter from the star above the correct number.

1. 

2. 

3. 

4. 

5. 

6. 

___ ___ ___   ___ ___ ___ ___ ___
3 5 1   2 5 3 4 6

Brainwork! Create a new flag design using only stars and stripes and three colors—red, white, and blue.

© Frank Schaffer Publications, Inc.

Name ____________________ Skill: Evaluating information

Getting to Know the Flag

Read the information on the flags below. Then read the sentences. Write **T** for **True** or **F** for **False** and the number of the flag that helped you decide.

1
The flag's thirteen stripes stand for the thirteen original colonies.

2
The fifty stars stand for the fifty states of the United States.

3
The words of our national anthem and the name **Star-Spangled Banner** came from a poem written by Francis Scott Key in 1814.

4
The color red stands for courage, the color white for liberty, and the color blue for justice.

	T or F	Flag Number
1. The thirteen stripes stand for the thirteen original countries.	F	1
2. The color red stands for liberty.	____	____
3. The name **Star-Spangled Banner** came from a poem written by Francis Scott Key.	____	____
4. The color white stands for courage.	____	____
5. Today the flag has forty-eight stars.	____	____
6. The color blue stands for justice.	____	____

Brainwork! Write the false sentences on the back of this page. Change a word in each sentence to make it true.

© Frank Schaffer Publications, Inc.

Name ______________________ Skill: Reading for details

Pledge to the Flag

President Harrison
(23rd president)

In 1892 President Benjamin Harrison wanted the public schools to celebrate the 400th anniversary of the discovery of America. To celebrate, the school children said the **Pledge to the Flag** for the first time. The pledge was written by Francis Bellamy.

Francis Bellamy

Original Pledge to the Flag

"I pledge allegiance to **my flag** and to the Republic for which it stands, one Nation, indivisible, with liberty and justice for all."

Today's Pledge to the Flag

"I pledge allegiance to **the Flag of the United States of America** and to the Republic for which it stands, one Nation **under God**, indivisible, with liberty and justice for all."

1. Who was the twenty-third president? ______________________
2. What did he want to celebrate? ______________________

   ____
3. Who wrote the Pledge to the Flag? ______________________
4. What year was the pledge first said in the schools? ______________________
5. Which eight words were added in place of **my flag**? ______________________

   ____
6. What other words have been added to the pledge we say today?

   ____

Brainwork! Write about how you feel when you say the **Pledge to the Flag**.

© Frank Schaffer Publications, Inc.

Name ______________________________ Skill: Sequencing

Flag-Flying Holidays

Our flag stands for the United States of America, its people, its government, and its beliefs. The flag is flown on holidays and special days, like those below, to honor the people and the events that are important to Americans.

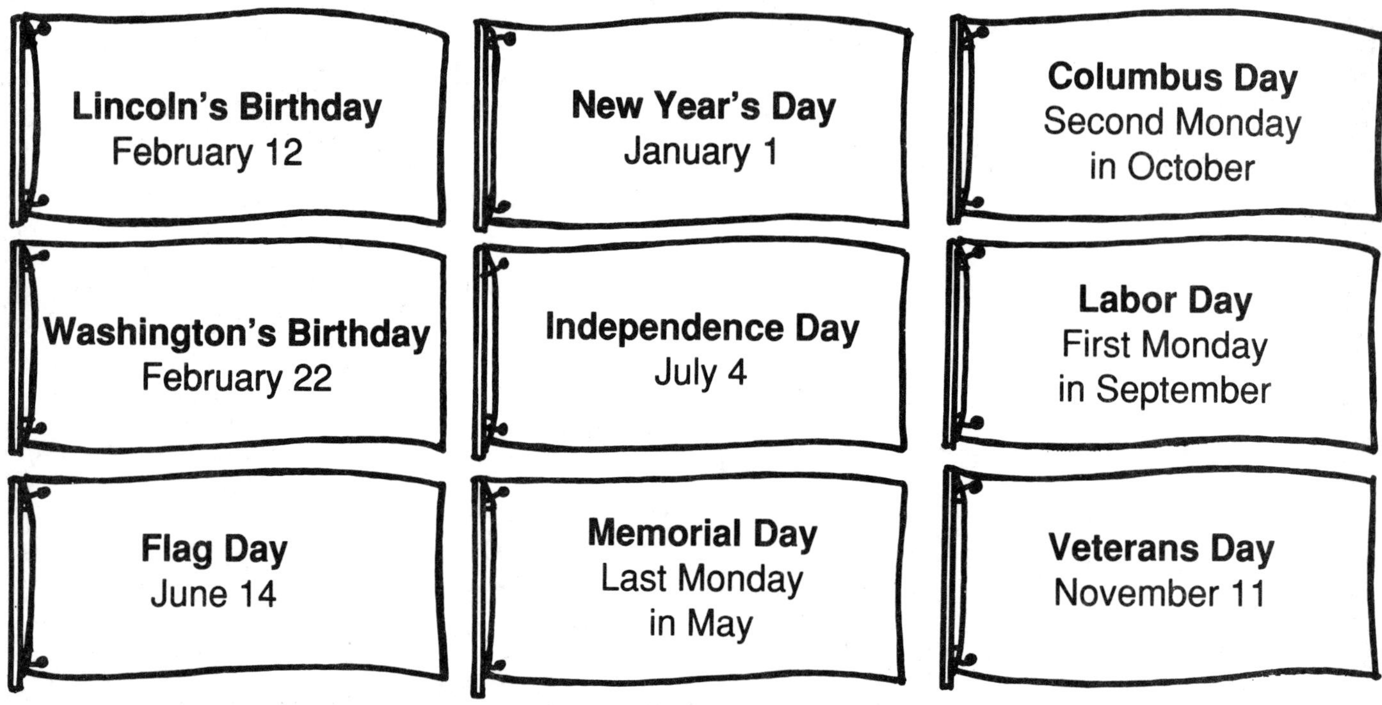

Read the flags. Write the boldfaced names of the holidays in calendar order. The **Months in Order** list will help you.

1. New Year's Day
2. ______________________________
3. ______________________________
4. ______________________________
5. ______________________________
6. ______________________________
7. ______________________________
8. ______________________________
9. ______________________________

Months in Order

January
February
March
April
May
June
July
August
September
October
November
December

Brainwork! Make up a name and date for a new holiday. Write five sentences about the holiday. Tell why the flag should be flown on the day.

© Frank Schaffer Publications, Inc.

Our Capital

Maryland

Washington, D. C.

Virginia

Our Capital

Our great capital city,
Long may it stand
As the seat of government
For all our land.

Name ______________________________

© Frank Schaffer Publications, Inc.

Name ______________________ Skill: Making a chart

Capital Places

For years, Congress (the lawmaking part of the government) met in different cities. (It even met in the same city three different times.) Each of the cities became the nation's capital while Congress was meeting there. Washington, D.C. became our permanent capital in 1791.

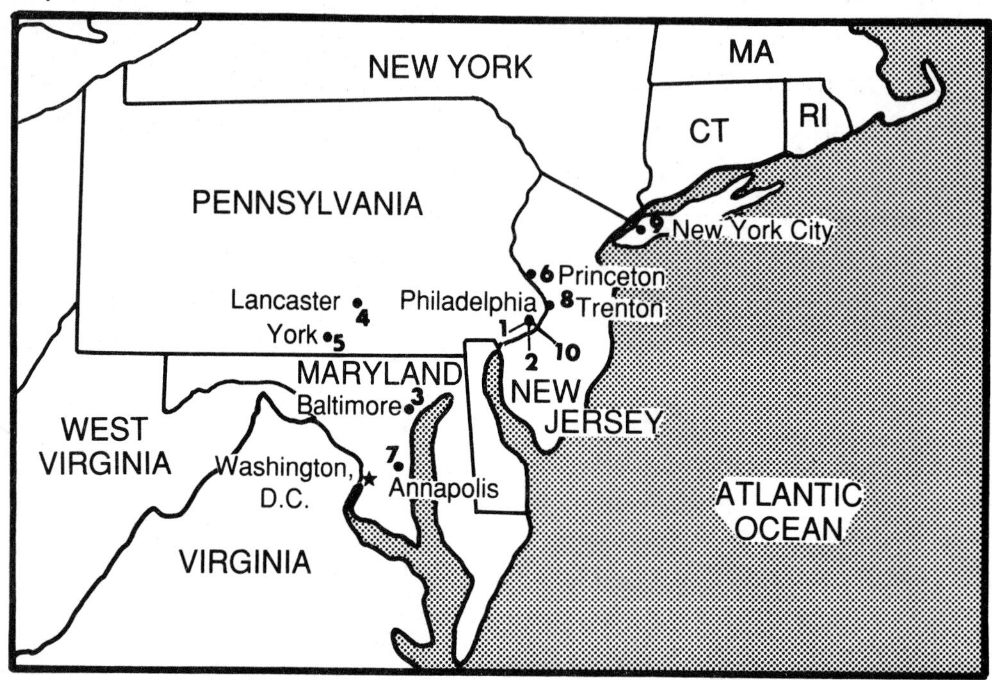

The map shows the cities and the order in which they became our nation's capital. List in order each city's name and its state.

City Where Congress Met	State Where the City Is Located
1. Philadelphia	Pennsylvania
2.	
3.	
4.	
5.	
6.	
7.	
8.	
9.	
10.	

Brainwork! Write the name of a city you'd choose as the capital and tell why.

© Frank Schaffer Publications, Inc.

Name ____________________ Skill: Comprehension

A Capital City

Read the story. Use the boldfaced words to help you do the puzzle.

In 1790 George **Washington** sat on the **veranda**, or porch, of his home—**Mount Vernon**. He looked at the **Potomac** River. He liked the river very much. He decided that America's capital city should be built on it, 18 miles upstream from Mount Vernon. The capital city was to be built on a 100-square-mile piece of land **donated** by two **states**. **Maryland** gave about 70 square miles and **Virginia** about 30 square miles. In 1846 Congress returned Virginia's land because it wasn't needed at that time. The land later became Arlington County.

Across

5. Person who decided the place for the capital
6. Maryland and Virginia
7. State that gave more land
8. A porch with a roof

Down

1. George Washington's home
2. To have given something
3. State whose land was returned by Congress
4. River by Mount Vernon

Brainwork! Name a make-believe city after yourself. Describe the city, where it's located, and what makes it a nice place to visit.

© Frank Schaffer Publications, Inc.

Name ______________________________ Skill: Reading for detail

Washington, District of Columbia

George Washington

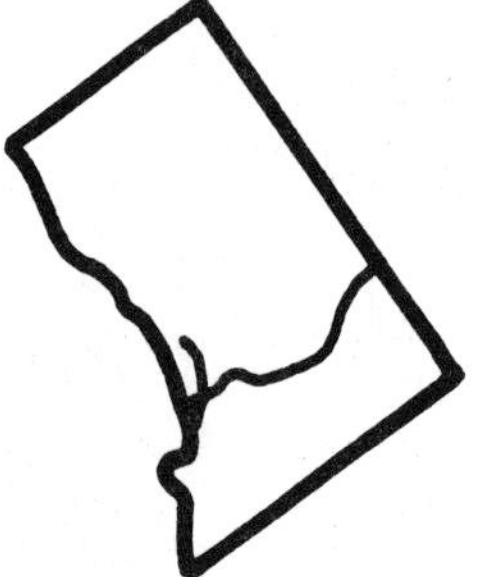

Washington, D.C.

Christopher Columbus

Washington, our capital city, is named after **George Washington**. The land around the city is called the **District of Columbia (D.C.).** This district is a special piece of land that belongs to the United States government. The name **Columbia** honors **Christopher Columbus**.

Over the years, the city of Washington has grown so large that it now fills the District of Columbia. Today the two names mean the same place.

1. Who owns the District of Columbia? ______________________________

____

2. What does **D.C.** stand for? ______________________________

____

3. What person does the name **Columbia** honor? ______________________________

____

4. What person does the the name **Washington** honor? ______________________________

____

5. What is Washington, D.C.? ______________________________

____

6. Why are the city and the district the same place today? ______________________________

____

____

Brainwork! Write why you think George Washington and Christopher Columbus deserve to have Washington, D.C. named after them.

© Frank Schaffer Publications, Inc.

Name ____________________ Skill: Following directions

What a Plan!

A young French engineer named Major Pierre Charles L'Enfant was chosen by President George Washington to plan the city of Washington.

In 1791 Major L'Enfant made a plan for the city. In the plan, the streets named with numbers ran north and south (↕), the streets named with letters ran east and west(↔), and the streets named after states of the United States ran diagonally (↖↘ ↗↙).

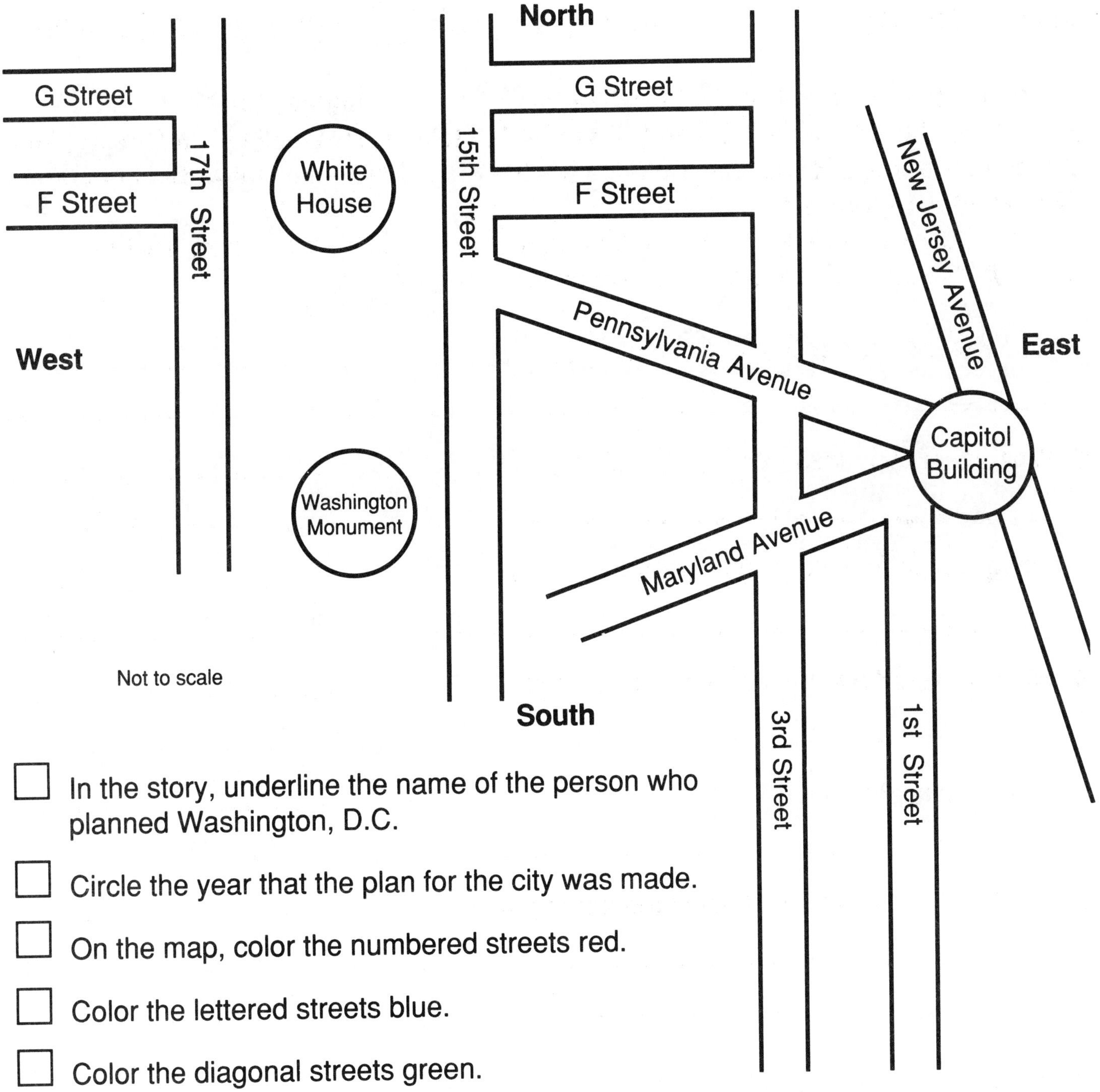

North

G Street
G Street
F Street
F Street
17th Street
15th Street
White House
Washington Monument
West
East
Pennsylvania Avenue
New Jersey Avenue
Capitol Building
Maryland Avenue
Not to scale
South
3rd Street
1st Street

- ☐ In the story, underline the name of the person who planned Washington, D.C.
- ☐ Circle the year that the plan for the city was made.
- ☐ On the map, color the numbered streets red.
- ☐ Color the lettered streets blue.
- ☐ Color the diagonal streets green.

Brainwork! Draw a plan showing your school and the streets around it.

© Frank Schaffer Publications, Inc.

Name ______________________________

A City in Four Parts

Washington, D.C. is divided into four sections: **NW** (**N**orth**w**est), **NE** (**N**orth**e**ast), **SE** (**S**outh**e**ast), and **SW** (**S**outh**w**est). This makes it easier to deliver mail. All addresses have either **NW**, **NE**, **SE**, or **SW** at the end of the street address.

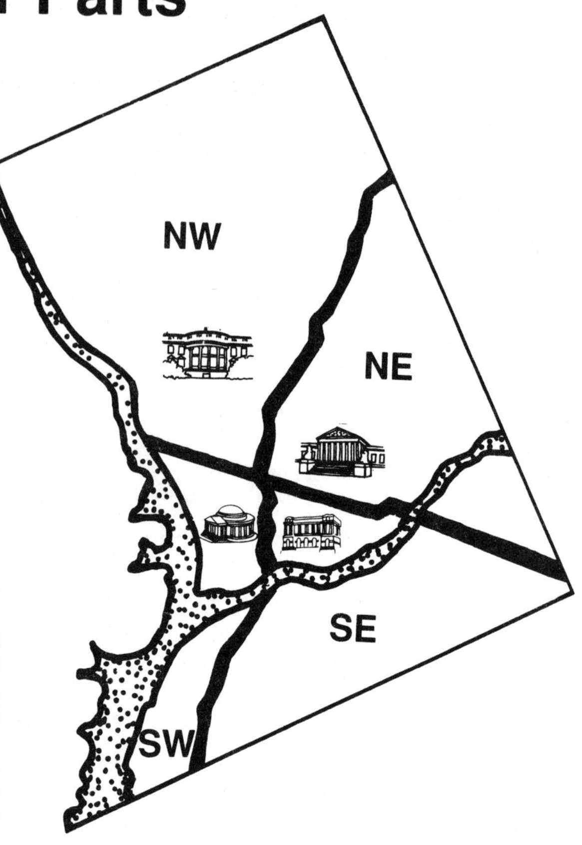

Choose and write the correct street address for each building pictured below. The map and addresses will help you.

Addresses:
- 1600 Pennsylvania Avenue, **NW**
- 14th Street, **SW**
- First and East Capitol Streets, **NE**
- First Street and Independence Avenue, **SE**

1. **The U.S. Supreme Court** (where laws are ruled on)

____

____

2. **The Jefferson Memorial** (honors Thomas Jefferson)

____

____

3. **The Library of Congress** ("America's Library")

____

____

4. **The White House** (home of the president)

____

____

Brainwork! Write on the back of this paper the name of the building you like best and why.

© Frank Schaffer Publications, Inc.

Name ____________________ Skill: Reading a chart

Weather—Washington, D.C. Style

Month	Average Monthly Temperature
January	37°
February	36°
March	46°
April	60°
May	70°
June	75°
July	82°
August	83°
September	77°
October	60°
November	49°
December	40°

Fahrenheit Thermometer

1. Which is the coldest month? ____________________
2. Which is the warmest month? ____________________
3. Which two months have the same average monthly temperature?

   ____
4. Which two months have average temperatures in the 80s?

   ____
5. When would you like to visit Washington, D.C.? Why?

   ____

   ____
6. Color the mercury in the thermometer red to show December's temperature.

Brainwork! On the back of this paper, write all the temperatures from highest to lowest starting with 83 degrees.

© Frank Schaffer Publications, Inc.

Our Government

The Constitution

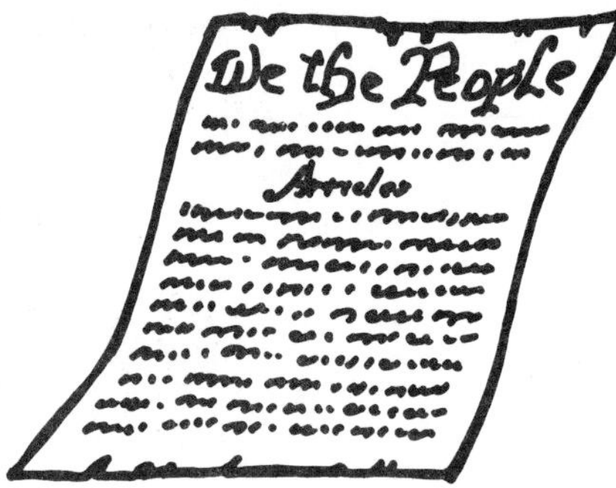

Congress
(House of Representatives and the Senate)

President

Supreme Court

The Capitol Building

The White House

The Supreme Court Building

The United States Government

The Constitution has laws and rights on its pages,
That govern our nation and people—all ages.
The President, Congress, and Supreme Court, too.
Uphold the Constitution for me and for you.

Name ______________________________

© Frank Schaffer Publications, Inc.

Name ____________________ Skill: Reading comprehension

Our Constitution

The Constitution is a document, or official paper. It tells about the government of the United States. It also tells about rights and freedoms of the American people.

In 1787 fifty-five of the country's leaders met at Independence Hall in Philadelphia, Pennsylvania, to write the Constitution.

The original Constitution is kept in the National Archives in Washington, D.C.

Independence Hall

National Archives

1. What is the Constitution? ____________________

____

2. What two things does the Constitution tell? ____________________

____

____

3. In what year was the Constitution written? ____________________

4. In what building was it written? ____________________

____

5. In what city and state was it written? ____________________

____

6. In what city and building is the original Constitution kept today? ____________________

____

____

Brainwork! Write a "Classroom Constitution." Put three rules in it that would help everyone in the class.

© Frank Schaffer Publications, Inc.

Name ______________________________ Skill: Reading for detail

The United States Government

The United States government runs the country. It has three parts.

1. **The Legislative**

House Senate

Congress makes the laws.

2. **The Executive**

The President makes sure the laws are carried out.

3. **The Judicial**

The Supreme Court settles questions about the laws.

Fill in the circle beside the correct answer.

1. Who runs the United States of America?

   (a) the Congress (b) the United States government (c) the President

2. Who settles questions about the laws?

   (a) the President (b) the Congress (c) the Supreme Court

3. Who makes sure the laws are carried out?

   (a) the Congress (b) the President (c) the Supreme Court

4. Who makes the laws?

   (a) the Supreme Court (b) the President (c) the Congress

5. What are the names of the three parts of the government?

   a. ______________________________

   b. ______________________________

   c. ______________________________

Brainwork! Write which part of the government you would like to work for and why.

© Frank Schaffer Publications, Inc.

Name ____________________ Skill: Following directions

The Lawmaking Legislature

Congress makes the laws for our country. Congress meets in the Capitol Building. Congress has two parts—the House of Representatives and the Senate.

Capitol Building

House of Representatives

Senate

Congress

People who work in the House of Representatives are called representatives. People who work in the Senate are called senators. Both representatives and senators are elected by the people of their states to work in Congress.

Check the box in front of each direction to show you followed the direction.

- ☐ Draw a yellow square around the word that tells how many parts Congress has.
- ☐ On the picture, draw a red circle around the House of Representatives.
- ☐ Draw a blue circle around the Senate.
- ☐ Underline the sentence in green that tells what Congress does.
- ☐ Write the name we call people who work in the House of Representatives. ____________________
- ☐ Write the name we call people who work in the Senate. ____________________

Brainwork! Write a law that you would help make if you were a representative or a senator.

© Frank Schaffer Publications, Inc.

Name ____________________ Skill: Sequencing

Pass the Bill!

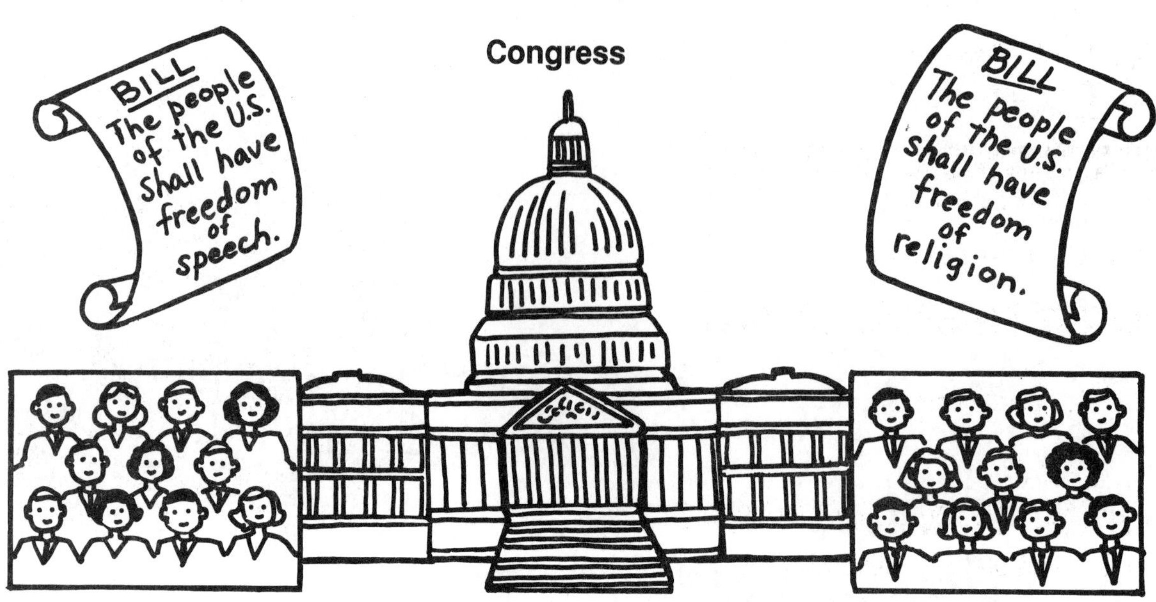

These things must be done to make a bill a law. First, a bill, or suggested law, is written. Next, the bill is voted on and passed by the House of Representatives. Then, the bill is voted on and passed by the Senate. Finally, the bill is signed by the president and becomes a law.

Number and write these sentences in the right order.

_____ The bill is voted on and passed by the House of Representatives.

_____ The bill is voted on and passed by the Senate.

_____ The bill is signed by the president and becomes a law.

_____ A bill is written.

1. ____________________
2. ____________________
____
3. ____________________
4. ____________________
____

Brainwork! Write a bill, or suggested rule, that you would like to have in your classroom.

© Frank Schaffer Publications, Inc.

The President

What qualifications are needed to be president?

Presidential Seal

What are some other names for the president of the United States?

What does the president of the United States do?

Read each sentence and write the number of its question.

___2___ The president is called the commander in chief of the army and navy.

________ The president must be at least 35 years of age.

________ The president is called the chief executive of the government.

________ The president sees that national laws are carried out and that new laws are made.

________ The president must have been born in the United States and have lived in the country for at least 14 years.

________ The president keeps the army and navy strong so they can defend the country.

Brainwork! Count the stars on the Presidential Seal. Why do you think the seal has that number of stars?

© Frank Schaffer Publications, Inc.

Name ____ Skill: Sequencing

Supreme Court Justices

The United States Supreme Court

The Supreme Court justices settle disagreements about laws and explain the Constitution.

These things must be done to appoint a Supreme Court justice. First, the Supreme Court needs a justice. Second, the president tells the Senate which person he wants. Next, the Senate votes on that person. Finally, if the Senate votes yes, the new justice takes his or her place on the Supreme Court.

Number and write these sentences in the right order.

_____ The president tells the Senate which person he wants.

_____ If the Senate votes yes, the new justice takes his or her place on the Supreme Court.

_____ The Supreme Court needs a justice.

_____ The Senate votes on that person.

Congress

House **Senate**

1. ____

2. ____

____

3. ____

4. ____

____

____

Brainwork! On this page, underline the sentence above that tells what the Supreme Court does.

© Frank Schaffer Publications, Inc.

Name ______________________________

Jane Addams
Nobel Peace Prize Winner

Jane Addams was the first American woman to win the Nobel Peace Prize. As a young woman, Jane visited Europe. There she visited a *settlement house*—a center that helped the poor people of the **community**. Jane **decided** she wanted to start a settlement house in America.

In Chicago she started Hull House—a community **center** with day care, a **gym**, and a playground. There was also a first-aid center and a **school**. Cooking and sewing classes were taught at the school. There young people could develop **talents** in music, art, and drama.

Write the words in dark print below their definitions.

1. building used for physical exercise

   ____

2. a group of people who live together in the same place

   ____

3. natural abilities or skills

   ____

4. made up one's mind

   ____

5. a place for teaching and learning

   ____

6. a main place or building

   ____

Write five sentences. In each sentence, use one of the words you wrote above.

1. ____

   ____

2. ____

   ____

3. ____

   ____

4. ____

   ____

5. ____

   ____

Brainwork! Illustrate and write about one of your own talents.

© Frank Schaffer Publications, Inc.

Name ______________________________ Skill: Vocabulary development

Marian Anderson
Singer

Marian Anderson was the first black singer to **appear** at New York City's Metropolitan Opera. She began singing as a child in her church choir. Church members paid for her singing **lessons**. Then her teacher gave her a **scholarship** for more lessons.

Her first **solo** performance was very successful. Marian studied and gave many **concerts** in Europe. Back in the United States, Marian Anderson sang for 75,000 people at the Lincoln Memorial. She had a rich and **beautiful** voice. People all over the world enjoyed her singing. She was given many awards and honors.

Write the words in dark print below their definitions.

1. music for one person to sing ____________
2. pleasing to hear ____________
3. performances of music ____________
4. come before the public ____________
5. a money gift to help a student ____________
6. classes or courses of study ____________

Write four sentences about Marian Anderson. In each sentence, use one of the words you wrote above.

1. ______________________________
2. ______________________________
3. ______________________________
4. ______________________________

Brainwork! List as many music words as you can. Begin with these words from the story: *choir, solo, concerts, voice.*

Name ________________________________ Skill: Read and answer the questions.

Maya Angelou
Author and Poet

Maya Angelou spent her childhood in a small Southern community. She attended an all-black school. Maya moved to San Francisco when she was a teenager. She studied drama, dance and music in San Francisco. Maya Angelou wrote about her childhood in the South and became a famous author. She also wrote poetry, plays and a TV series.

1. Where did Maya Angelou spend her childhood?

2. What kind of school did Maya Angelou attend?

3. Where did Maya move when she was a teenager?

4. What subject did Maya Angelou write about when she became famous?

5. What other kinds of writing did Maya Angelou do?

© Frank Schaffer Publications, Inc.

Name ______________________________

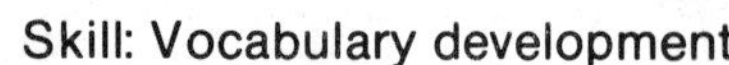
Skill: Vocabulary development

Susan B. Anthony
Women's Rights Leader

Susan B. Anthony worked her **entire** life so that women could **vote**. She lived over one-hundred years ago. Once she tried to vote but was fined. Susan B. Anthony refused to pay the **fine** but worked even harder to win women the **right** to vote.

She became an **effective** writer and speaker. She wrote for a journal called *The Revolution* that called for the **emancipation** of women. With some other women, she started the National American Woman Suffrage Association. Fourteen years after she died, the "Susan B. Anthony Amendment" to the U.S. Constitution gave women the right to vote.

Write the words in dark print below their definitions.

1. to decide by ballot ______________
2. freedom ______________
3. whole, complete ______________
4. lawful claim, privilege ______________
5. making a strong impression ______________
6. money paid as a penalty ______________

Write four sentences. In each sentence, use one of the words you wrote above.

1. ____

____

2. ____

____

3. ____

____

4. ____

____

Brainwork! Make a word search puzzle using the six words above.

© Frank Schaffer Publications, Inc.

Name ______________________________ Skill: Sequencing

Mary McLeod Bethune

Black Teacher

Read the sentences at the bottom of the page.
Write them in the correct order next to the pictures.

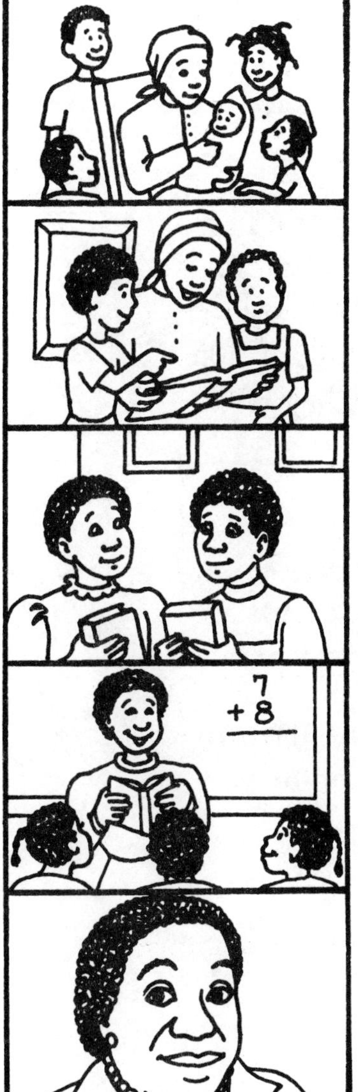

1. ______________________________

2. ______________________________

3. ______________________________

4. ______________________________

5. ______________________________

- As a young child, Mary learned to read at school and taught her family at home.
- Mary McLeod Bethune was born into a large family.
- When she was 13 years old, Mary went to college.
- In her later years, Mrs. Bethune was given many awards and medals for teaching.
- After college, Mary McLeod Bethune became a teacher and started her own school.

Brainwork! Young Mary wanted to learn to read more than anything else. Write three sentences about something you want to learn more than anything else.

Name ______________________ Skill: Read and find the answers.

Guion Bluford

Astronaut

Guion Bluford was the first black American in space. He was a mission specialist on the third flight of the space shuttle **Challenger**. He did experiments to study space sickness. He also did tests for new treatments for diabetes and other diseases.

Word Box		
Challenger	space	sickness
diseases	third	specialist

1. Guion Bluford was the first black American astronaut in ______________________.

2. His job was mission ______________________.

3. He was on the ______________________ flight of the space shuttle ______________________.

4. He studied space ______________________ and a new treatment for ______________________.

Name ______________________ Skill: Read and find the answers.

Ralph Bunche
Winner of Nobel Peace Prize

Ralph Bunche was the first black American to win the Nobel Peace Prize. He studied other governments, helped start the United Nations and helped countries to be peaceful. He said that peace is more than not fighting; he said peace is when children have enough food, homes, schools and happiness.

Word Box		
United Nations	peaceful	Peace
happiness	fighting	first

1. Ralph Bunche was the ____________ black American to win the Nobel ____________ Prize.
2. Ralph Bunche helped start the ________________________.
3. He also helped countries to be ________________________.
4. Ralph Bunche said that peace is more than not ____________.
5. He said that peace is when children have enough food, homes, schools and ________________________.

© Frank Schaffer Publications, Inc.

Name ______________________________ Skill: Read and answer the questions.

George Washington Carver

Scientist

George Washington Carver made scientific discoveries that helped farmers in the South. He taught farmers to grow peanuts, soybeans and sweet potatoes. He also taught them to rotate crops in order to renew the soil.

1. Who was helped by the discoveries of George Washington Carver?

2. What kind of discoveries did he make?

3. What three crops did Carver teach farmers to grow?

4. What else did George Washington Carver teach farmers?

5. Why did Carver teach farmers to rotate crops?

© Frank Schaffer Publications, Inc.

Name ______________________ Skill: Read and find the answers.

Ray Charles
Musician

Ray Charles is well-known for introducing soul music. He said soul music was a combination of gospel, blues and jazz played with deep feeling. Charles became blind at age seven but later he became famous as a creative singer, pianist, saxophonist and composer.

Word Box		
soul music	jazz	singer
deep	blind	famous

1. Ray Charles is well-known for introducing ______________________.

2. He said soul music was a combination of gospel, blues and ______________ played with ______________ feeling.

3. Charles became ______________ at age seven.

4. Charles became ______________ as a creative ______________, pianist, saxophonist and composer.

© Frank Schaffer Publications, Inc.

Name ______________________ Skill: Read and answer the questions.

Shirley Chisholm
Member of Congress

Shirley Chisholm was the first black woman to be a member of the United States Congress. Before becoming a member of Congress, she was a teacher and director of a child-care center. In 1972 she ran for the nomination of United States President.

1. Shirley Chisholm was the first black woman to be a member of what group?

____

2. What are the two jobs she had before becoming a member of Congress?

____

____

3. What did she run for in 1972?

____

4. When did Shirley Chisholm run for the presidential nomination?

____

© Frank Schaffer Publications, Inc.

Name ______________________ Skill: Read and find the answers.

Duke Ellington
Jazz Musician

Duke Ellington was a composer and a musician. He pioneered modern jazz. His band was the first to give jazz concerts regularly. He composed nearly 1,000 songs.

Word Box

jazz	composer	musician
1,000	concerts	band

1. Duke Ellington was a ______________________

   and a ______________________ .

2. He pioneered modern ______________________ .

3. His ______________________ was the first to give jazz

   ______________________ regularly.

4. He wrote nearly ______________________ songs.

© Frank Schaffer Publications, Inc.

Name ______________________________ Skill: Read, color, cut and staple to make a book.

Dr. Martin Luther King, Jr.
Civil Rights Leader

As a child Martin Luther King loved to play games and read.
2

Martin felt uncomfortable when white people were unfriendly to him.
3

In high school Martin decided to be a minister like his father.
4

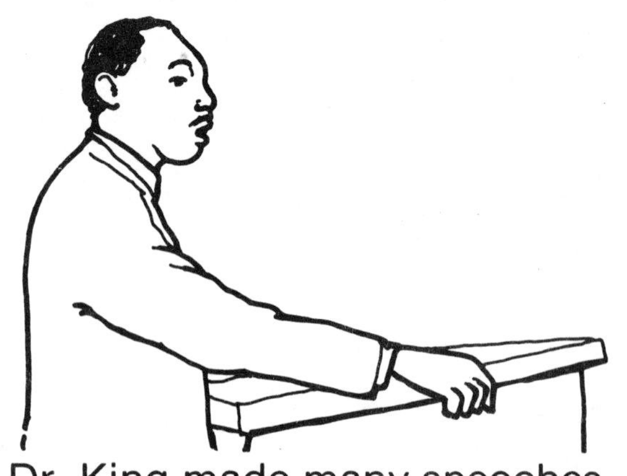

Dr. King made many speeches. He wanted equality for all people.
5

In 1964 Dr. King won the Nobel Peace Prize for working to change unfair laws in non-violent ways.
6

© Frank Schaffer Publications, Inc.

Name ____ Skill: Sequencing

Emma Lazarus

Poet

Read the sentences at the bottom of the page.
Write them in the correct order next to the pictures.

1. ____

2. ____

3. ____

4. ____

5. ____

- When she was eighteen, Emma's poems were printed in a book.
- As a young child, Emma Lazarus liked to write poems and stories.
- After Emma died, words of her famous poem were placed on the base of the statue.
- As a young woman, she wrote about making America a land of "liberty and justice for all."
- Emma Lazarus wrote a poem, "The New Colossus," to help raise money for the base of the Statue of Liberty.

Brainwork! Emma's famous poem "The New Colossus" was written as if the statue were talking to new immigrants. Learn part of the famous poem: "Give me your tired, your poor, your huddled masses yearning to breathe free ..."

© Frank Schaffer Publications, Inc.

Name ______________________ Skill: Read and answer the questions.

Thurgood Marshall

United States Supreme Court Justice

Thurgood Marshall was the first black American to be a justice of the Supreme Court. Before he became a justice, he had been a lawyer. Thurgood Marshall had worked for integrating public schools. Integrating meant the end of separate schools for blacks and whites.

1. Who was the first black American to be a Supreme Court justice?

2. What was Thurgood Marshall before he became a justice of the Supreme Court?

3. What did Thurgood Marshall work to accomplish?

4. What did integrating mean?

© Frank Schaffer Publications, Inc.

Name ______________________________ Skill: Sequencing

María Martínez
Native American Potter

Read the sentences at the bottom of the page.
Write them in the correct order next to the pictures.

1. ______________________________

2. ______________________________

3. ______________________________

4. ______________________________

5. ______________________________

- As a young woman, María Martínez showed talent for making well-shaped pottery.
- As an older woman, María taught her granddaughter and many others to make pottery.
- As a child, María Martínez learned how to make pottery from her aunt.
- As a young married woman, she was encouraged when two scientists bought her pottery.
- María Martínez's pottery became famous when her husband discovered how to fire it black.

Brainwork! Write five sentences about events in your own life. Put them in the order they happened.

Name ____ Skill: Reasoning, Decoding

Liliuokalani

Queen of Hawaii

Queen Liliuokalani was the last member of the royal family to rule Hawaii. Her father and brother had been kings before her. As a child she learned to read and speak English. She also studied music. When the United States took over Hawaii, she worked hard to save Hawaiian ways of life. She wrote songs about the native Hawaiian ways of life.

a	b	c	d	e	f	g	h	i	j	k	l	m
2	4	6	8	10	12	14	16	18	20	22	24	26
n	**o**	**p**	**q**	**r**	**s**	**t**	**u**	**v**	**w**	**x**	**y**	**z**
28	30	32	34	36	38	40	42	44	46	48	50	52

Use the code above to write the answer to each clue.

Queen Liliuokalani's English name was Lydia. As a child Lydia enjoyed special feasts called ___ ___ ___ ___ ___ (24 42 2 42 38). At luaus food was served in big bowls made from gourds called ___ ___ ___ ___ ___ ___ ___ ___ ___ ___ (6 2 24 2 4 2 38 16 10 38). Luaus included a storyteller, or ___ ___ ___ ___ ___ ___ (22 2 16 42 28 2). The kahuna chanted as ___ ___ ___ ___ (16 42 24 2) dancers swayed to the music of drums. Lydia wore a flower necklace called a ___ ___ ___ (24 10 18). She greeted her friends with the word ___ ___ ___ ___ ___ (2 24 30 16 2) which meant both "hello" and "good-bye." Lydia usually remembered to say "thank you," or ___ ___ ___ ___ ___ ___ (26 2 16 2 24 30).

Brainwork! Write and illustrate the seven Hawaiian words you decoded above.

© Frank Schaffer Publications, Inc.

Name ______________________________ Skill: Sequencing

Julia Morgan

Architect

Read the sentences at the bottom of the page.
Write them in the correct order next to the pictures.

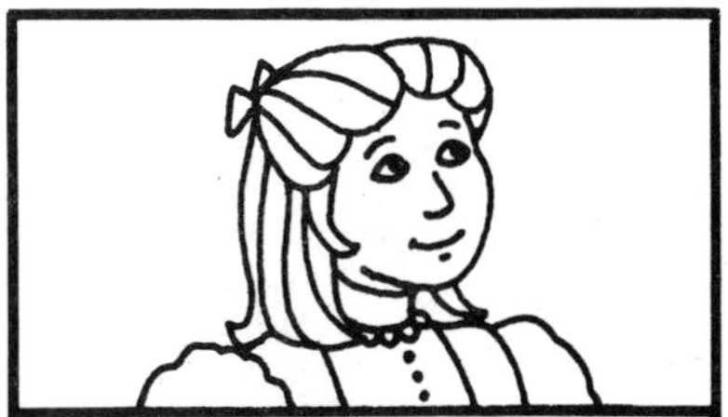

1. ______________________________

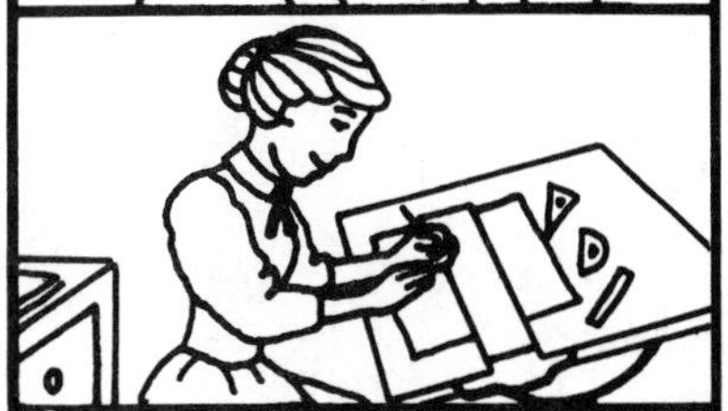

2. ______________________________

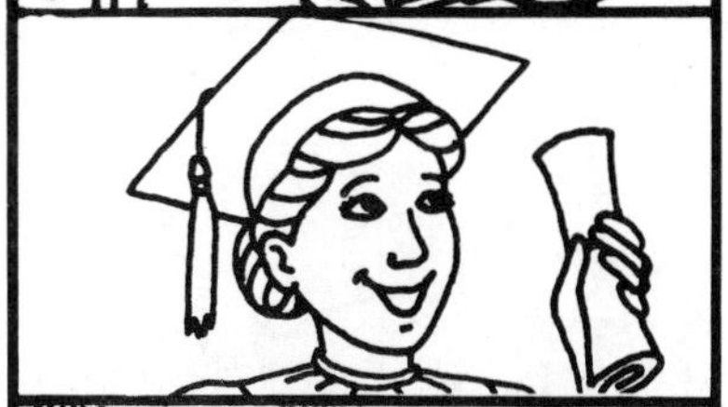

3. ______________________________

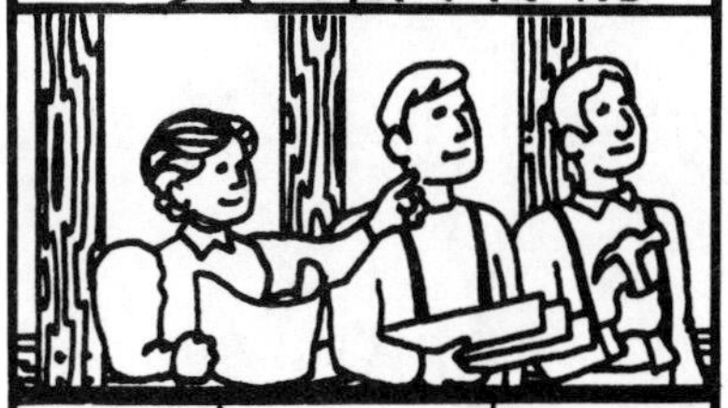

4. ______________________________

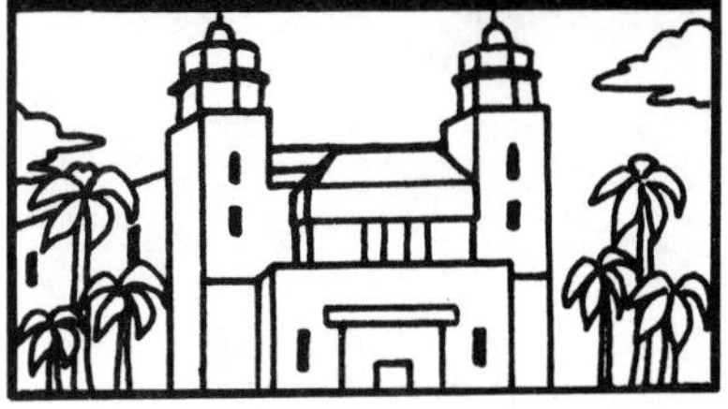

5. ______________________________

- At college there were no architecture classes, so she became a civil engineer.
- After college she became the first woman graduate of a famous architecture school in Paris.
- As a girl in the early 1900s, Julia Morgan wanted to be an architect.
- When she died, she had designed nearly 800 buildings including the famous Hearst Castle.
- As an architect, she designed both simple, inexpensive homes and elaborate, expensive homes.

Brainwork! Hearst Castle had its own zoo, library, art collection, and outdoor pool. Draw your own castle on the back of this paper.

Name ____ Skill: Reasoning, Decoding

Justice Sandra Day O'Connor

First Woman on the Supreme Court

Sandra Day O'Connor is the first woman member of the United States Supreme Court. She became an associate justice of the Supreme Court in 1981. President Reagan chose her for this important job. Before she became an associate justice, Sandra Day O'Connor was a lawyer and a judge. She works extremely hard to know the laws and how they've been used before.

a	b	c	d	e	f	g	h	i	j	k	l	m
26	25	24	23	22	21	20	19	18	17	16	15	14
n	o	p	q	r	s	t	u	v	w	x	y	z
13	12	11	10	9	8	7	6	5	4	3	2	1

Use the code above to write the answer to each clue.

1. Sandra Day O'Connor is the first woman member of the United States Supreme ___ ___ ___ ___ ___.
   24 12 6 9 7

2. She was chosen by President ___ ___ ___ ___ ___ ___.
   9 22 26 20 26 13

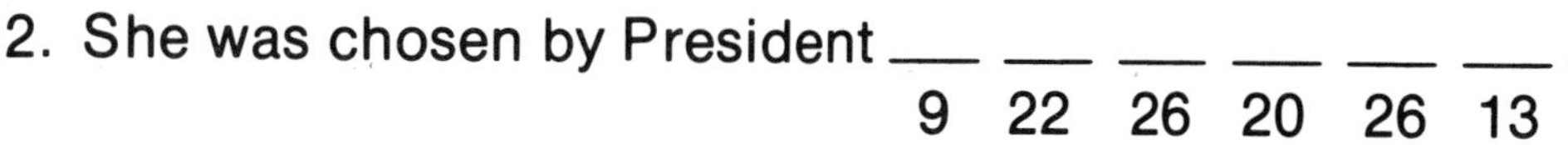

3. Associate justice of the Supreme Court is a job that is very ___ ___ ___ ___ ___ ___ ___ ___ ___.
   18 14 11 12 9 7 26 13 7

4. Another word for *chose* is ___ ___ ___ ___ ___ ___ ___ ___ ___.
   26 11 11 12 18 13 7 22 23

5. Sandra Day O'Connor has been a ___ ___ ___ ___ ___ ___
   15 26 4 2 22 9

   and a ___ ___ ___ ___ ___.
   17 6 23 20 22

6. She works hard to know the ___ ___ ___ ___.
   15 26 4 8

Brainwork! Capitalize the two decoded words needing capitals.

© Frank Schaffer Publications, Inc.

Name ______________________ Skill: Read and find the answers.

Jessie Owens
Record-Breaking Athlete

Jessie Owens held world records in track and field events. On one day he set three world records and tied another. The records he set were in sprinting, hurdling and jumping. Jesse Owens won four gold medals in the 1936 Olympic Games.

1. In what category did Jesse Owens hold world records?

2. How many world records did Owens set in one day?

3. In what three track and field events were the three world records?

4. When did Jesse Owens win four gold medals?

5. Where did Jesse Owens win four gold medals?

© Frank Schaffer Publications, Inc.

Name ______________________________

Eleanor Roosevelt

Human Rights Leader

Eleanor Roosevelt worked all her life for human rights—fair treatment for everyone. As the wife of President Franklin D. Roosevelt, she was a very active first lady. She helped her husband who had polio. As his partner, she made many fact-finding trips for him.

She was chosen a **delegate** to the United Nations. As a delegate, she helped **draft** and pass the **Universal** Declaration of Human Rights. The **declaration** states all persons are born **free** and equal in **dignity**. Eleanor Roosevelt worked very hard to get all countries to support the declaration.

Write the words in dark print below their definitions.

1. independent, at liberty ______________
2. outline, make a plan ______________
3. concerning everyone ______________
4. public statement or proclamation ______________
5. representative ______________
6. pride and self-respect ______________

Write five sentences. In each sentence, use one of the words you wrote above.

1. ____

2. ____

3. ____

4. ____

5. ____

Brainwork! Make a crossword puzzle using the six words above and their definitions.

© Frank Schaffer Publications, Inc.

Name ______________________ Skill: Read, color, cut and staple to make a book.

Wilma Rudolph

Record-Breaking Athlete

Wilma Rudolph had a crippling disease and was not able to walk until she was eight years old.

2

After having therapy, she threw away her special shoes. When she was 11, she became active in sports.

3

She was an outstanding basketball player in high school, setting a state record for girls' scoring.

4

In the 1960 Olympics, she became the world's fastest woman runner and won three gold medals.

5

Later Wilma Rudolph broke other world track records.

6

© Frank Schaffer Publications, Inc.

Name ____ Reasoning, Decoding

Sacagawea

Famous Guide and Translator

Sacagawea became famous as a guide and translator on the Lewis and Clark expedition. She was a Shoshone Indian and the only woman on the expedition. She helped the men by teaching them about the land she knew and translating their words to the Indians. Sacagawea guided the men to the Pacific Ocean. She carried her baby son on her back.

a	b	c	d	e	f	g	h	i	j	k	l	m
1	2	3	4	5	6	7	8	9	10	11	12	13
n	**o**	**p**	**q**	**r**	**s**	**t**	**u**	**v**	**w**	**x**	**y**	**z**
14	15	16	17	18	19	20	21	22	23	24	25	26

Use the code above to write the answer to each clue.

1. Sacagawea's name means

   ___ ___ ___ ___ ___ ___ ___ ___ ___.
   2 9 18 4 23 15 13 1 14

2. Sacagawea belonged to the Indian group

   ___ ___ ___ ___ ___ ___ ___ ___.
   19 8 15 19 8 15 14 5

3. Sacagawea worked as a ___ ___ ___ ___ ___.
   7 21 9 4 5

4. Sacagawea traveled with

   ___ ___ ___ ___ ___ and ___ ___ ___ ___ ___.
   12 5 23 9 19 3 12 1 18 11

5. Sacagawea helped the men reach the ___ ___ ___ ___ ___.
   15 3 5 1 14

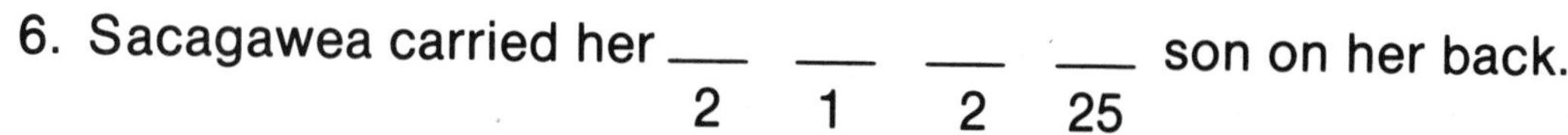

6. Sacagawea carried her ___ ___ ___ ___ son on her back.
   2 1 2 25

Brainwork! Three of the decoded words above need capitals. Find them and capitalize them.

© Frank Schaffer Publications, Inc.

Name ______________________________

Skill: Reasoning, Decoding

Maria Tallchief
Prima Ballerina

Maria Tallchief began piano and ballet lessons before she was five years old. She practiced several hours each day. At 12 she gave a concert. She played the piano and danced. At 17 she decided she wanted to be a dancer more than anything else. She worked very hard to become a great dancer. Maria became one of the best ballerinas in the world.

a	b	c	d	e	f	g	h	i	j	k	l	m
Z	Y	X	W	V	U	T	S	R	Q	P	O	N
n	o	p	q	r	s	t	u	v	w	x	y	z
M	L	K	J	I	H	G	F	E	D	C	B	A

Use the code above to write the answer to each clue.

Maria Tallchief was a ___ ___ ___ ___ ___ ___ ___ ___ ___ Native American
Y V Z F G R U F O

dancer. She became ___ ___ ___ ___ ___ ___ when she danced in a
U Z N L F H

___ ___ ___ ___ ___ ___ named *The Firebird.* This ballet had been created
Y Z O O V G

___ ___ ___ ___ ___ ___ ___ ___ ___ ___ for her. She danced the part of
V H K V X R Z O O B

a ___ ___ ___ ___ bird with ___ ___ ___ ___ ___ ___ ___ powers. She
D R O W N Z T R X Z O

___ ___ ___ ___ ___ ___ ___ ___ ___ her audience with very
H F I K I R H V W

___ ___ ___ ___ ___ ___ ___ ___ ___ steps.
W R U U R X F O G

Brainwork! A *prima ballerina* means the leading female dancer in a ballet company. Write *prima ballerina* using the code above.

© Frank Schaffer Publications, Inc.

Name ______________________ Skill: Read and answer the questions.

Sojourner Truth
Anti-slavery Speaker

Sojourner Truth was born a slave. She ran away from her owner shortly before slaves were freed by law. Sojourner Truth traveled to make speeches against slavery. She was a well-liked speaker because she told the sad story of being a slave. Sojourner Truth made speeches for women's voting rights, too.

1. Who was born a slave?

2. What did Sojourner Truth do shortly before slaves were freed?

3. Why did she travel?

4. Why was Sojourner Truth a well-liked speaker?

5. What other speeches, besides anti-slavery, did Sojourner Truth give?

© Frank Schaffer Publications, Inc.

Name ______________________________ Skill: Vocabulary development

Harriet Tubman
Runaway Slave

Harriet Tubman was born a slave but became a **leader** of the antislavery **struggle**. She began working in the fields as a young **child** so she never learned to read or write. After she had escaped to the North and **freedom**, she helped other slaves escape. Harriet Tubman was the most famous leader of the "Underground Railroad." The "Underground Railroad" gave black people a **quick** and **secret** way to escape to the North and Canada. Over 300 slaves were helped to freedom by Harriet Tubman. On one of her nineteen trips, she helped her parents escape.

Write the words in dark print below their definitions.

1. a person who guides

   ____

2. hidden; kept from being known

   ____

3. to make a great effort

   ____

4. a young girl or boy

   ____

5. done with speed; rapid

   ____

6. able to move and act as one wishes

   ____

Write four sentences about Harriet Tubman. In each sentence, use one of the words you wrote above.

1. ____

   ____

2. ____

   ____

3. ____

   ____

4. ____

   ____

Brainwork! *Antislavery* means against slavery. Find and list three other words that begin with the prefix *anti*.

© Frank Schaffer Publications, Inc.

Name ______________________ Skill: Read and find the answers.

Booker T. Washington

Educator for Black Americans

Booker T. Washington helped improve the lives of black Americans. He believed education, more jobs and better income would help to improve their lives the most. He started a school to train black teachers, farmers, brick makers and carpenters. His ways of teaching by doing were later used by other Americans.

Word Box

education	improve	jobs
doing	school	income

1. Booker T. Washington helped ______________ the lives of black Americans.
2. He believed ______________, more ______________ and better ______________ would help black Americans the most.
3. He started a ______________.
4. His way of teaching by ______________ was used in other American schools.

© Frank Schaffer Publications, Inc.

Name ______________________ Skill: Read and answer the questions.

Whitney Young, Jr.
Civil Rights Leader

Whitney Young, Jr. helped many black Americans obtain civil rights. He worked as director of the National Urban League. Whitney Young started on-the-job training programs, Head Start programs in schools for young children and tutoring centers for older children.

1. Who helped many blacks obtain civil rights?

2. What was Whitney Young's job?

3. What did he help many black Americans get?

4. What did Whitney Young start for young children?

5. What did Whitney Young start for older children?

© Frank Schaffer Publications, Inc.

Name ________________________________ Skill: Compare and contrast

Two Famous Women of Flight

Amelia Earhart

Sally Ride

Amelia Earhart is remembered as the first lady of the air. She loved to fly, bought her own plane, and was the first woman to fly solo across the Atlantic Ocean. Besides being a pilot, Amelia Earhart was an author, fashion designer, photographer, poet, and painter.

Sally Ride will be remembered as America's first woman in space. She flew on the space shuttle *Challenger* as a mission specialist. Dr. Ride is an astronaut and scientist. While growing up, Sally Ride was a nationally ranked junior tennis player.

Decide which famous woman of flight the statement below describes. Write the correct name.

1. America's first woman in space ________________
2. first woman to fly solo across Atlantic Ocean ________________
3. owned her own airplane ________________
4. famous woman pilot ________________
5. flew on space shuttle ________________
6. tennis player ________________
7. was a fashion designer ________________
8. famous woman astronaut ________________

Brainwork! Write three ways Amelia Earhart and Sally Ride are alike.

© Frank Schaffer Publications, Inc.

Name ______________________________ Skill: Compare and contrast

Two Famous Women Educators

Helen Keller

Helen Keller became deaf and blind very young. Anne Sullivan worked hard to teach Helen. Finally Helen learned the word *water* when Anne spelled it in one of Helen's hands while Helen felt water in the other hand. After that Helen learned quickly. She spent her life showing that people with disabilities could learn.

Anne Sullivan

Anne Sullivan was chosen to teach Helen because she, too, had been blind. She had gone to a special school for the blind and deaf. Before Helen learned the word *water,* Anne had spelled out many other words. Finally Helen learned that words were names for things and actions. Anne was pleased when Helen spelled T-E-A-C-H-E-R.

Decide which famous woman educator the statement below describes. Write the correct name.

1. was deaf and blind very young

   ____

2. worked hard to teach Helen

   ____

3. was pleased when Helen spelled T-E-A-C-H-E-R

   ____

4. finally learned that words were names for things and actions

   ____

5. went to a special school

   ____

6. spelled out many words for Helen

   ____

7. learned the word *water* after a long time

   ____

8. learned very quickly once she learned words were names.

   ____

Brainwork! Close your eyes and pretend you are blind. Imagine how you would eat dinner. Write three sentences to tell how you would do it differently than now.

© Frank Schaffer Publications, Inc.

Name ____________________ Skill: Compare and contrast

Two Famous Scientists

Rachel Carson

Rachel Carson grew up loving the outdoors, reading, and writing stories. In college she studied to be a writer and a scientist. She became the first woman scientist in the Department of Fisheries in 1936. Carson's books told people to care for the world around them. These books made her famous.

Dixy Lee Ray

Dixy Lee Ray grew up loving the sea, climbing mountains, and earning money by putting on puppet shows. In college she studied to be a scientist. As a TV teacher, she made science exciting. Dixy Lee Ray was the first woman to head the Atomic Energy Commission. In 1976 she was elected governor of Washington State.

Decide which famous woman scientist each statement describes. Write the correct name.

1. first woman to head Atomic Energy Commission

   ____

2. first woman scientist in Department of Fisheries

   ____

3. wrote books about caring for world around us

   ____

4. governor of Washington state

   ____

5. TV teacher who made science exciting

   ____

6. writing books made her famous

   ____

7. loved outdoors, reading, and writing stories

   ____

8. put on puppet shows

   ____

Brainwork! Rachel Carson was ten years old when her first story was printed. Dixy Lee Ray was twelve years old when she climbed the highest mountain in America. Write your age now and compare yourself with one of the women above.

© Frank Schaffer Publications, Inc.

Name ________________________________ Skill: Compare and contrast

Two Famous Women in Medicine

Elizabeth Blackwell

Elizabeth Blackwell was born in England and later became the first woman medical student in the United States. She became the first U.S. woman doctor. She started a hospital staffed only by women and a women's medical college. She is remembered for her ideas on cleanliness and ways to prevent illness.

Clara Barton

Clara Barton and some friends started the Red Cross in the United States. She was its first president. During wars the Red Cross helped wounded soldiers. Later the Red Cross began to help victims of floods, tornadoes, earthquakes, and disease. The Red Cross gave materials to rebuild homes and plant crops.

Decide which woman in medicine the statement below describes. Write the correct name.

1. first woman medical student

   ____

2. first president of Red Cross

   ____

3. helped start Red Cross

   ____

4. first woman doctor in U.S.

   ____

5. worked to expand Red Cross

   ____

6. started hospital staffed only by women

   ____

7. started women's medical college

   ____

8. remembered for ideas on cleanliness

   ____

Brainwork! Write three sentences telling how these two women in medicine were alike.

© Frank Schaffer Publications, Inc.

Name ______________________________ Skill: Compare and contrast

Two Famous American Artists

Mary Cassatt

Mary Cassatt was the first great American woman artist. As a child she visited museums and galleries in France. It was then she decided to be a painter. People all over the world liked her paintings with their short brush strokes and rich, bright colors. She often painted mothers and children.

Georgia O'Keeffe

Georgia O'Keeffe was a well-known American woman artist. She created an original style of painting by enlarging one object. Often the object filled an entire canvas. The design was clear and exact. She painted single flowers or the skulls of animals. Many of her paintings showed the beauty of the desert.

Decide which famous woman artist the statement below describes. Write the correct name.

1. first great American woman artist

   ____

2. created original style of painting

   ____

3. decided to be painter when a child

   ____

4. painted mothers and children

   ____

5. paintings showed beauty of the desert

   ____

6. enlarged one object to fill canvas

   ____

7. painted with bright colors

   ____

8. painted flowers and skulls

   ____

Brainwork! Would you rather have a painting in your room by Mary Cassatt or Georgia O'Keeffe? Why? Write your answers.

© Frank Schaffer Publications, Inc.

Name ______________________________ Skill: Compare and contrast

Two Famous Women Authors

Laura Ingalls Wilder

Laura Ingalls Wilder became famous when she wrote a series of children's books. The nine "Little House" books told of her family's pioneer life. Laura didn't begin writing until she was 65 years old. In 1954 she won the first Laura Ingalls Wilder Award given for outstanding written or artistic work.

Harriet Beecher Stowe

Harriet Beecher Stowe became famous for her book, *Uncle Tom's Cabin*. She was the first American author to write about black people and slavery. Her book told of the horrible lives of slaves. This story caused many people to work to free the slaves. It also hurried the beginning of Civil War.

Decide which famous woman author the statement below describes. Write the correct name.

1. wrote *Uncle Tom's Cabin*

   ____

2. wrote "Little House" series

   ____

3. first to write about black people

   ____

4. first to win Laura Ingalls Wilder Award

   ____

5. wrote about slavery

   ____

6. wrote about pioneer life

   ____

7. began writing at 65

   ____

8. caused people to work to free the slaves

   ____

Brainwork! Make a list of how these two famous American authors are alike.

© Frank Schaffer Publications, Inc.

Name ______________________________ Date ______________

First Americans: The Indians

The first people in America were the Indians. No one is sure when they first came, or from where they came. We think they came from Asia. Long ago there may have been a land "bridge" between Russia and Alaska. They could have walked across. Some stayed in Alaska. Others traveled to all parts of North and South America.

There were many tribes of Indians. Each tribe wanted to be left alone. They lived simple lives. They did not build towns with schools. They did not have books. They learned from older people in the tribe.

The Indians had many good ways. They loved the land. They only took whatever they needed from it. They shared with each other. They were free.

1. Who were the first Americans?

____

2. From where could they have come?

____

3. How could they have come over here?

____

4. What did they not have?

____

5. Write one good thing about Indian ways.

____

TO DO: Begin a book on America. Find out more about the Indians. Draw Indian pictures. How do you think the Indians felt when the white men came? Pretend you were an Indian then. Write how you felt. Find Asia, Russia and Alaska on a map. See how the Indians might have come.

© Frank Schaffer Publications, Inc.

Name ______________________ Date ____________

Columbus Finds America

Christopher Columbus lived in Italy. He liked ships. He wanted to sail when he grew up. Some people still thought the world was flat. Columbus wanted to sail around the world. Then he could prove it was round.

One day he went to the King and Queen of Spain. They wanted to find a shorter way to sail to India. They wanted Columbus to find gold. Columbus asked for ships to sail. He was given three. He got a crew together. They sailed many weeks. It was long and hard. Some of the men wanted to go back. Columbus said, "No! We must sail on!" Then, on October 12, 1492, Columbus landed near South America. He had found the Americas!

1. How did Columbus think the world was shaped?

____

2. Who gave ships to Columbus?

____

3. What did Columbus say to his men?

____

4. What was Columbus sent to find?

____

5. When did he find the Americas?

____

TO DO: Look at a world map. Find Italy and Spain. See how far Columbus sailed. He was brave. Have you ever been brave? Write a story about it. Save it for your book.

© Frank Schaffer Publications, Inc.

Name ______________________________ Date ______________

Many Explorers

Columbus was an explorer. An explorer puts his flag in the ground when he lands. This means that the land is discovered and claimed by his country. Columbus sailed for Spain. He planted the Spanish flag on the shore.

After Columbus, other Spanish explorers came. They started little towns in South America. Then they went to the southwestern part of the United States. They put up their flags. They pushed the Indian aside. They forgot that he was there first.

Rulers of other lands heard about the Americas. They sent explorers too. Soon there were flags of France, Holland, and England in the new land.

1. What must explorers do when they find a new land?

____

2. What does this mean?

____

3. Columbus was born in Italy. Why did he have a Spanish flag?

____

4. What other lands sent explorers?

____

5. What part of the United States was discovered?

____

TO DO: Look at a world map. Find these lands: France, Holland, Spain. Draw their flags. Label them. Put them in your book.

© Frank Schaffer Publications, Inc.

Name ________________________________ Date ________________

Jamestown

When you claim a new land, you need more than just a flag in the ground. Your people must live there too. The King of England wanted English people in this new land. He didn't think the land belonged to the Indians.

In 1607 three ships left England for America. They came here to live. They came to get rich. They chose a place and called it Jamestown. They named it for their king, James.

They began to look for gold. Then they ran out of food. Many people got sick. Some died. These were hard times.

Then they saw that the land was good. So they began farming. The people of Jamestown did not find gold. But they got rich from the fine land.

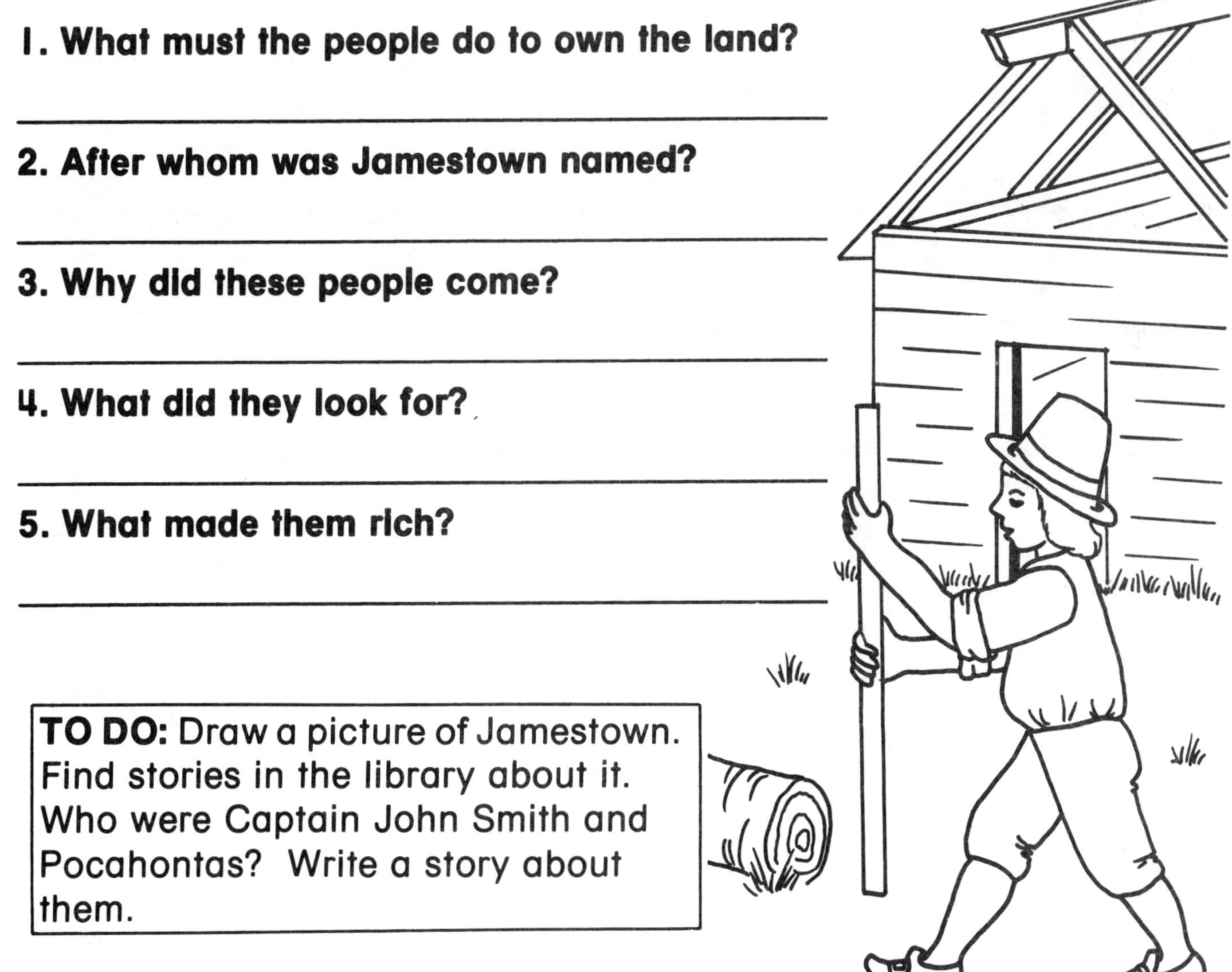

1. What must the people do to own the land?

____

2. After whom was Jamestown named?

____

3. Why did these people come?

____

4. What did they look for?

____

5. What made them rich?

____

TO DO: Draw a picture of Jamestown. Find stories in the library about it. Who were Captain John Smith and Pocahontas? Write a story about them.

© Frank Schaffer Publications, Inc.

Name ______________________ Date ____________

Black Americans

Most people came to America because they wanted to come. Some came to be free. Some came to get rich. But some came as slaves.

Many people started farms in what are now the southern states of America. The farms grew very large. More workers were needed. So men from America sailed to Africa. They captured many of the black people who lived in Africa. They brought the slaves to America. The slaves were forced to work on the farms. They were treated very badly. Black people were slaves in America for many years. Slavery in America ended when Abraham Lincoln made it against the law to own slaves.

Today all Americans are free. Free Americans are every color!

1. Where did the black Americans come from?

____

2. Why were they brought here?

____

3. Where were the large farms?

____

4. Who set them free?

____

5. What color are Americans today?

____

TO DO: Find Africa on a world map. Look in the library for books about slavery. Pretend you lived in Africa and were forced to go to America on a ship. How would you feel? Write a story. Talk about freedom. What does it mean to be "free"?

© Frank Schaffer Publications, Inc.

Name ______________________ Date ______________

Pilgrims And The Mayflower

There were some unhappy people in England. The King said they had to go to his church. They wanted to go to their own churches. Someone said, "Let's go to America. There we can be free to worship as we wish."

About 100 Pilgrims left England on the Mayflower. It was a small ship. The sea was stormy. People got sick. It was a hard trip.

They were to go to Jamestown. They got to America, but not to Jamestown. The wind blew them farther north. They landed at Plymouth Rock in December of 1620.

1. What did the King want the people to do?

____

2. Why were the Pilgrims unhappy?

____

3. What was the name of their ship?

____

4. What made the trip hard?

____

____

TO DO: Draw a picture of the Mayflower. Find out more about this little ship. If you had left your home to sail across a big ocean, how would you feel? Pretend you were a Pilgrim. Write a story.

© Frank Schaffer Publications, Inc.

Name ______________________ Date ______________

The First Thanksgiving

It was winter when the Pilgrims landed. They slept on the Mayflower at night. They chopped down trees in the daytime. They made houses and a fort. The Pilgrims made beds and tables. It was a long, hard winter. They ran out of food. Many Pilgrims got sick and died.

In the spring they met a kind Indian named Squanto. He showed them how to plant and grow food.

In the fall the Pilgrims picked lots of food from their gardens. They were very thankful. They asked the Indians to come for a big dinner. This was the first Thanksgiving.

1. What did the Pilgrims make?

____

2. Tell something about the first winter.

____

3. What did Squanto teach them?

____

4. Who came to dinner?

____

5. Why were the Pilgrims thankful?

____

TO DO: Draw a picture of the first Thanksgiving. Find out more about Squanto. The Pilgrims were thankful. For what are you thankful? Make a list. Put it in your book.

© Frank Schaffer Publications, Inc.

Name ______________________ Date ____________

Thirteen Colonies

More and more people came to America. Most of them were from England. Some came because they wanted freedom to worship in their own way. Some came to make money. Many people landed in the north. Some people lived down south. They all settled on the Atlantic coast.

Each group began with a town. Soon there were many towns. They called each group of towns a colony. A colony was not free to make its own laws. The King of England ruled them all. Soon there were thirteen colonies.

1. From where did most people come?

____

2. Why did they come?

____

3. What ocean were they near?

____

4. What were the groups of towns called?

____

5. Who ruled them?

____

TO DO: Look at the map on page 62. Now look at a United States map. Do you find the names of the 13 colonies on it? Find England on a world map. Write a list of the colonies for your book.

© Frank Schaffer Publications, Inc.

Name ______________________ Date ____________

The American Colonies

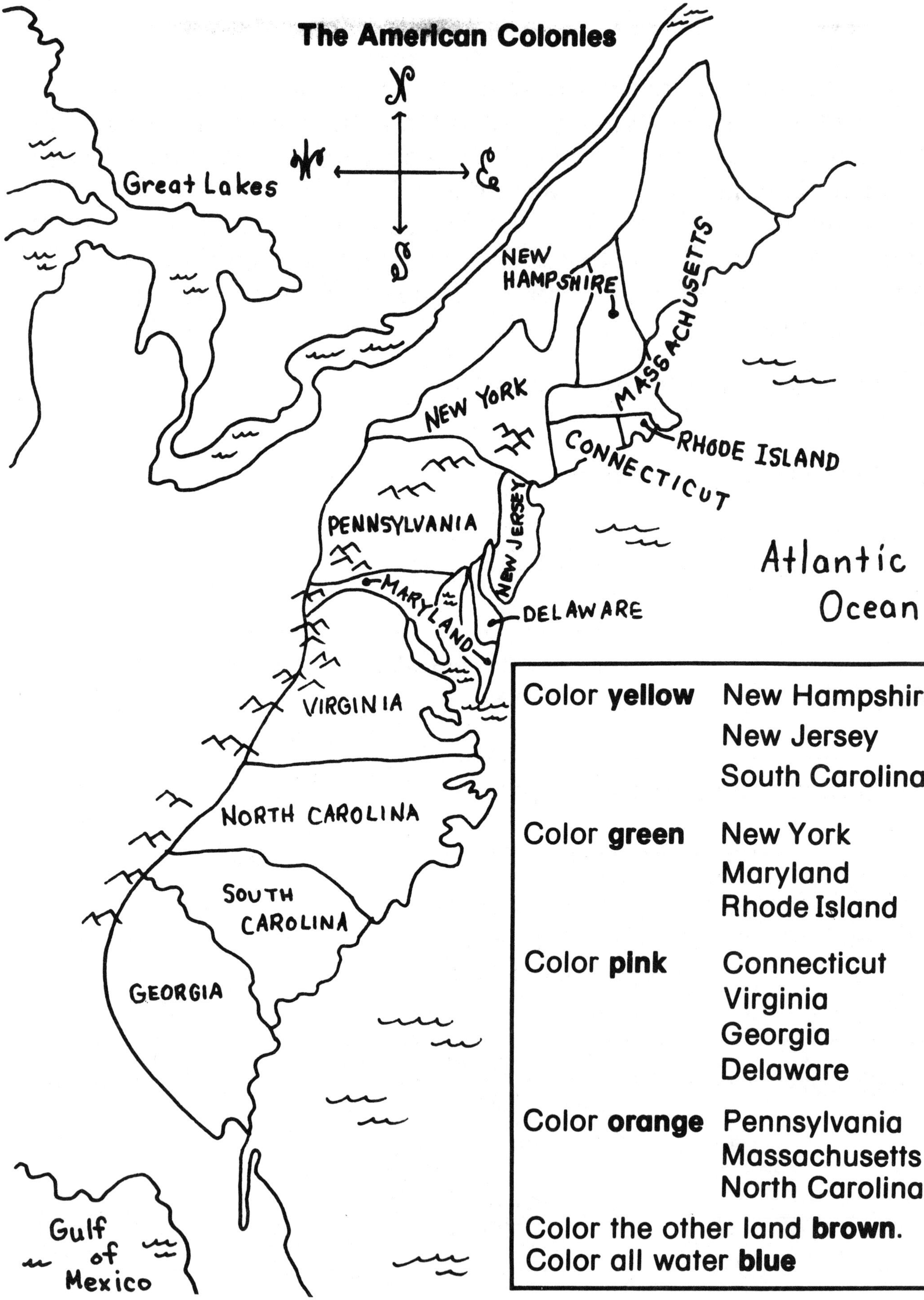

Color **yellow**	New Hampshire New Jersey South Carolina
Color **green**	New York Maryland Rhode Island
Color **pink**	Connecticut Virginia Georgia Delaware
Color **orange**	Pennsylvania Massachusetts North Carolina

Color the other land **brown**.
Color all water **blue**

© Frank Schaffer Publications, Inc.

Name ______________________ Date ______________

Life in the Colonies

Life in the early colonies was hard. The people had to chop down trees. They had to make everything they needed. They slept on straw mats. They had to grow their own food. Animals were hunted for meat and fur. Many people were sick. Many died.

As years went by, life got better. The colonists built ships. They sailed to England to buy things. They built better homes. Many people slept on soft feather beds. The colonies were growing, happy places.

1. What did the people have to make?

____

2. Where did they get the wood?

____

3. Where did they get their food?

____

4. How did they get soft beds and better homes?

____

____

5. Where did they get their ships?

____

TO DO: Pretend you lived in a colony. If you had to make everything you needed, what would you make first? Then what? List six or eight things.

Name ______________________ Date ____________

The French-Indian War

The colonies kept growing. People began to move west. They crossed some mountains to find more land. The land had been claimed by France. The French did not want to live there. They just wanted to trap animals for their furs. They would sell the furs to make money. They did not want the English to live there either. They began to fight.

The King of England sent over some soldiers. The Indians helped the French fight. They fought for 75 years! At last it was over. England took the land.

1. Why did the English cross the mountains?

____

2. Who claimed this land?

____

3. What would the French do with the furs?

____

4. How long did they fight?

____

5. Who got the land?

____

TO DO: Draw a picture for your book. Look in the library for stories about this war. What did George Washington have to do with it? Write a story.

Name ______________________________ Date ______________

The Boston Tea Party

The French-Indian War cost England a lot of money. The King thought the colonists should help pay for the war. He put a tax on tea and other goods from England that the colonists would buy. This tax would help pay for the war.

The colonists were angry. They said, "It is not fair! We did not vote for this. We will not pay a tax we did not vote for!" The King said, "You will!" The colonists said, "We won't!"

One night some colonists dressed up like Indians. They went to the harbor. They got on an English ship. They threw all the boxes of tea into the water. They called it "The Boston Tea Party."

1. Why did the King put a tax on things?

____

____

2. Why were the colonists angry?

____

3. How did the colonists dress up?

____

4. Was "Boston Tea Party" a good name? Why?

____

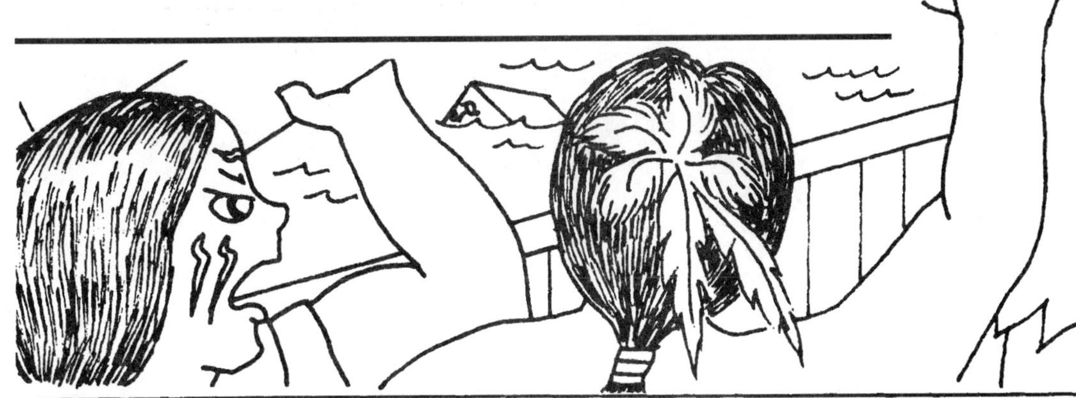

TO DO: Draw a picture of this "party." The English and the colonists did not agree. Set up chairs facing each other. Some students be colonists, some be English. Tell why you feel you are right.

© Frank Schaffer Publications, Inc.

Name ______________________ Date ______________

The Colonists Want To Be Free!

The colonists tried and tried to talk to the King. They asked him to let them help make their laws. The King would not hear of it!

Near Boston there was a battle between some colonists and some English soldiers. Men were killed on both sides.

Then the King hired some German soldiers to come fight the colonists. There was going to be a war.

Leaders from the colonies met. Thomas Jefferson wrote an important paper. It told the world that the colonies were going to become one free country. The date was July 4, 1776, which is now called the birthday of our country.

1. What did the colonists want?

____

2. Who did the King hire to fight the colonists?

____

3. Who wrote an important paper?

____

4. What did the paper say?

____

5. When is our country's birthday?

____

TO DO: Do you think the colonists had the right to help make their laws? If you had been Thomas Jefferson, what would you have said? Think carefully, then write it down.

© Frank Schaffer Publications, Inc.

Name ______________________________ Date ________________

A New Flag

Each colony had its own flag. But now they would be fighting as a team. They wanted one flag for all!

George Washington was made the leader of the colonial army. They needed a flag to follow. They needed a flag to fly over their camps and to carry into battle.

It is said that Betsy Ross made our first flag. Washington wanted 13 stripes for the 13 colonies. He wanted them to be red and white. Betsy Ross put a square of blue in the corner. On the blue was a circle of 13 stars.

The leaders of the colonies liked the new flag. They voted for it on June 14, 1777. Now June 14 is called Flag Day.

1. Who was the leader of the colonial army?

____

2. Why did they want a new flag?

____

3. How many stripes and stars were on the first flag?

____

4. What colors did Washington want?

____

5. When is Flag Day?

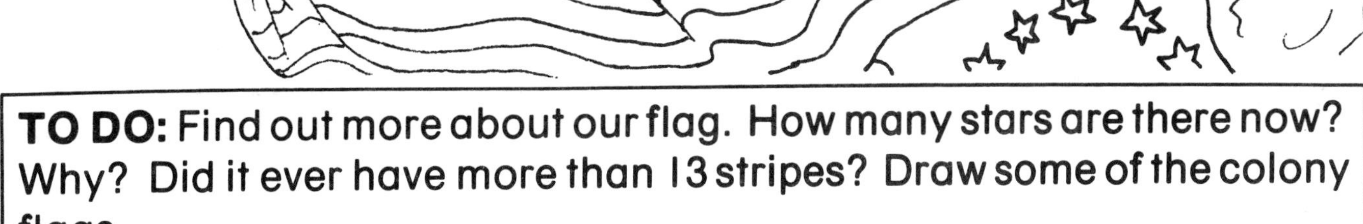

TO DO: Find out more about our flag. How many stars are there now? Why? Did it ever have more than 13 stripes? Draw some of the colony flags.

© Frank Schaffer Publications, Inc.

Name ____________________ Date ____________

How To Make A Star

Here is how to make a star. Make 13 white ones. Now get some red, white, and blue paper. Make the first American flag.

1.

2.

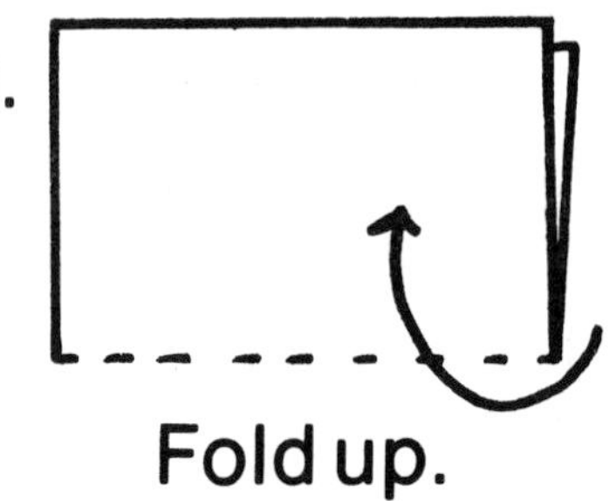

Fold up.

3.

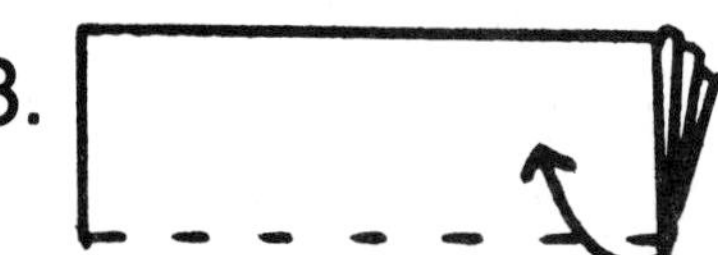

Fold up again.

4. Open to Step 2.

5.

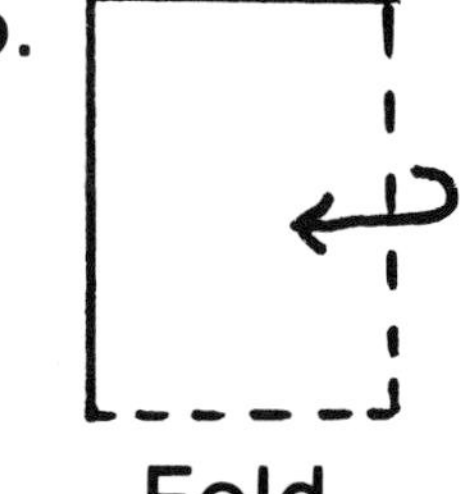

Fold.

6.

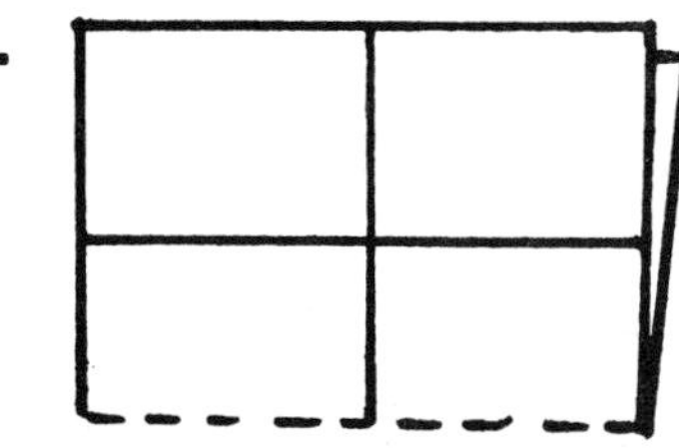

Open to Step 2.

7.

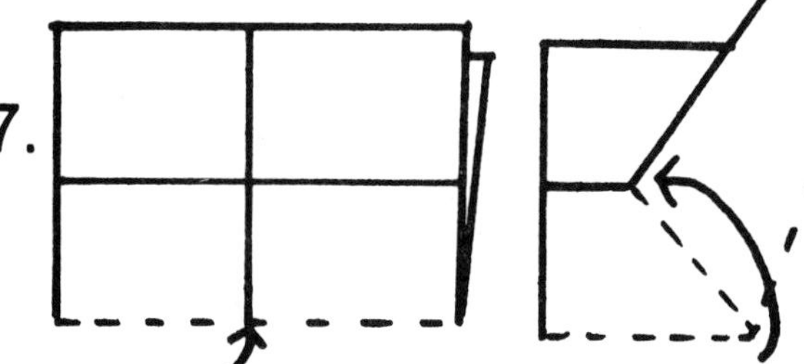

Put finger here.

Touch corner to fold line.

8.

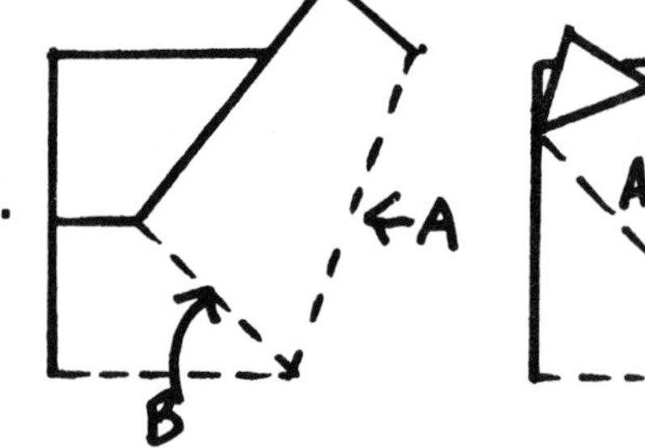

Fold **A** over to line up with **B**.

9.

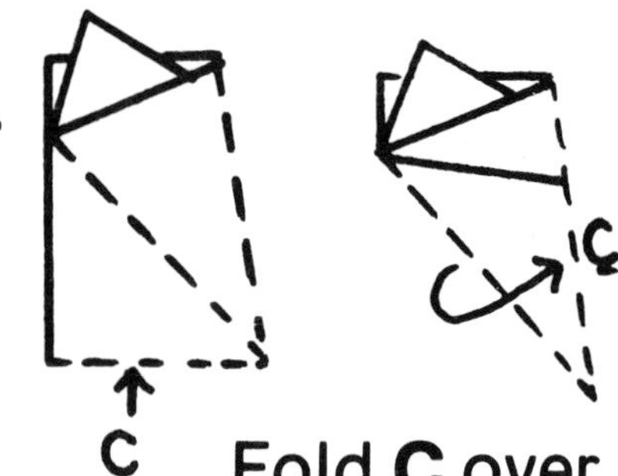

Fold **C** over.

10.

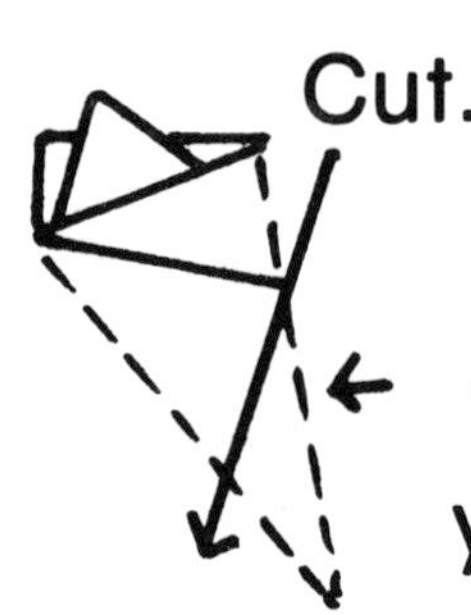

Cut.

Unfold. This is your star!

© Frank Schaffer Publications, Inc.

Name ______________________ Date ______________

The Fight For Freedom

The Revolutionary War began. For a long time it looked like the colonists would never win. The English soldiers were stronger. They had better guns and training.

One winter was very bad. The colonial army was out of food. They were sick. They were cold. Snow was on the ground and some soldiers had no shoes.

George Washington was a good leader. He bought food with his own money. He tried to cheer up the men.

Then the people of France decided to help the colonists. With the help of the French soldiers, the colonists won the war. There was now a new free country: the United States of America!

1. Why were the English winning?

____

____

2. What made Washington a good leader?

____

____

3. What country helped the colonists?

____

4. What was the new country's name?

____

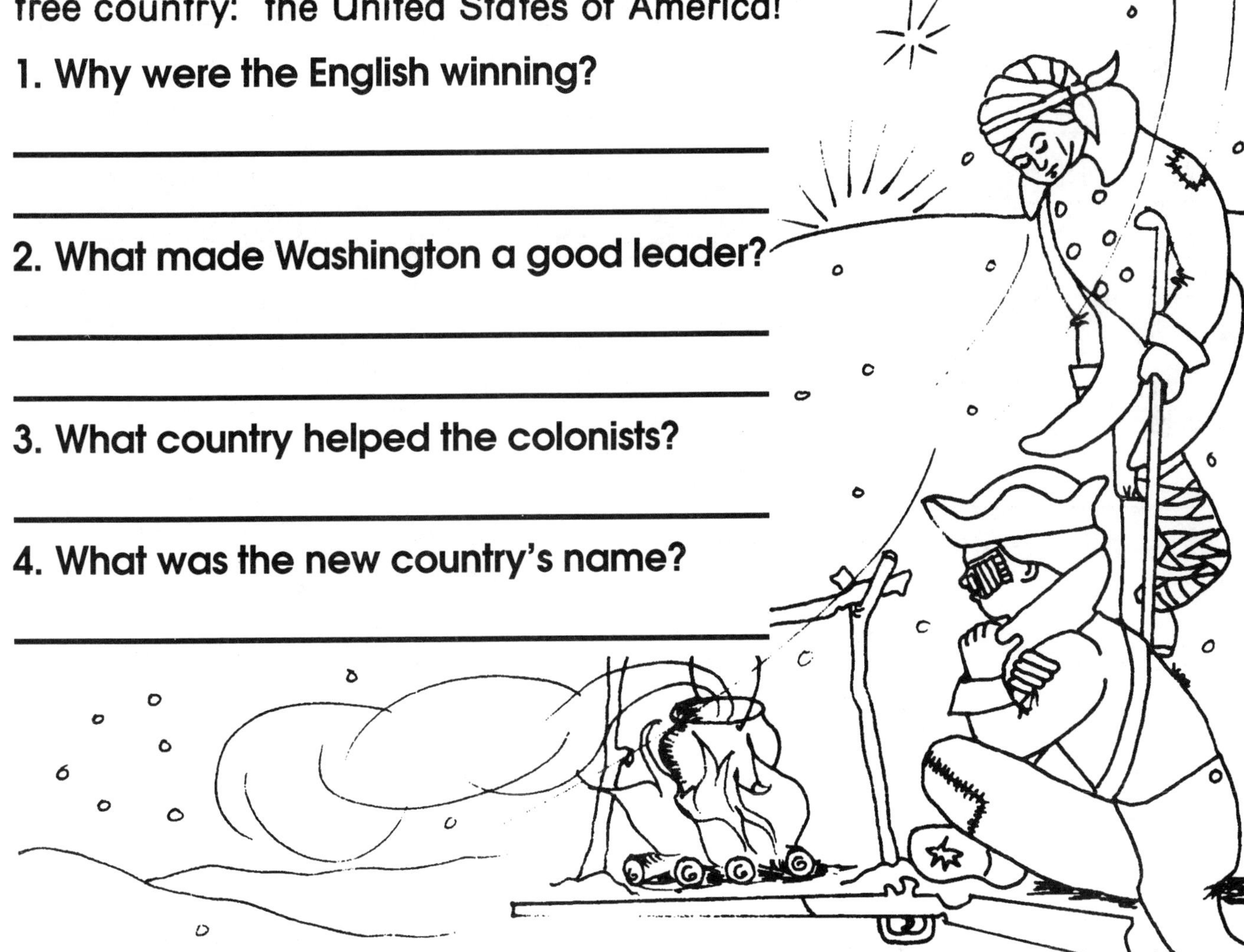

TO DO: Use your library. Find books about this war. Who were some of the leaders besides Washington? Make a list or write a story.

© Frank Schaffer Publications, Inc.

Name ______________________ Date ______________

A New Government

A new country had been born. Now the colonies were called states. George Washington and others were wise. They knew the states needed a new kind of government. They called together leaders from all the states.

For many days the men worked. They wrote a wonderful plan. This plan has helped our country grow faster than any other country in the world! They made sure there would be no king giving orders. They made sure the people had the right to vote. They made sure there were many freedoms.

The people all agreed on the plan. Then they chose George Washington to be their president.

1. What did the colonies become?

____

2. What did the states need?

____

3. Who wrote this plan?

____

4. Name something good about the plan.

____

5. Who became the first president?

____

TO DO: The new government gave us many freedoms. Look in the library. Talk to others. Then write down a list of our freedoms. What would it be like without them? Think about it.

© Frank Schaffer Publications, Inc.

Name ______________________ Date ______________

A Great American

Many great men worked hard for the colonies' freedom. One of the greatest was George Washington. He is called "the father of his country."

George Washington was born in the colony of Virginia. He liked to ride horses and play outside. He learned how to get along in the woods. This helped him to be a good soldier.

George Washington was a great leader in the war for freedom. When the war was over, he helped write the new government's laws. Then he was president for eight years. He was a very good president. The people loved him. He was a great American!

1. Who is the father of our country?

____

2. Where was he born?

____

3. Name something great he did.

____

4. How long was he president?

____

5. How did the people feel about him?

____

TO DO: Read about George Washington. Write a story about some part of his life. George was a great leader. What makes a good leader? Talk about it. Now get your book in order. Make a red, white and blue cover. Give it a good name. Let your friends read it.

Name ______________________________ Skill: Following directions

Which Way?

A compass shows **N** for North, **S** for south, **E** for east, and **W** for west. It also has an arrow which always points north. The compasses below are missing arrows and some of their directions. Write in the missing directions. Here are hints to help you.

1. The compass arrow always points north.
2. If you face north, east is always on the right.
3. If you face east, west is behind you.

1. N, S

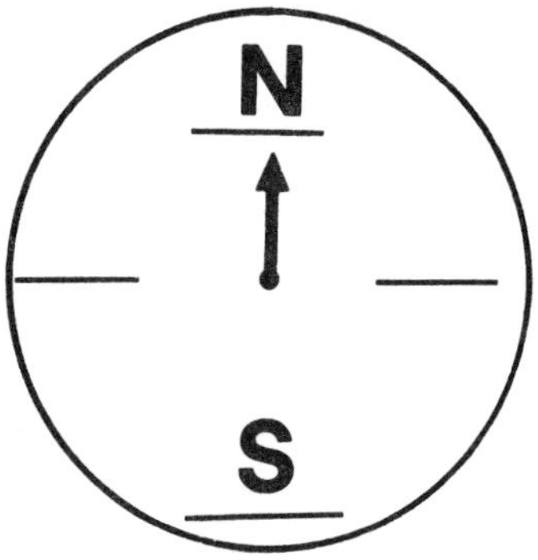

2. S, W

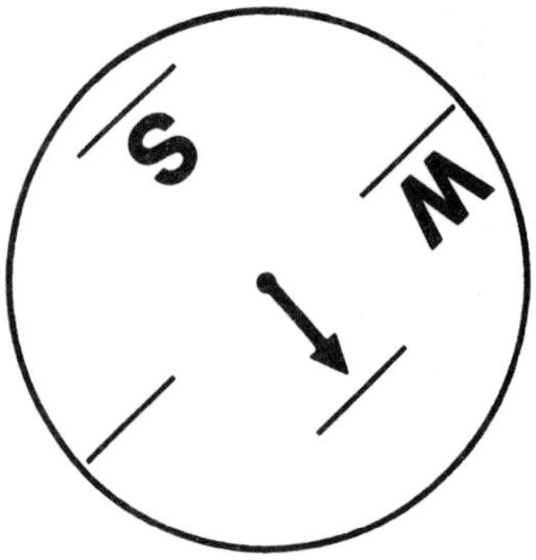

3. N, E

4. W, E

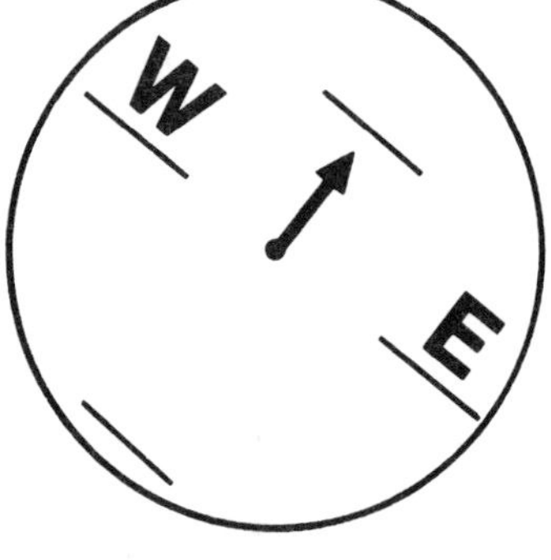

5. S

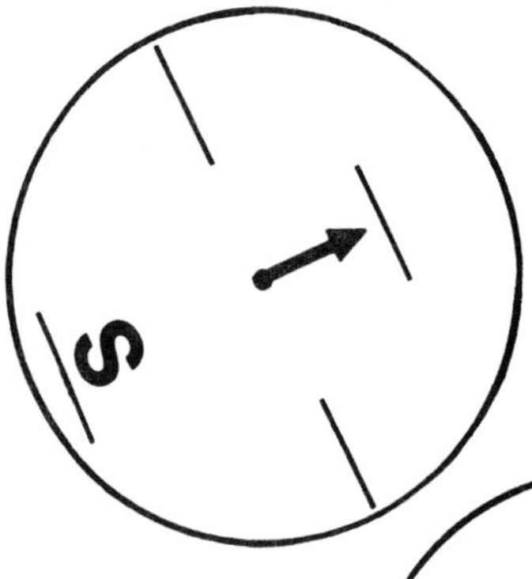

6. E

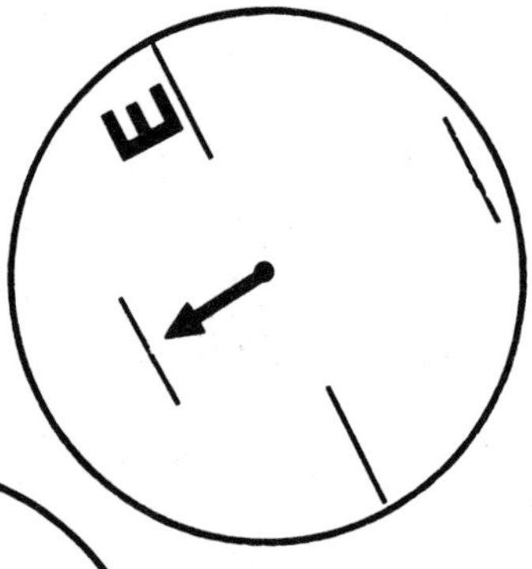

7. Make this circle into a compass. Mark the four directions and draw an arrow pointing north.

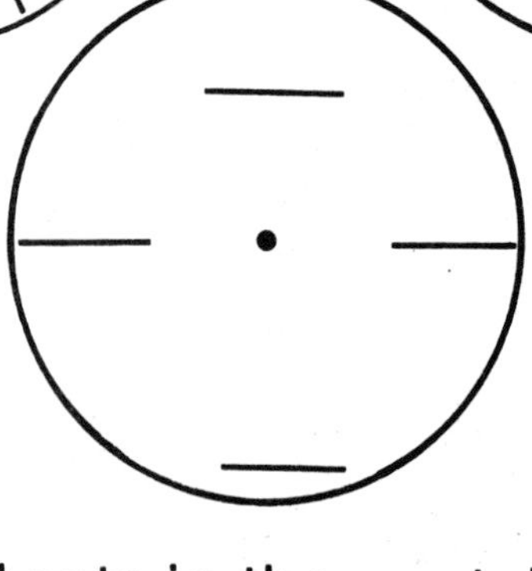

Brainwork! The sun rises in the east and sets in the west. Find out which way your house faces. Draw a top view of your house. Label north, south, east, and west on your picture.

© Frank Schaffer Publications, Inc.

Name ______________________ Skill: Using direction words

The Compass Rose

Most maps have a sign that shows you which way is north. Sometimes that sign is an arrow that points north. Sometimes it is a **compass rose** which shows the directions of north, south, east, and west.

Write the correct direction name from the compass rose to complete each sentence below.

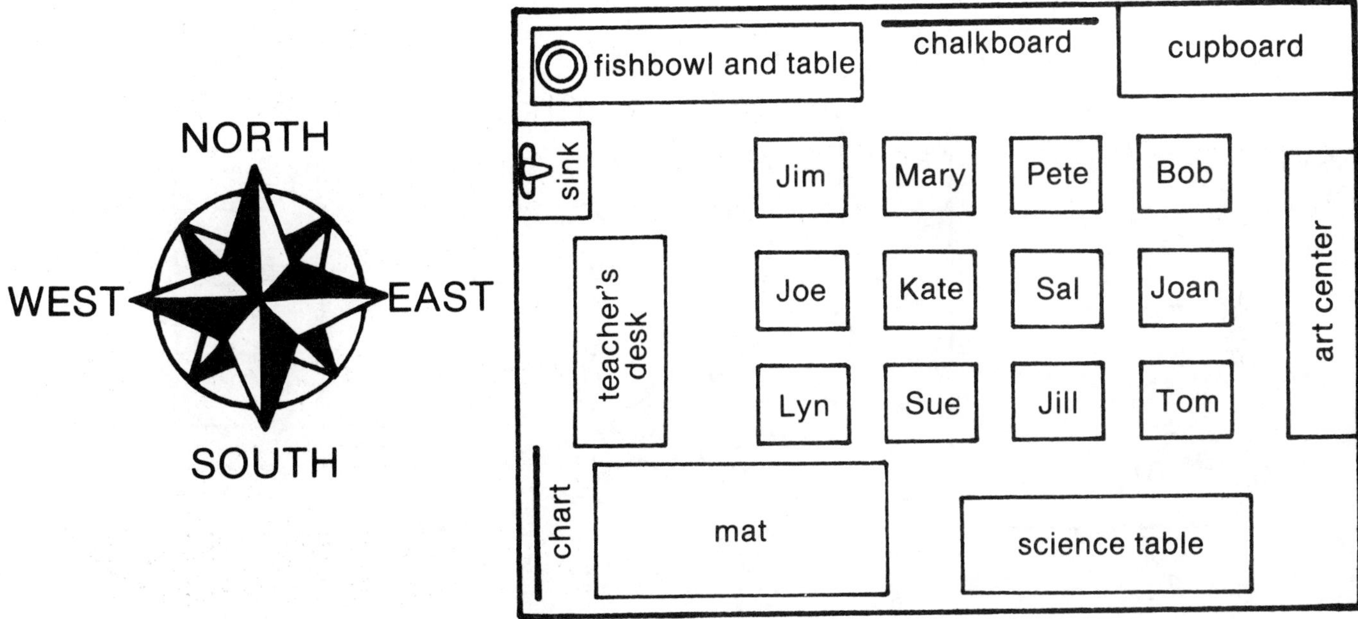

1. The teacher's desk is on the ______________ side of the room.
2. Lyn's desk is ______________ of Jim's desk.
3. The science table is ______________ of the mat.
4. The chalkboard is ______________ of Pete's desk.
5. The art center is on the ______________ side of the classroom.
6. Jill will walk south and turn ______________ to read the chart.
7. When Joe feeds the fish, he will walk west then turn ______________.
8. Sal will walk north then ______________ to reach the cupboard.

Brainwork! Draw a map of your classroom. Draw a compass rose on your map to show where north, south, east, and west are.

© Frank Schaffer Publications, Inc.

Name ______________________________ Skill: Using map symbols

Important Places in the City

Symbols are drawings which stand for important things on a map. Here are some symbols you might find on a map.

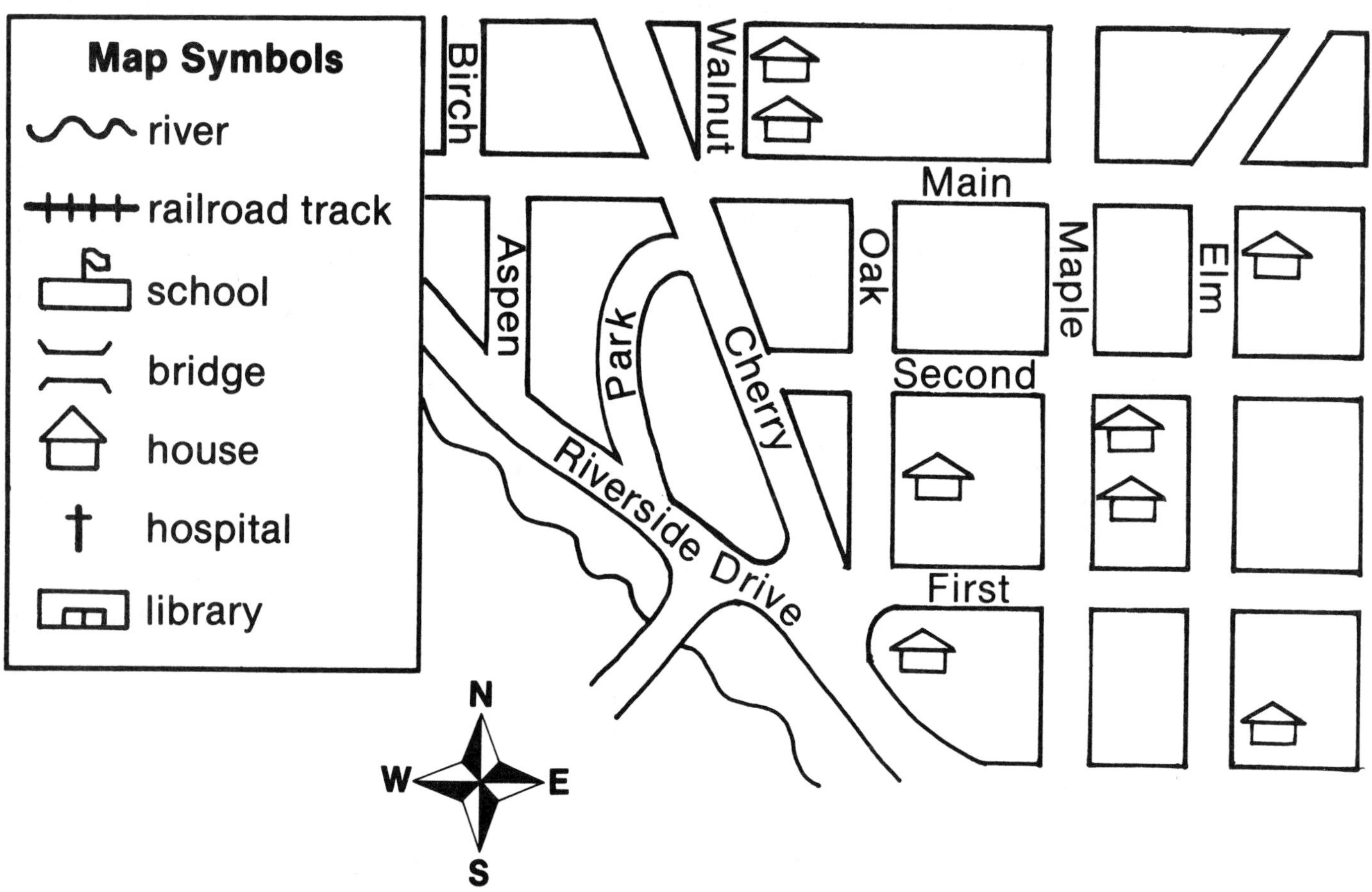

Follow the directions below to draw the correct symbols where they belong on this map.

1. Draw the school symbol on the east side of Elm between First and Second.
2. Draw the hospital symbol on Main between Birch and Cherry.
3. Draw the railroad track symbol down the middle of Maple.
4. Draw the bridge symbol on Main where it crosses over the railroad tracks.
5. Draw the library symbol on Cherry between Second and Main.

Brainwork! Make up symbols for the important things around your school. Show these symbols on a map of your school.

© Frank Schaffer Publications, Inc.

Name ______________________________

What Is It?

The symbols on a map and what they mean are shown inside of a **legend**. Looking at the legend will help you read the symbols on a map.

Find the legend for this map. Then write what the symbol stands for on each numbered line.

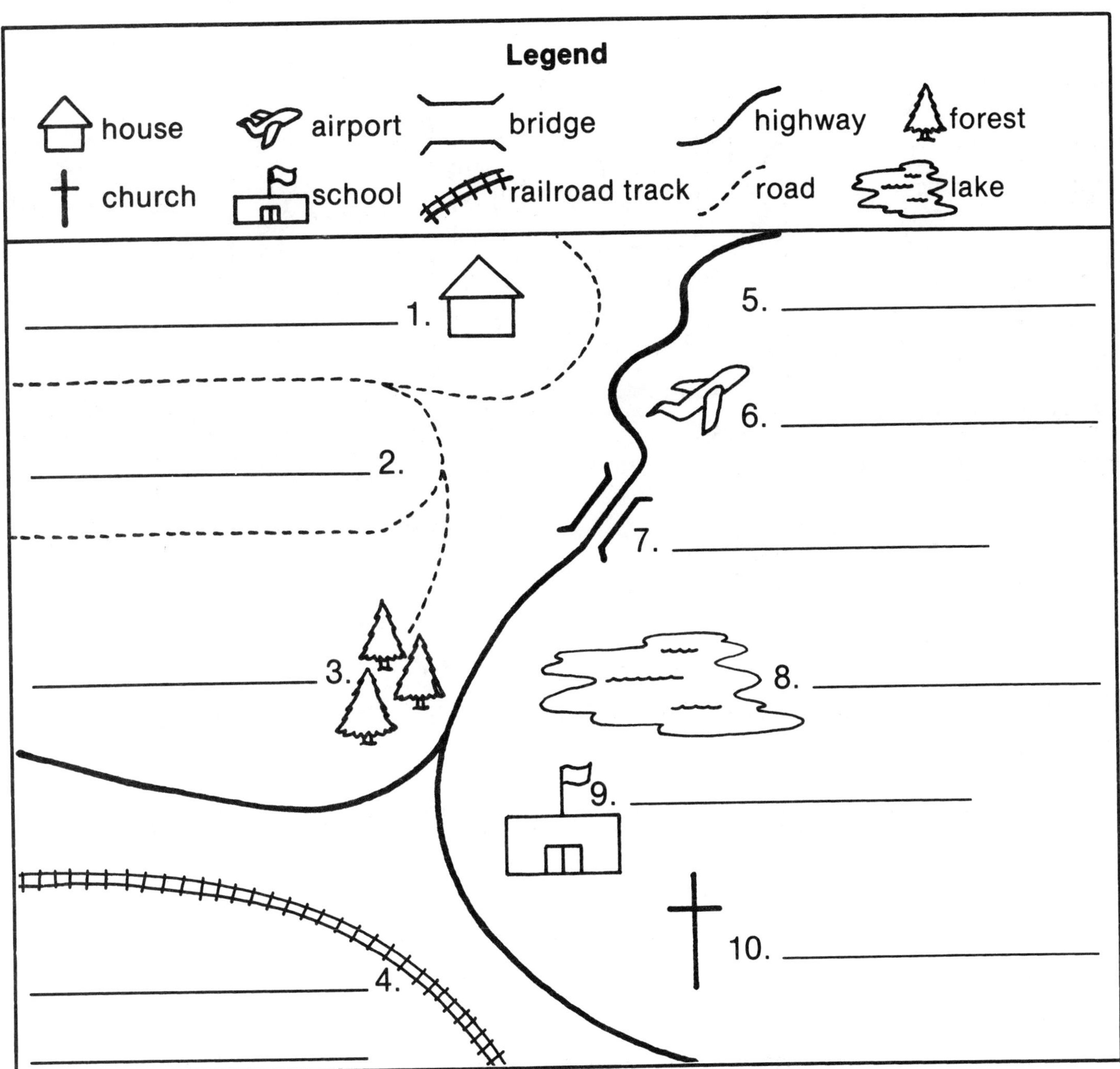

Brainwork! Draw a map of a make-believe city. Make a legend to show what symbols you will use on your map.

© Frank Schaffer Publications, Inc.

Name ______________________ Skill: Following directions

How Do We Get There?

Jim and Jenny are invited to a party at Clara's house. They have planned a route to walk to the party. Read their directions. Draw a line on the map below to show where Jim and Jenny will walk.

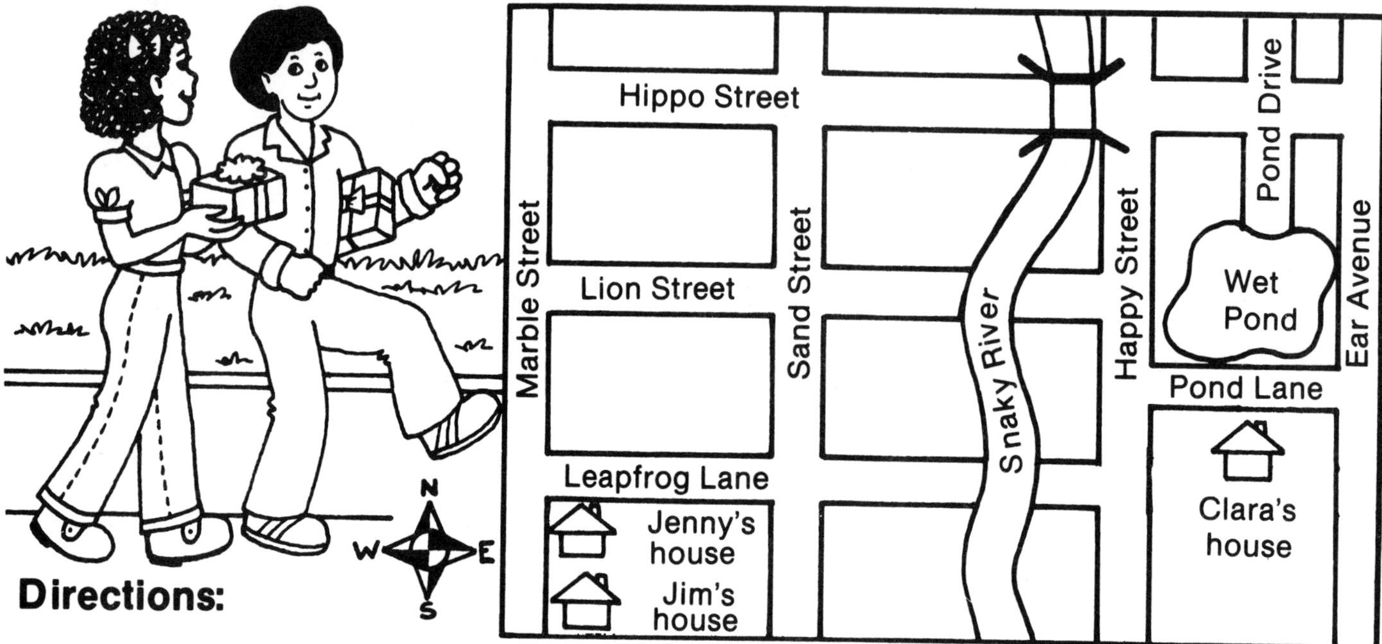

Directions:

1. Start at Jenny's house on Leapfrog Lane.
2. Go east one block.
3. Turn north on Sand Street and walk two blocks.
4. Turn east on Hippo Street and walk to the bridge.
5. Cross the bridge and walk two more blocks east.
6. Turn south on Ear Avenue and go to Pond Lane.
7. Go west on Pond Lane to Clara's house.

8. There is a shorter way to Clara's house **after** Jim and Jenny go across the bridge. Write the steps here. ______________________

____

____

____

____

Brainwork! Imagine you live on the corner of Hippo and Marble. Draw your house and your route to Clara's house.

© Frank Schaffer Publications, Inc.

Name ____

Point Me in the Right Direction

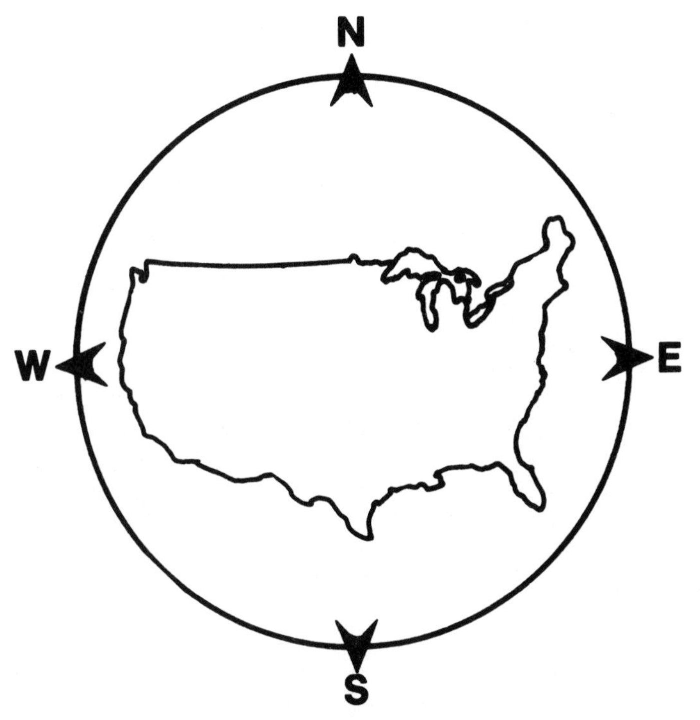

There are four main directions on a map: **n**orth, **e**ast, **w**est and **s**outh. Fill in the missing capital letter. On a map:

_____ orth is toward the top.

_____ ast is toward the right.

_____ est is toward the left.

_____ outh is toward the bottom.

Look at the letters you just wrote.

What word do they spell?

_____ _____ _____ _____

There are four other directions on a map. They are northeast, southeast, southwest and northwest. They come between the main directions. (Northeast is halfway between north and east.) Complete the blanks below by filling in the words **northeast, southeast, southwest** and **northwest** in the correct spaces.

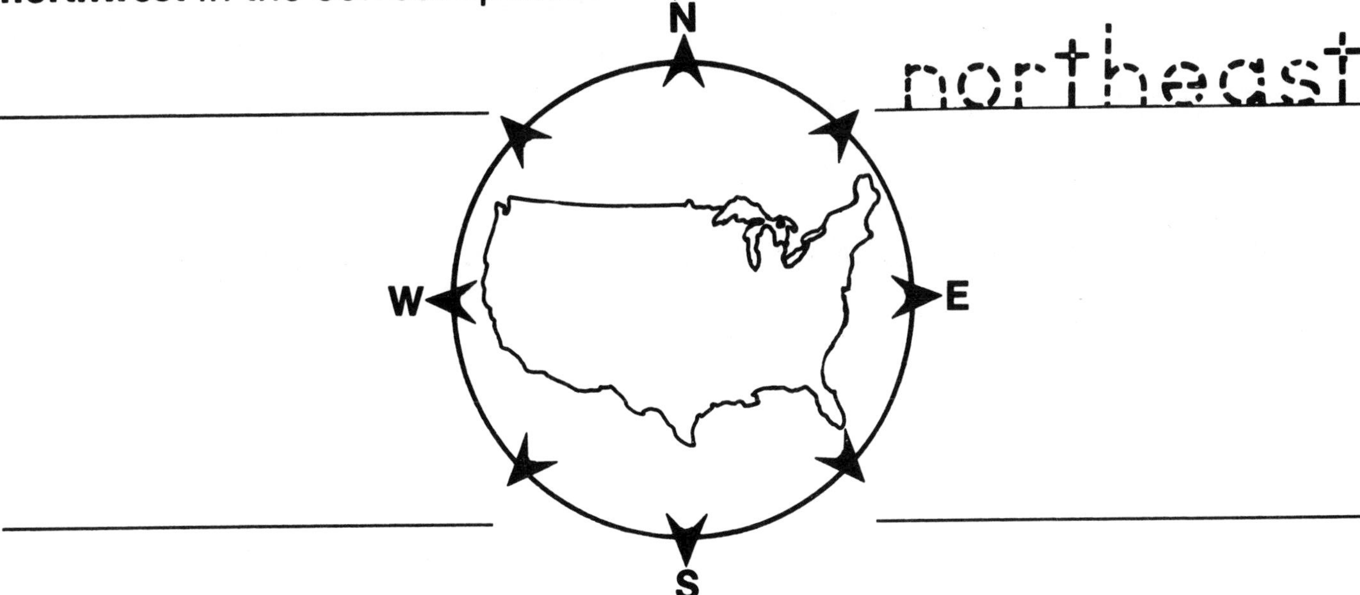

Brainwork! Find Alaska on a map. What country lies west of Alaska? What direction is your state from Alaska?

© Frank Schaffer Publications, Inc.

Name ______________________ Skill: Using direction names

Which Way Is North?

The **compass rose** can show eight direction names. Use the compass rose below to answer the following questions.

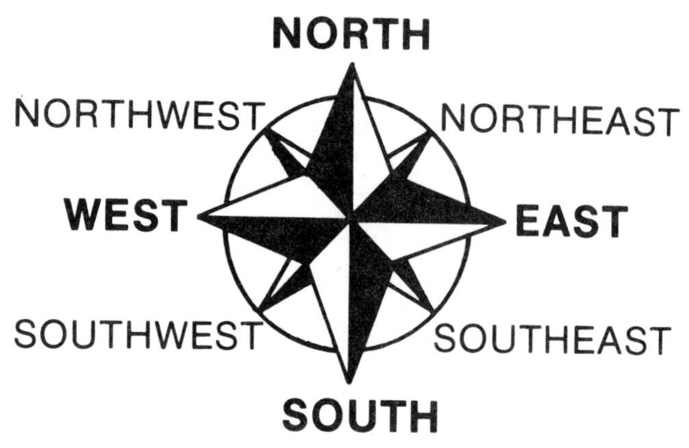

1. Which direction is between **north** and **east**? ______________
2. Which direction is between **west** and **south**? ______________
3. **Northwest** is between which two directions? ______________ and ______________
4. Which direction is between **south** and **east**? ______________

Write the direction names from the compass rose to complete the sentences below about the map of Marie's neighborhood.

MARIE'S NEIGHBORHOOD

ZOO
MARIE'S HOUSE
POST OFFICE
FIRE STATION
MARIE'S CHURCH
SCHOOL
PARK
POOL
LIBRARY
FRED'S HOUSE

5. When Marie's dad walks home from the fire station, he goes ______________ .
6. When Marie goes home from church, she walks ______________ .
7. When Fred meets Marie at the park, he must walk ______________ .
8. If Marie goes to the library after school, she walks ______________ .
9. Marie will walk ______________ to Fred's house.
10. Marie's class must walk ______________ to go on a field trip to the park.

Brainwork! Write three more sentences about the map above. Use direction words in each section.

Name ______________________________

Where in the World Are We?

You know that the earth is not flat. It is a very big ball, or sphere. Imagine being able to cut the earth in half, in the same way that you can cut an orange.

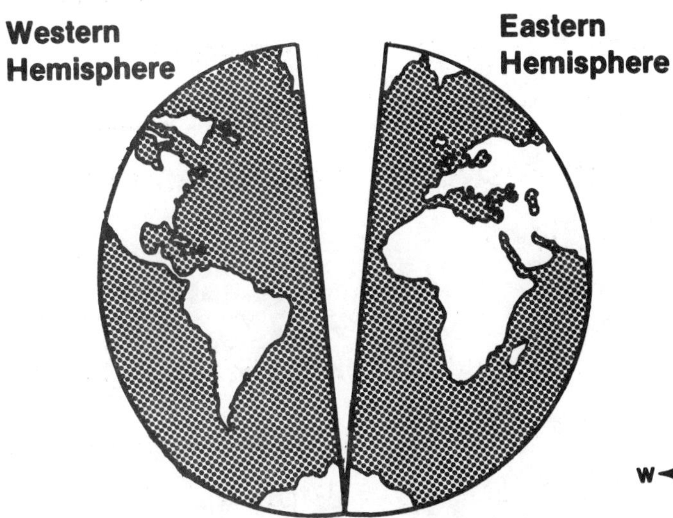

If you imagine cutting the earth in half, as shown in this picture, you would have two halves. The halves are called **hemispheres**. Hemisphere means "half-ball." Divided this way, the United States is in the Western Hemisphere.

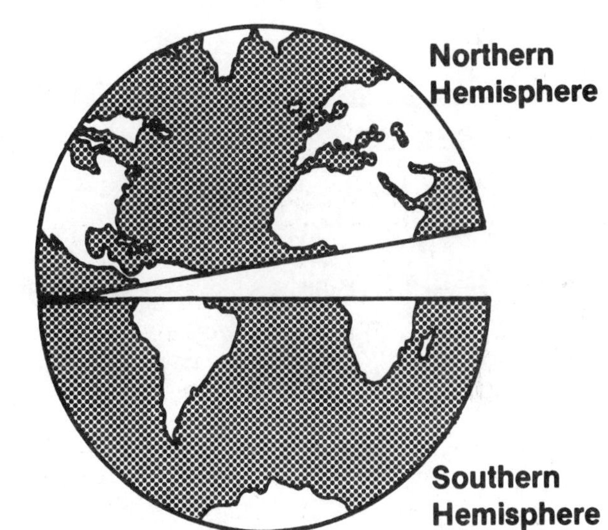

If you now imagine cutting the earth in half, as shown in this picture, you would still have two halves. They would still be called hemispheres but divided this way, the United States is in the Northern Hemisphere.

Write **yes** if the sentence is true, or **no** if it is not true.

1. __________ The earth is flat.
2. __________ A sphere is another name for a ball.
3. __________ The earth can really be cut in half.
4. __________ Hemisphere means "half-ball."
5. __________ The United States is in the Western Hemisphere.
6. __________ The United States is in the Northern Hemisphere.

Brainwork! Draw and label three common objects that are spheres and three that are hemispheres.

© Frank Schaffer Publications, Inc.

Name ______________________ Skill: Identifying regions in North America

North America, A Colorful Continent

Choose a different color for each place listed on the key and color the boxes next to each name. Then color the land areas on the map to match the key.

1. What country is north of the United States? ______________
2. What country is south of the United States? ______________
3. What large island is north of Canada? ______________

Brainwork! Make a map key to include the nine other North American countries which are south or east of Mexico.

© Frank Schaffer Publications, Inc.

Name ______________________________ Skill: Continents

Around the Globe

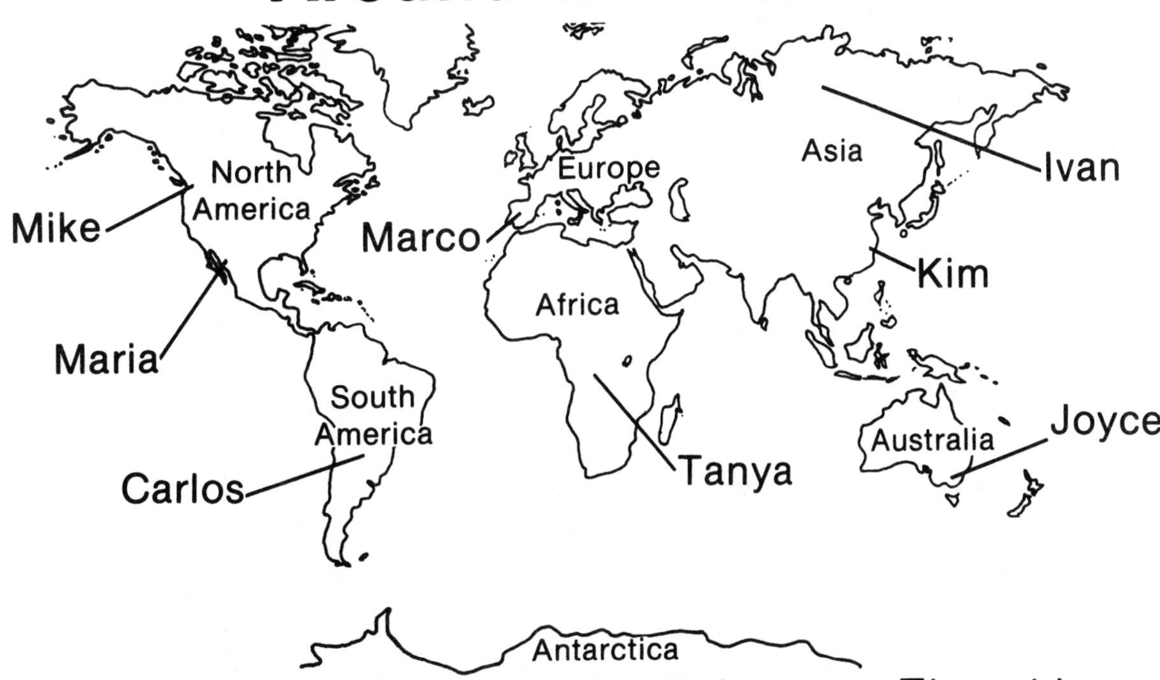

The world is divided into seven large land masses. These big areas are called **continents**. Their names are Asia, Africa, Europe, North America, South America, Australia, and Antarctica. Asia is the largest continent. More than half of the world's people live there. No one lives on Antarctica because it's too cold!

The map shows where some students were born. Fill in the table below with the correct continent names.

Names	Continents Where They Were Born
Carlos	
Ivan	
Tanya	
Mike	
Kim	
Marco	
Maria	
Joyce	

Brainwork! Draw a picture of the continent where you were born.

© Frank Schaffer Publications, Inc.

Name ________________________________ Skill: Reading a world map

Sail With Magellan

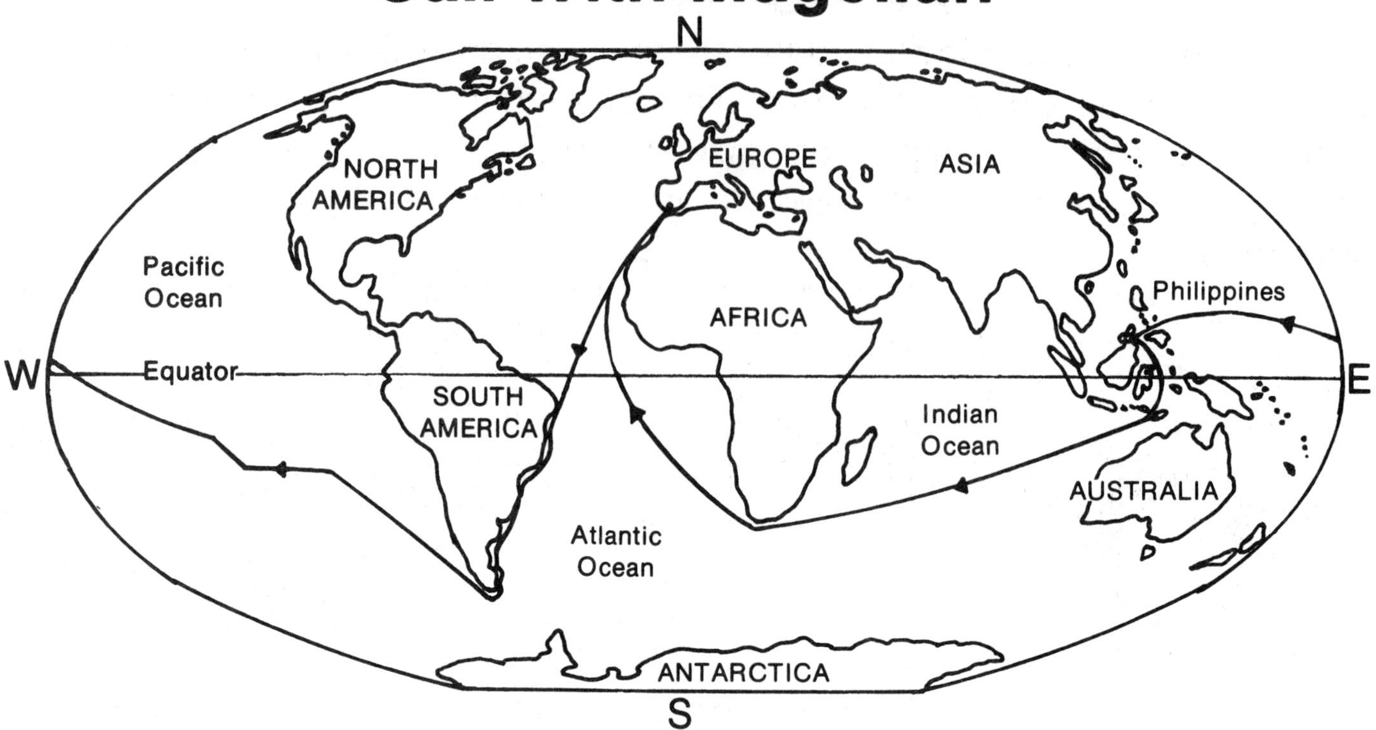

Magellan was the first person ever to lead ships around the world. Use the map to complete the sentences below.

1. The continent of ______________________ is south of North America. Magellan sailed around it first.
2. The first ocean he sailed on was the ______________ Ocean.
3. Magellan named the peaceful waters west of North America, the ______________________ .
4. Magellan died in the Philippine Islands. They are north of the continent called ______________________ .
5. The Indian Ocean is south of the continent called ____________ .
6. The continent of ______________________ is south of Europe. Magellan's men sailed around it to go back home.
7. Only one of Magellan's five ships and a few sailors finished the journey back to the continent of ______________ . It is ______________ of North America.

Brainwork! Draw something you'd like to sail in around the world.

© Frank Schaffer Publications, Inc.

Name ______________________________ Skill: Using coordinates

Mapping Out the Zoo!

Many maps have letters and numbers called **coordinates**. They are found along the sides of the map. The letters and numbers name each square. Coordinates help locate places and things on a map. For example, to find the gorilla cage on the zoo map below look inside square 3A.

Use the map to answer these questions.

1. What animal is inside of square 1A? ______________
2. In what square is Monkey Island? ______________
3. What animal is inside of square 3B? ______________
4. What square has a "Do Not Touch" sign? ______________
5. What animal is inside of square 3C? ______________
6. What square shows you how to cross the river? ______________
7. What animal is inside of square 1E? ______________
8. What should you feed the animal inside of square 2C? ______________
9. In what square is the drinking fountain? ______________

Brainwork! Draw an animal inside of square 1B, a pond inside of square 3D, and a picnic table inside of square 2A.

© Frank Schaffer Publications, Inc.

Name ______________________________

Skill: Using a map grid, Following directions

Find the Treasure

A treasure is hidden on this map **grid**. A grid is a set of lines. Along the margins of this grid are letters and numbers called **coordinates**. These letters and numbers name each square. (The horse is inside square B4.)

Follow these directions. Draw a line to show your path.

1. Start at the **X** in A1.
2. Go to the haystack in B2.
3. Walk around the hay and you will see an old house in A4. Go there.
4. Don't go in. That house is haunted. Run to the car in E5.
5. Whoops! There are no car keys. Cross over the bridge in E4.
6. Jump over the pond in D3.
7. Go north to C3. Walk over the log between C3 and C2.
8. Go to B1. Peek in the barn.
9. Now go straight south to the next square.
10. You have found the treasure! It is in the ______________.

Brainwork! Draw a map with a grid and pictures like the one above. Write directions to a treasure. Let a friend try to find your treasure!

© Frank Schaffer Publications, Inc.

Name ______________________ Skill: Recognizing types of maps

What Can You Tell From a Map?

Different maps of the same place tell different things about it.

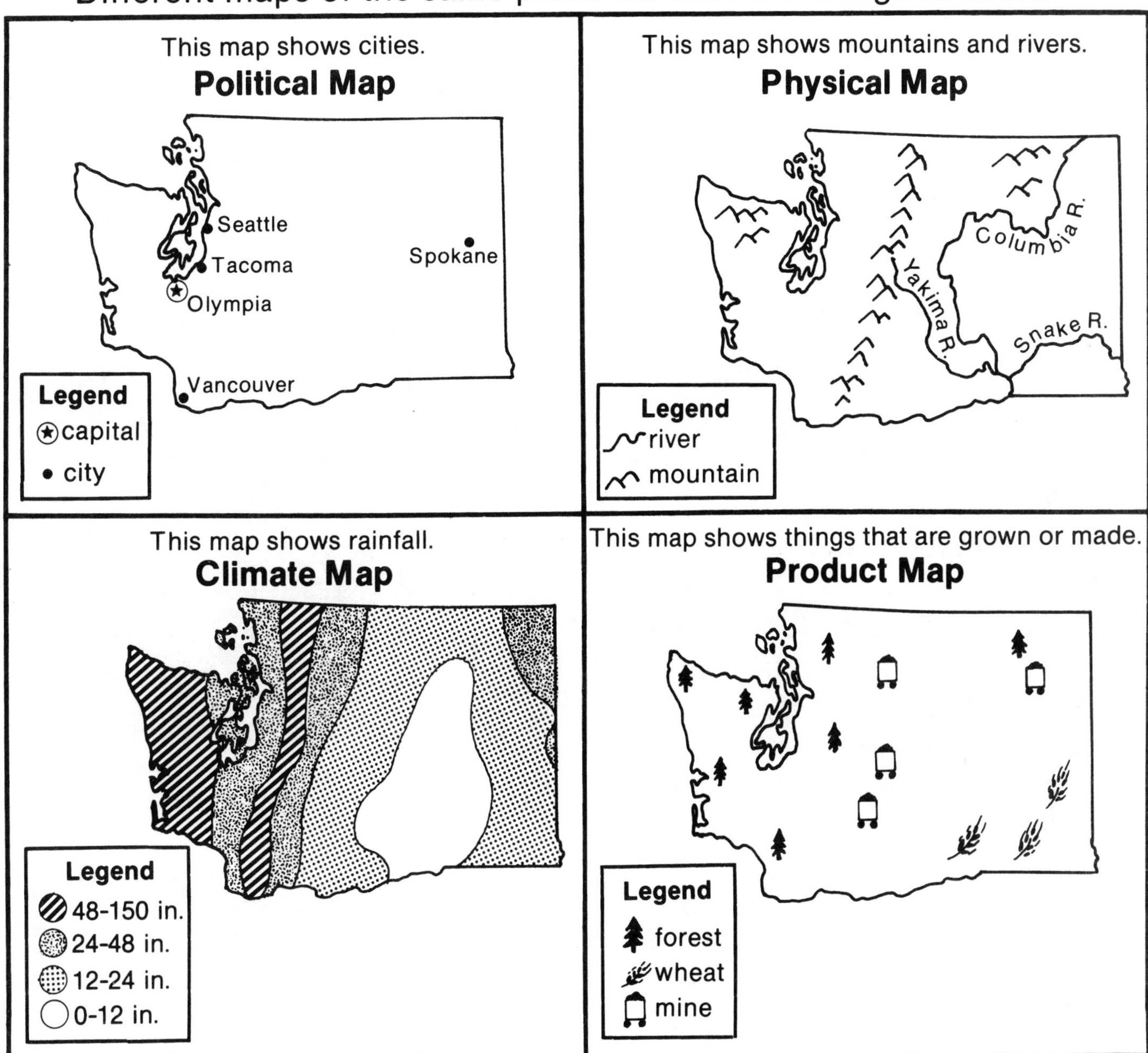

Write the name of the map that you could use to:

1. Find out where two major rivers cross. ______________________
2. Find the capital city of a state. ______________________
3. See how much it rains in a certain place. ______________________
4. Find out where forests are grown. ______________________
5. Learn where mountains are located. ______________________

Brainwork! Write five questions that can be answered with the maps above.

© Frank Schaffer Publications, Inc.

Name ________________________________ Skill: Understanding scale

Let's Take a Field Trip!

Each map has a **scale** that tells you the distance on the map that is equal to the real distance on earth. This map shows where some important buildings in a city are found. This is the scale for this map.

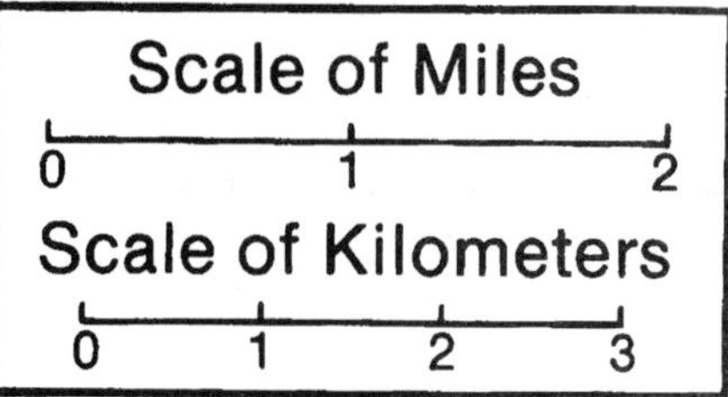

A class in Mulberry School would like to go to a place near the school for a field trip. The school's principal said the students cannot go more than one mile from school. Using the scale of miles, measure to find out which places are one mile or less from the school. Then complete the table below.

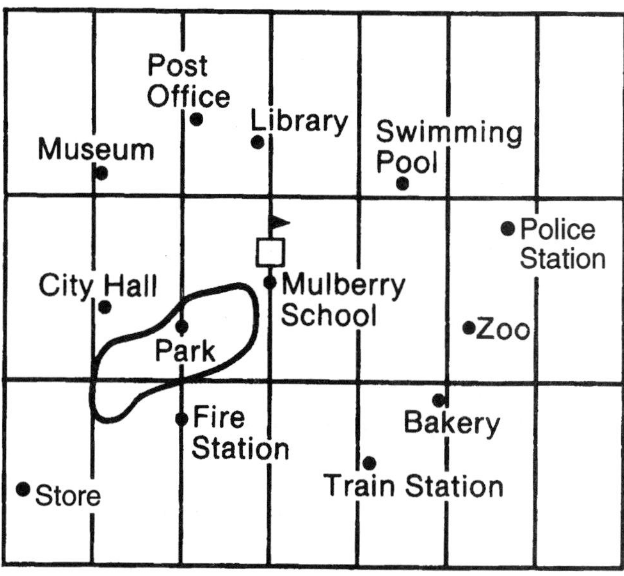

Places the Class Can Go	Places the Class Cannot Go

Brainwork! Find a map. Use its scale to write the distance between two places.

Name ______________________________ Skill: Using a scale

How Far Is It?

Use the scale on the map to answer the questions below. The entrance for each ride is shown by the [entrance symbol].

For example: How far is it from the park's main entrance to the entrance for the Double Ferris Wheel ride? 50 yards

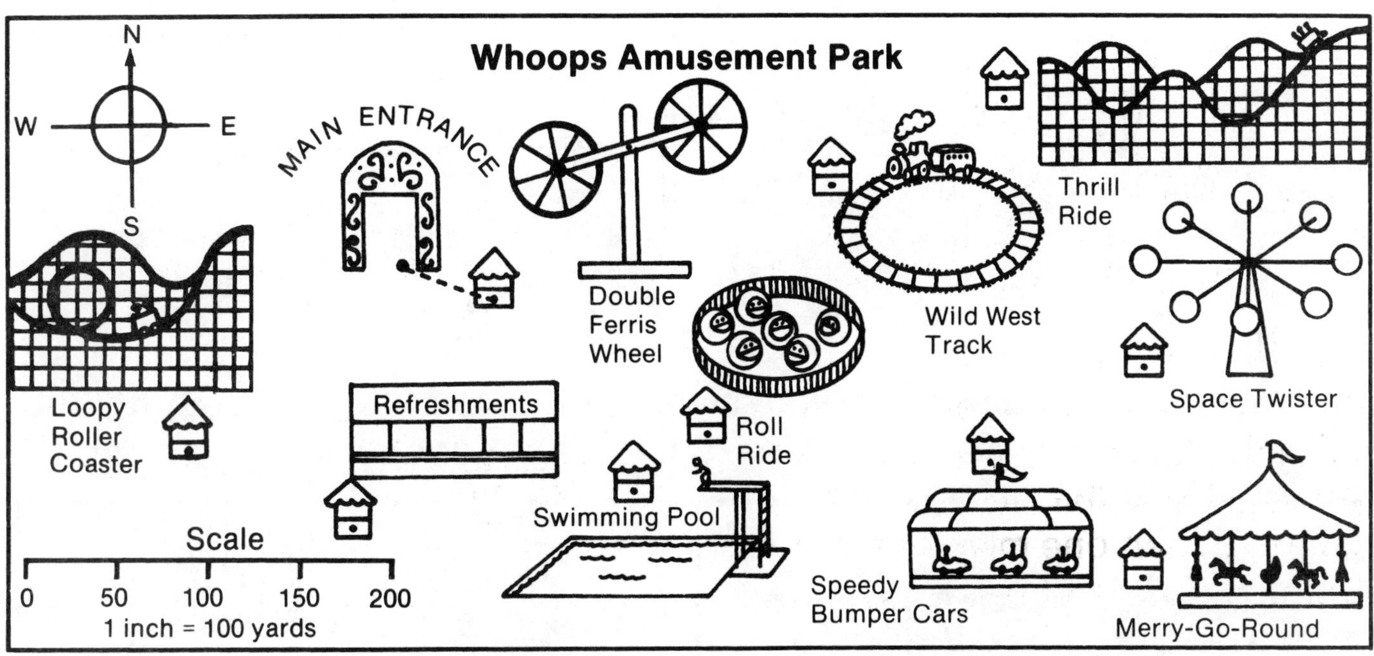

1. I want to go on the Loopy Roller Coaster first. How far is it from the park's main entrance? ______________________

2. I'm thirsty. How far do I have to go from the Loopy Roller Coaster to buy something to drink? ______________________

3. The Roll Ride looks like fun! How far is the ride from the refreshment stand? ______________________

4. How far is the swimming pool from the Roll Ride? ______________________

5. After a swim, I want to ride the Speedy Bumper Cars and the Space Twister. How far will I have to walk to ride both? ______________________

Brainwork! Which three rides would you like to go on? How far is each of them from the main entrance of the park?

© Frank Schaffer Publications, Inc.

Name ______________________________ Skill: Recognition of areas by configuration

Regions of the United States

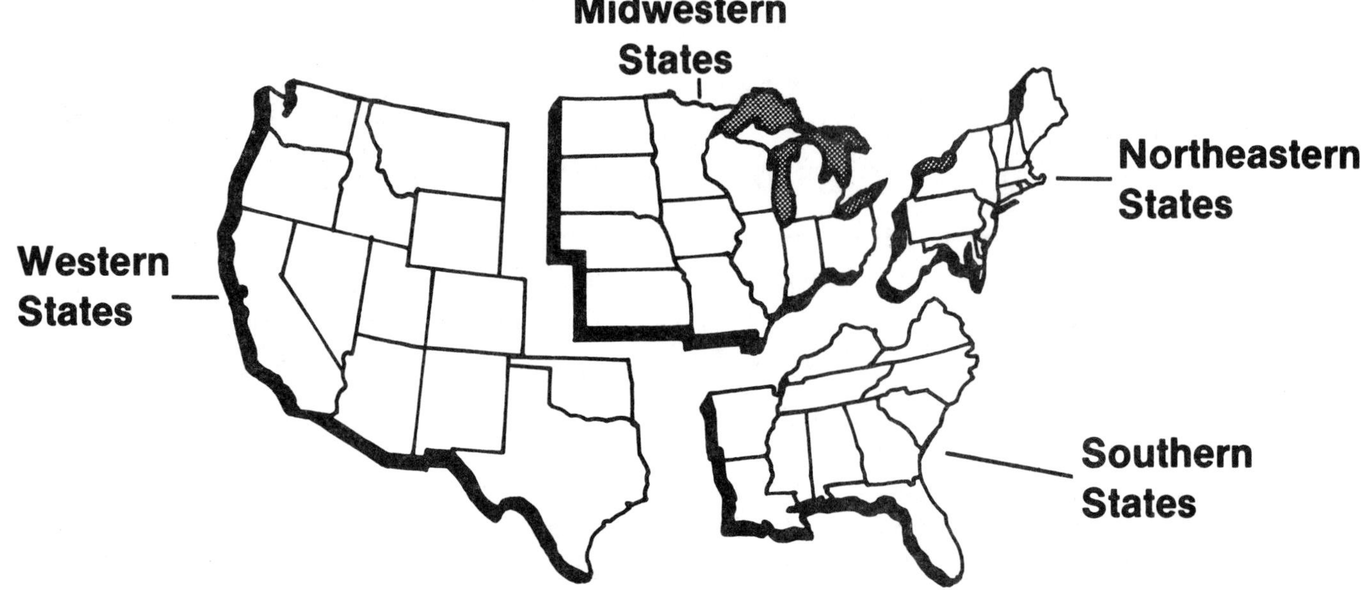

The map shows one way the states can be divided into areas. Study the shapes. Then write the name of the dark area shaded on each map below.

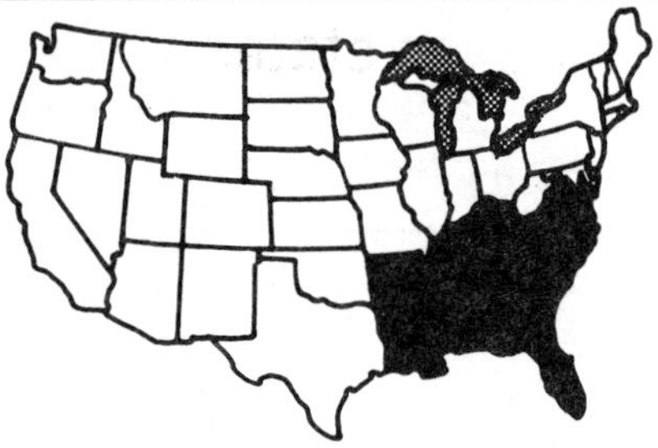

____

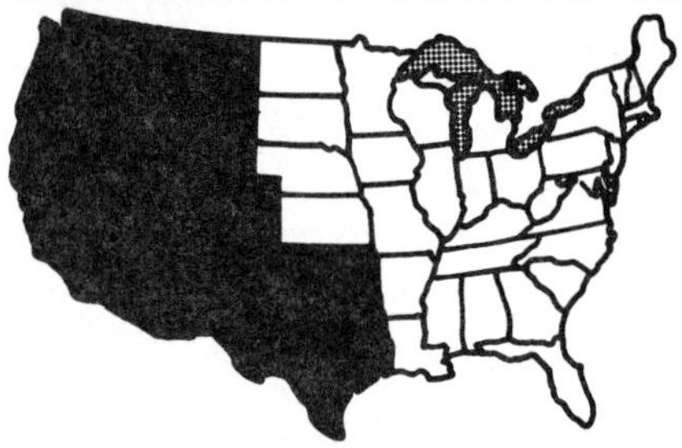

____

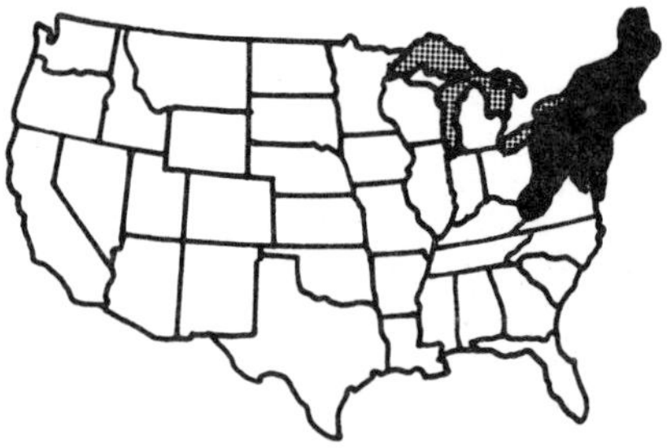

____

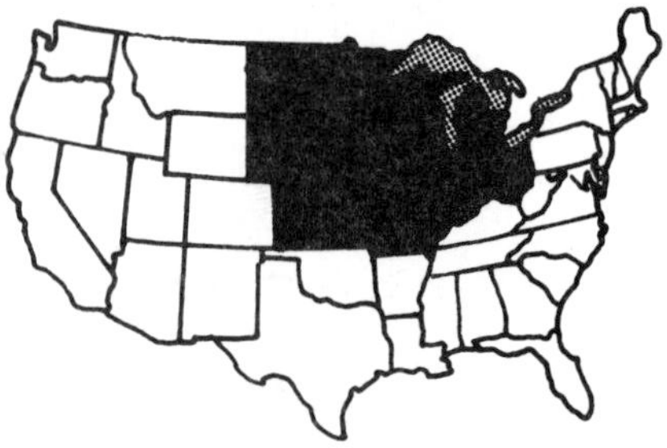

____

Brainwork! Write the area your state is in. List your state and all the other states in that area.

© Frank Schaffer Publications, Inc.

Name ______________________________ Skill: Visual discrimination

States in Sets

Use the large map to find and color the sets of states below.

1. Color the southern states green.

2. Color the midwestern states orange.

3. Color the western states yellow.

4. Color the northeastern states blue.

Brainwork! What two western states are not shown on this map? (Clue: They are not connected to the rest of the U.S.) Draw their shapes.

Name ______________________________ Skill: Recognizing configuration

United States Assembly

Cut out the puzzle pieces. Fit them together to make a map of the United States. Then glue them onto paper.

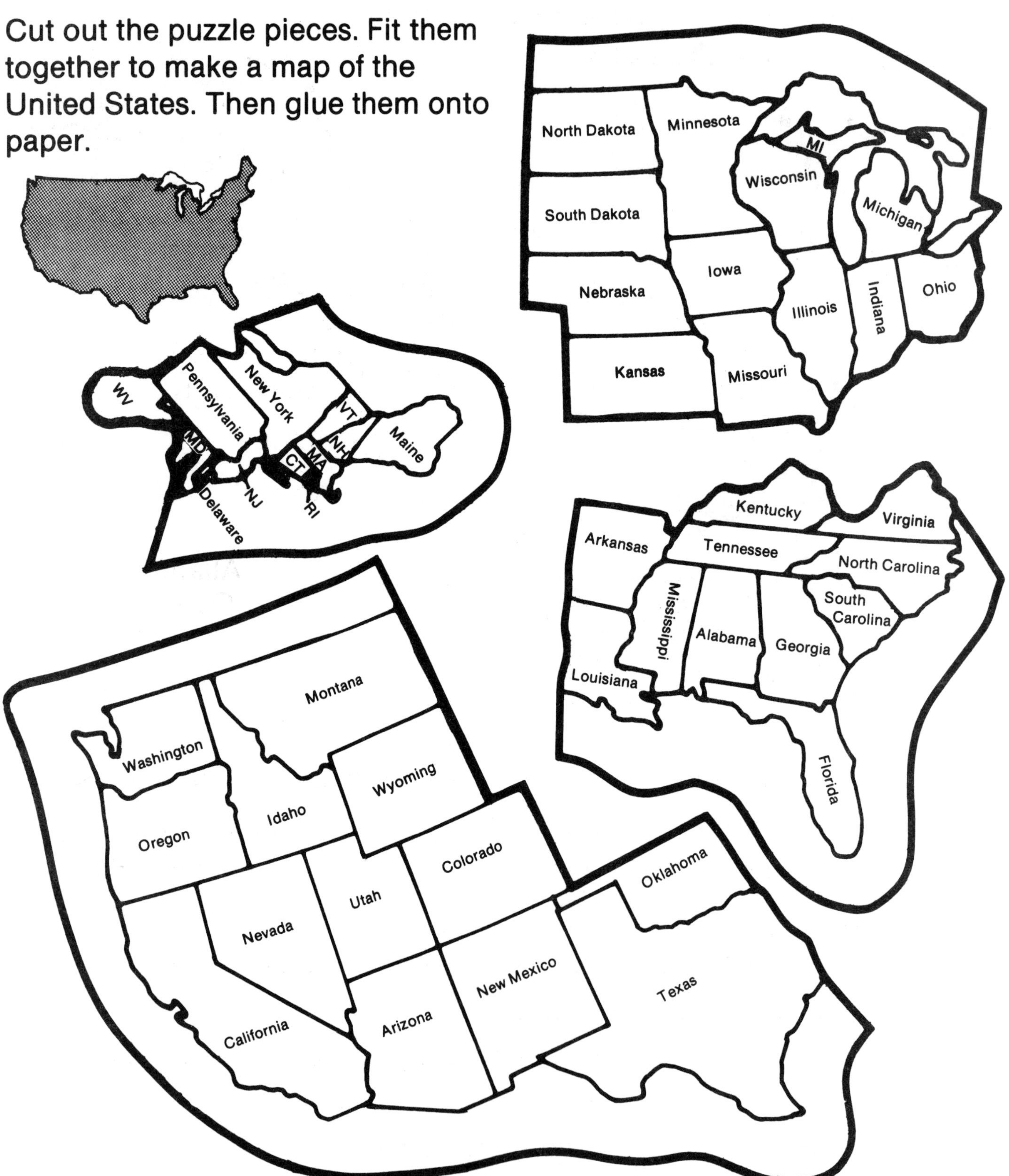

Brainwork! Color your state red.

Name ______________________________ Skill: Map reading

The Northeastern States

Use this map of the northeastern United States to help you do the activities below.

N W E S

Canada

Maine

Vermont

L. Ontario

New York

New Hampshire

Massachusetts

L. Erie

Rhode Island

Connecticut

Pennsylvania

New Jersey

Atlantic Ocean

West Virginia

Maryland

Delaware

1. How many states are part of the northeastern United States? ______
2. Which state is farthest north and east? ______________________
3. Which state do you think has a name that means "Penn's woods?"

   ____

4. The **L.** in **L. Ontario** stands for **Lake**. What state touches Lake Ontario? ______________________
5. Color all the northeastern states that do not touch the Atlantic Ocean **green**.
6. Color the smallest state, Rhode Island, **red**.

Brainwork! Write the names of the northeastern states in ABC order.

Name ____________________ Skill: Map reading

The Southern States

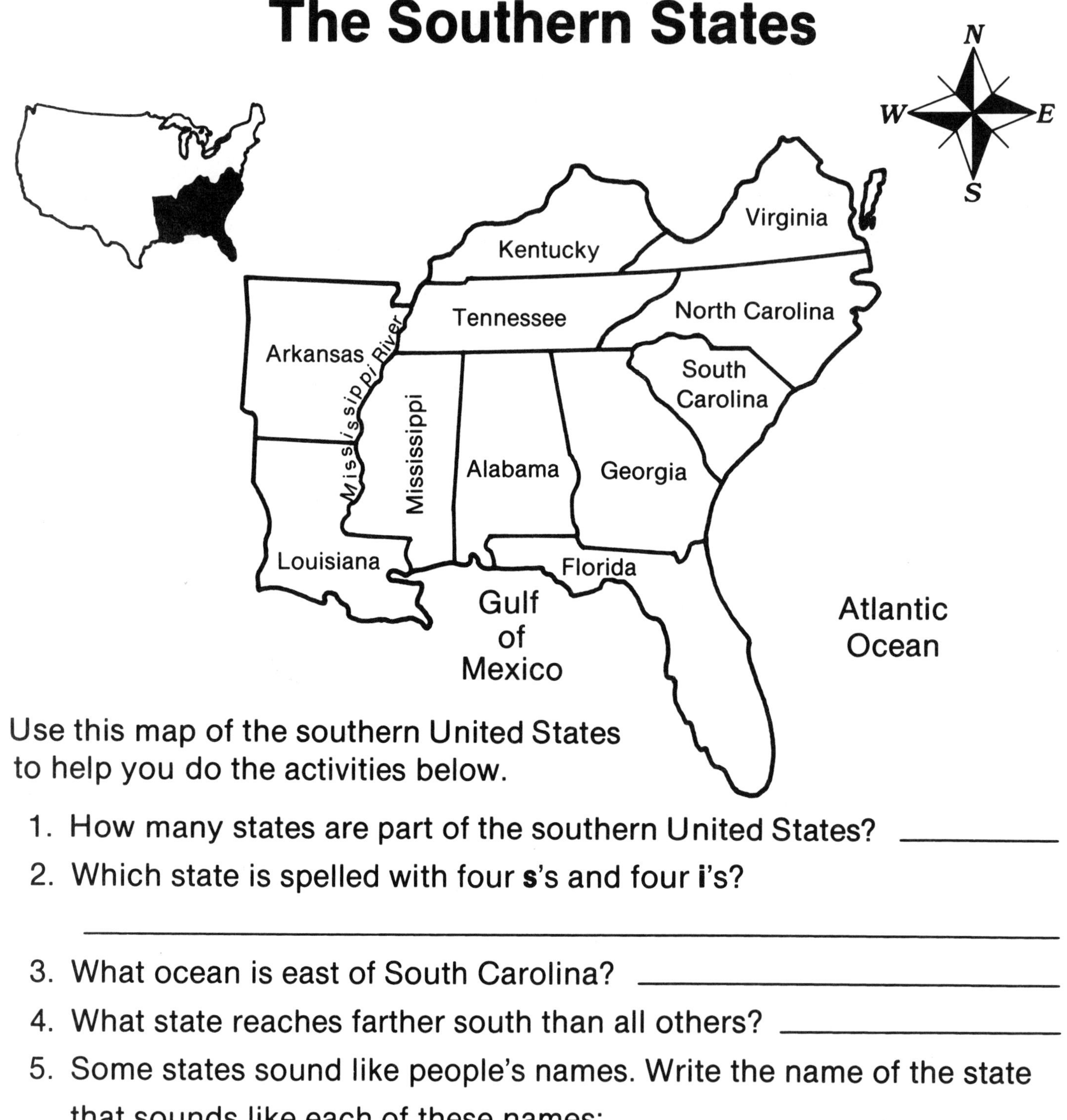

Use this map of the southern United States to help you do the activities below.

1. How many states are part of the southern United States? ________
2. Which state is spelled with four **s**'s and four **i**'s?

   ____
3. What ocean is east of South Carolina? ____________
4. What state reaches farther south than all others? ____________
5. Some states sound like people's names. Write the name of the state that sounds like each of these names:

   George ____________ Carol ____________

   Louise ____________ Ken ____________

Brainwork! Georgia is known for its peanut crop. Find out what president came from Georgia and raised peanuts! Write three facts about him.

© Frank Schaffer Publications, Inc.

Name ______________________________ Skill: Map reading

The Midwestern States

Use this map of the midwestern United States to help you do the activities below.

1. How many states are part of the midwestern United States? ______
2. The **L.** in **L. Michigan** stands for **Lake.** How many states touch Lake Michigan? ______________
3. Two rivers are shown on the map. What are their names? ________ ______________________________
4. Name a state that touches both rivers. ______________________
5. What state has two parts separated by a lake? ________________
6. What state is south of Minnesota? ______________________
7. Color the four lakes shown on the map **blue**.
8. Color the states whose names begin with vowels **orange**.

Brainwork! Find out what these midwestern cities have to do with cars: Indianapolis, Indiana and Detroit, Michigan. Write your findings.

© Frank Schaffer Publications, Inc.

Name ______________________ Skill: Map reading

The Western States

Use this map of the western United States to help you do the activities below.

1. How many states are part of the western United States? ________
2. What ocean is west of California? ________
3. What state is a group of islands? ________
4. What state on the map begins with I? ________
5. How many states shown begin with C? ______ A? ______ O? ______
6. If you were driving from Arizona to Utah, which direction would you be driving? ________
7. Which state has the name of a president? ________

Brainwork! In what states would you find each of these things: polar bear, lei, the Grand Canyon, and Sequoia trees?

© Frank Schaffer Publications, Inc.

Name ____________________ Skill: State abbreviations—western U.S.

USA for Short

Each state is numbered. Find it on the map. Write the state's two-letter abbreviation next to its name.

1
AK
not to scale

2
HI
not to scale

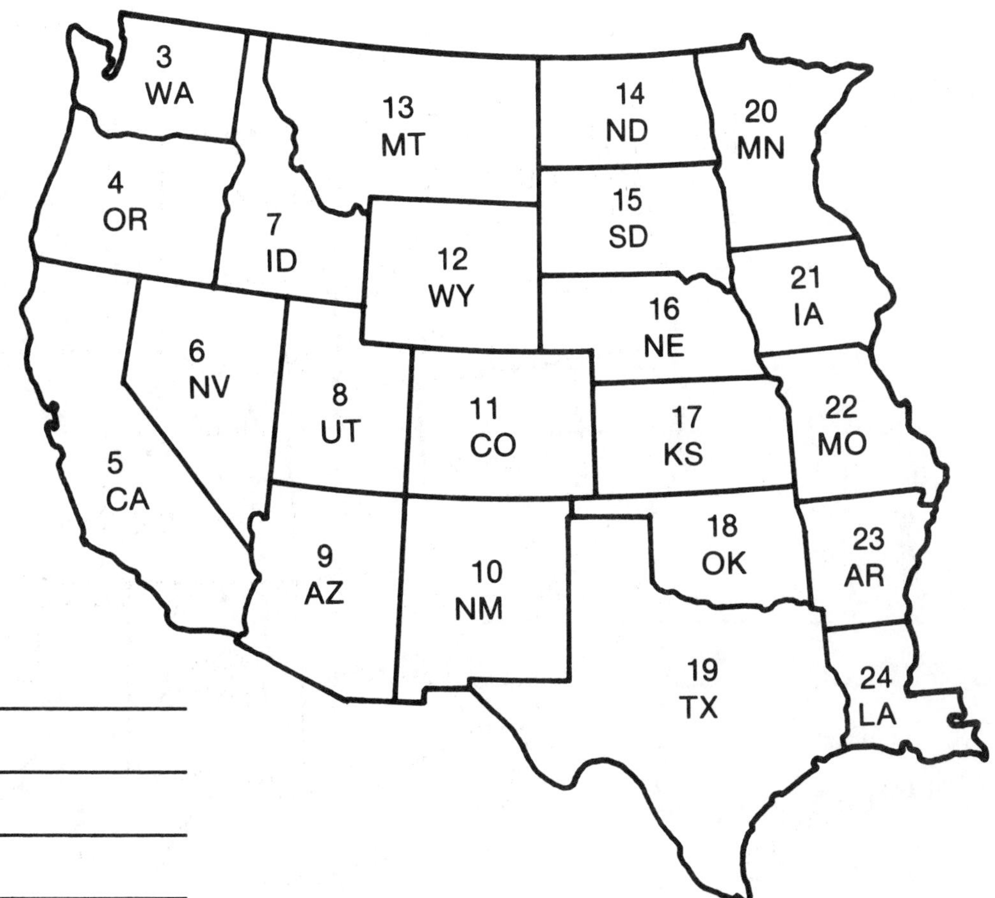

1. Alaska ________
2. Hawaii ________
3. Washington ________
4. Oregon ________
5. California ________
6. Nevada ________
7. Idaho ________
8. Utah ________
9. Arizona ________
10. New Mexico ________
11. Colorado ________
12. Wyoming ________
13. Montana ________
14. North Dakota ________
15. South Dakota ________
16. Nebraska ________
17. Kansas ________
18. Oklahoma ________
19. Texas ________
20. Minnesota ________
21. Iowa ________
22. Missouri ________
23. Arkansas ________
24. Louisiana ________

Brainwork! Color the ten states that have the first two letters of their name as their abbreviations.

© Frank Schaffer Publications, Inc.

Name ______________________ Skill: State abbreviations—eastern U.S.

USA for Short

Each state is numbered. Find it on the map. Write the state's two-letter abbreviation next to its name.

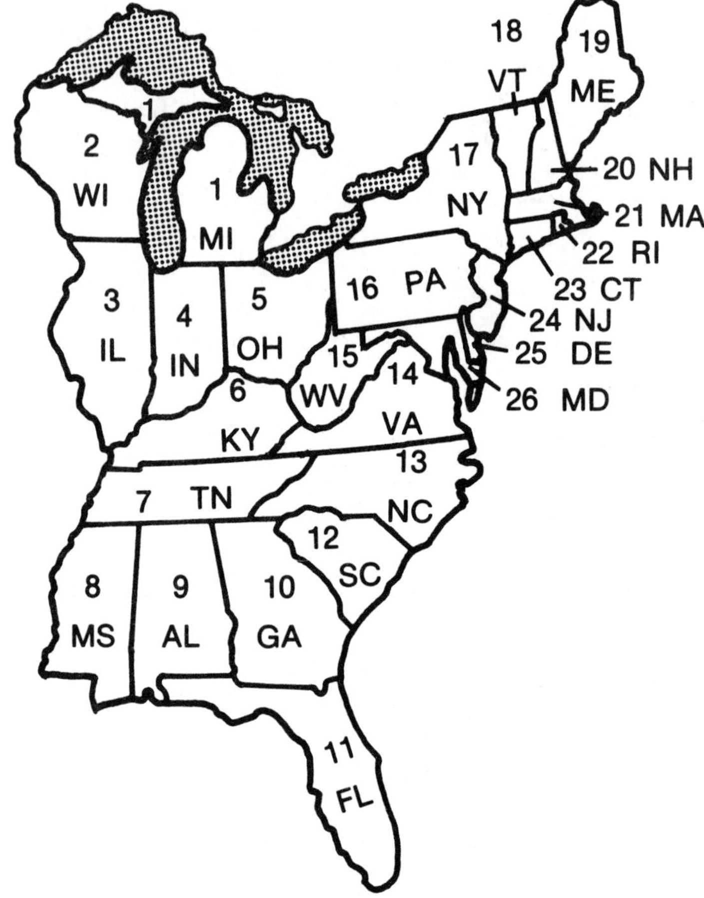

1. Michigan __________
2. Wisconsin __________
3. Illinois __________
4. Indiana __________
5. Ohio __________
6. Kentucky __________
7. Tennessee __________
8. Mississippi __________
9. Alabama __________
10. Georgia __________
11. Florida __________
12. South Carolina __________
13. North Carolina __________
14. Virginia __________
15. West Virginia __________
16. Pennsylvania __________
17. New York __________
18. Vermont __________
19. Maine __________
20. New Hampshire __________
21. Massachusetts __________
22. Rhode Island __________
23. Connecticut __________
24. New Jersey __________
25. Delaware __________
26. Maryland __________

Brainwork! Color the eight states whose abbreviations are the first and last letters of their names.

© Frank Schaffer Publications, Inc.

Name ______________________

Major City Hunt

Each • on the map stands for a city. Read the clues below. Write the clue number in the box by the city it tells about.

1. **Washington, D.C.** is the capital ⊛ of the U.S. The president lives there. It lies between Maryland and Virginia.

2. **Los Angeles** is the largest city in California. It is next to the Pacific Ocean in the west.

3. **Chicago** lies on the tip of Lake Michigan in the midwestern state of Illinois.

4. **New York City** is at the tip of New York State on the Atlantic Ocean. This eastern city is the largest city in the U.S.

5. **Dallas**, Texas, is one of the fastest growing cities in the U.S.

6. In the northwest state of Washington is **Seattle**.Its nearby forests have many trees.

Brainwork! Write five sentences that tell about a real or imaginary trip that includes five different states.

© Frank Schaffer Publications, Inc.

Name ______________________ Skill: Drawing conclusions

What State Am I?

Read the clues. Write the name of the state.

States
Hawaii, Rhode Island
Florida, Texas
California, Alaska

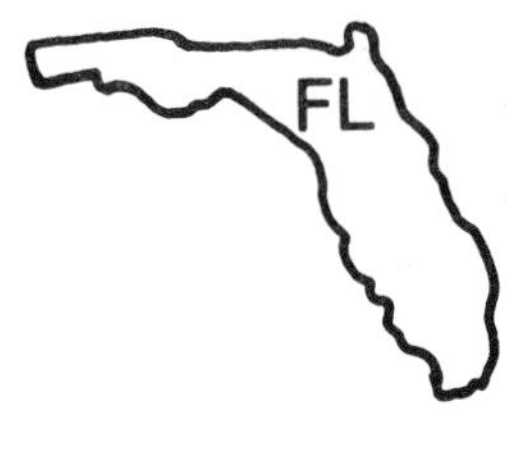

1. I am a southern state. One of my cities is Miami. I have ocean on three sides.

I am the state of

____

2. I am the largest state and the farthest north. It is cool or cold most of the time here.

I am the state of

____

3. I am the smallest state. I am found on the east coast. My name is tricky because I am not really an island.

I am the state of

____

4. People first rushed to me to look for gold. I am on the west coast. You can visit Disneyland here.

I am the state of

____

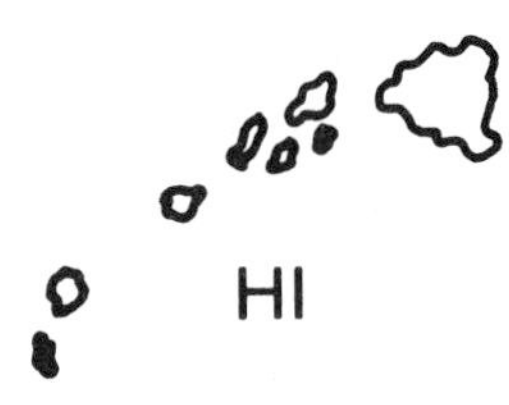

5. I am the only state that is a group of islands. You can visit me in the Pacific Ocean.

I am the state of

____

6. I am a big state. Mexico lies just south of me. Dallas is one of my cities.

I am the state of

____

Brainwork! Write a riddle about another state.

© Frank Schaffer Publications, Inc.

Name ________________________________ Skill: Using a map index

Know Your State Capitals!

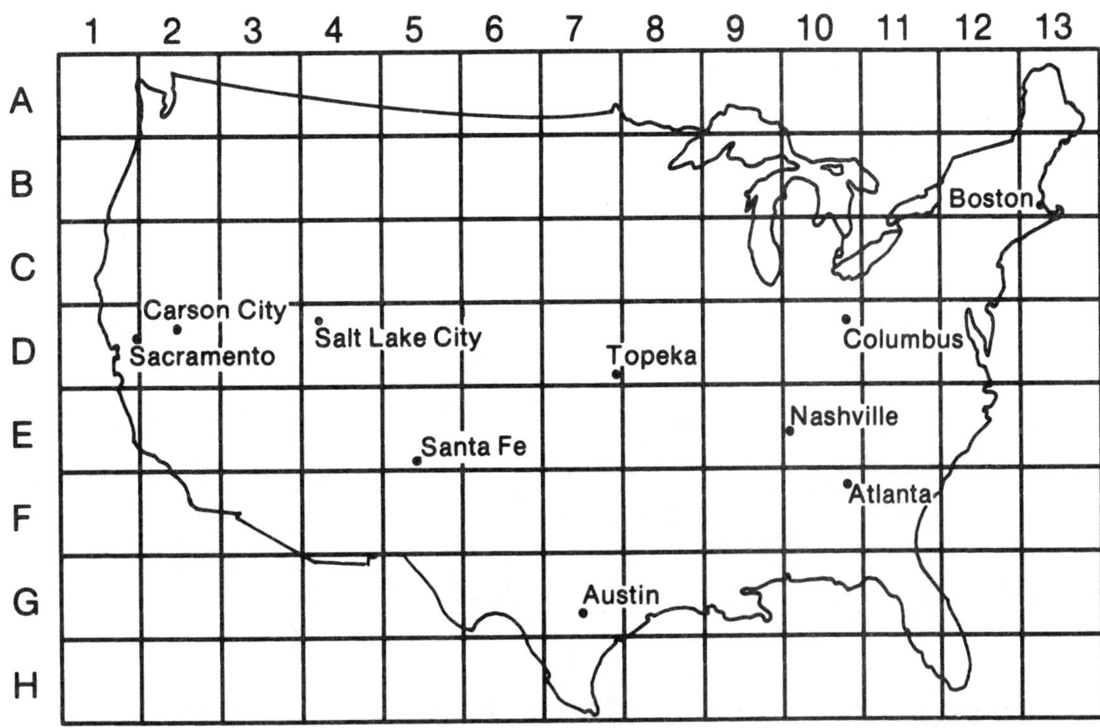

The **map index** below lists certain states. The letter and number after each state tell you in which square you'll find its capital city. The letter and number pairs are called **coordinates**. Write the name of the capital city before its state name on the map index below.

1. ________________________ (Utah) D4
2. ________________________ (California) D1
3. ________________________ (Massachusetts) B13
4. ________________________ (Georgia) F10
5. ________________________ (Nevada) D2
6. ________________________ (New Mexico) E5
7. ________________________ (Tennessee) E10
8. ________________________ (Ohio) D10
9. ________________________ (Kansas) D7
10. ________________________ (Texas) G7

Brainwork! Use a United States map to locate and write the names of three other state capitals on the map above.

© Frank Schaffer Publications, Inc.

Name ______________________ Skill: Unscramble state names

Scrambled States

The names of twelve states are spelled correctly on the map. Unscramble the mixed-up words below to spell the names of these states.

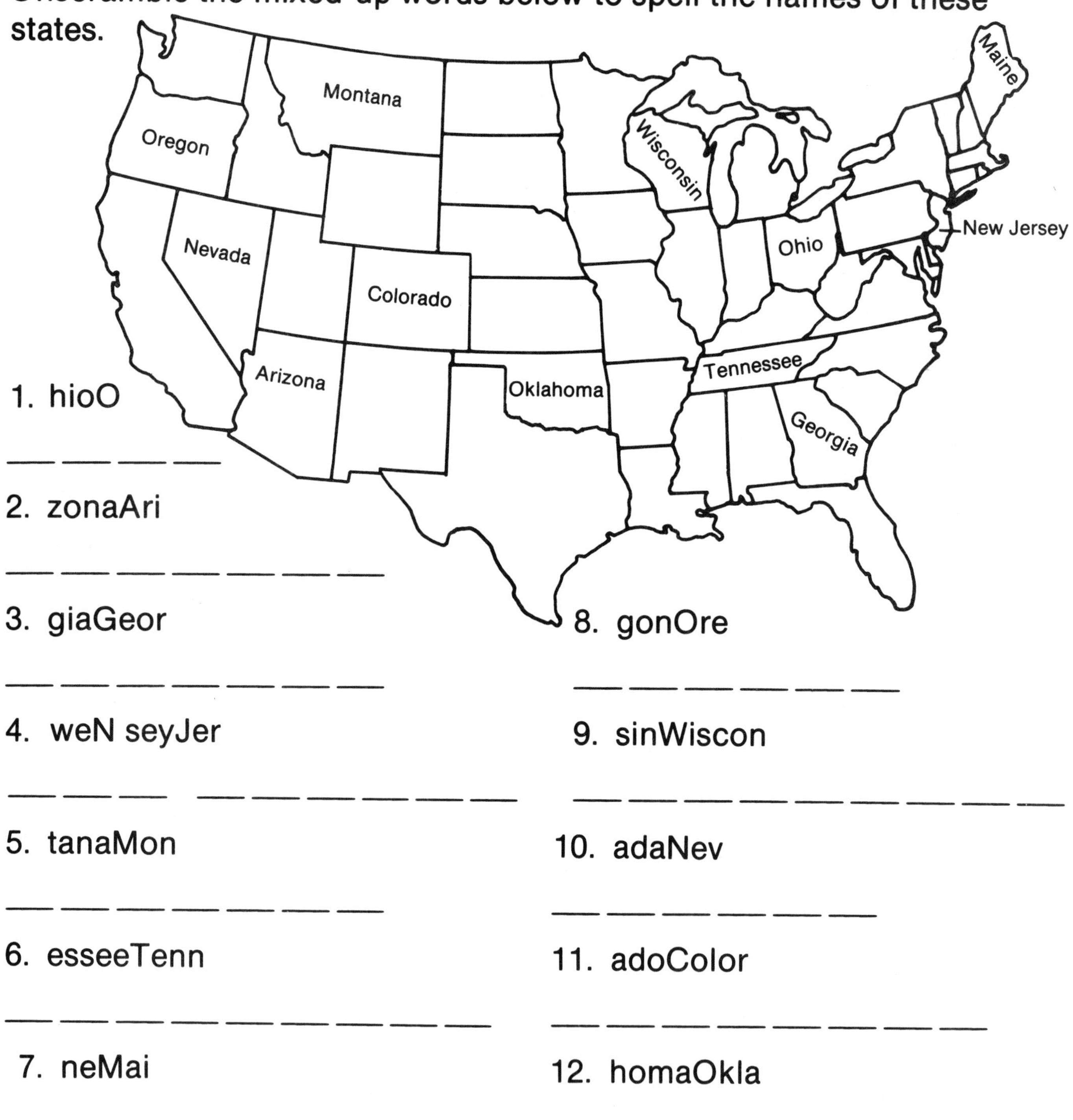

1. hioO

__ __ __ __

2. zonaAri

__ __ __ __ __ __ __

3. giaGeor

__ __ __ __ __ __ __

4. weN seyJer

__ __ __ __ __ __ __ __ __

5. tanaMon

__ __ __ __ __ __ __

6. esseeTenn

__ __ __ __ __ __ __ __ __

7. neMai

__ __ __ __ __

8. gonOre

__ __ __ __ __ __

9. sinWiscon

__ __ __ __ __ __ __ __ __

10. adaNev

__ __ __ __ __ __

11. adoColor

__ __ __ __ __ __ __ __

12. homaOkla

__ __ __ __ __ __ __ __

Brainwork! Scramble the names of five other states. Give them to a friend to unscramble.

© Frank Schaffer Publications, Inc.

Name ______________________ Skill: Recognition of state names

A State or Not?

If a block has the name of a state, color the block **blue**. If it has the name of another place, color the block **red**.

Missouri
Maryland
North America
Chicago
Los Angeles
Delaware
Vermont
Connecticut
Miami
Germany
Massachusetts
Michigan
Dallas
Greenland
Iowa
Mexico
Illinois
New Mexico
Japan
Utah
Louisiana
Idaho
Pacific
Alabama
Boston
Atlantic
U.S.S.R.
New Hampshire
Arkansas

Brainwork! Write the names of other countries you found in the puzzle.

© Frank Schaffer Publications, Inc.

Name ______________________________ Skill: Sequencing

Trip Through the States

Nancy will tell about her cross-country trip. Her stops are correctly numbered on the map, but her sentences are out of order. Cut apart the sentences and paste them in the correct order on another paper.

It seemed like we had been driving a long time. When we stopped at a hotel the first night, we were in Chicago, Illinois.

From Chicago we drove northwest. We stopped in South Dakota to see Mt. Rushmore.

Our trip began in Pittsburgh, Pennsylvania. We were ready to travel west.

To end our trip, we went all the way to the west coast, to see the redwood trees in northern California. The ocean was great.

Next, we drove southwest to Salt Lake in Utah. The water is so salty in the lake that it was easy to keep afloat.

© Frank Schaffer Publications, Inc.

Name ________________________ Skill: Application of information

Know Your State

Find and color your state on this map. Answer the questions.

1. In what area is your state located? (Northeast, South, West, Midwest)

   ____

2. What other states does your state touch? ________________________

   ____

3. Name a big city in your state. ________________________
4. What is the abbreviation of your state? ____________
5. What special place can people visit in your state?

   ____

6. What is your state famous for? ________________________

   ____

7. What do you like best about your state?

   ____

Brainwork! Write the name of your state bird, flower, and song.

© Frank Schaffer Publications, Inc.

Name ______________________________ Skill: Report writing

My State Report

State Shape

State Flag

Name of state ______________________________

State nickname ______________________________

Capital city ______________________________

Location of state ______________________________

Facts about the land: ______________________________

____

Facts about the people: ______________________________

____

Historical facts: ______________________________

____

A famous person from the state ______________________________

State Flower

State Bird

Brainwork! Make a travel poster advertising your state.

© Frank Schaffer Publications, Inc.

Answer Key

Our Flag

This page may be used as a book cover.

The Flag of the United States

Fifty white stars
On a field of blue;
Seven red stripes,
And six white ones, too.

Name ______________________

Page 1

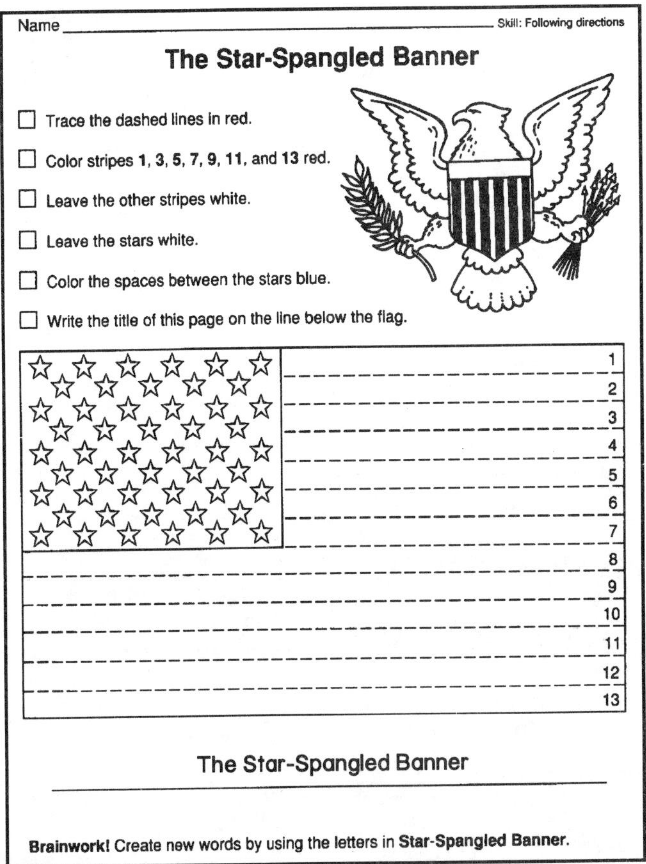

Name ______________________ Skill: Following directions

The Star-Spangled Banner

☐ Trace the dashed lines in red.

☐ Color stripes **1**, **3**, **5**, **7**, **9**, **11**, and **13** red.

☐ Leave the other stripes white.

☐ Leave the stars white.

☐ Color the spaces between the stars blue.

☐ Write the title of this page on the line below the flag.

1 2 3 4 5 6 7 8 9 10 11 12 13

The Star-Spangled Banner

Brainwork! Create new words by using the letters in **Star-Spangled Banner.**

Page 2

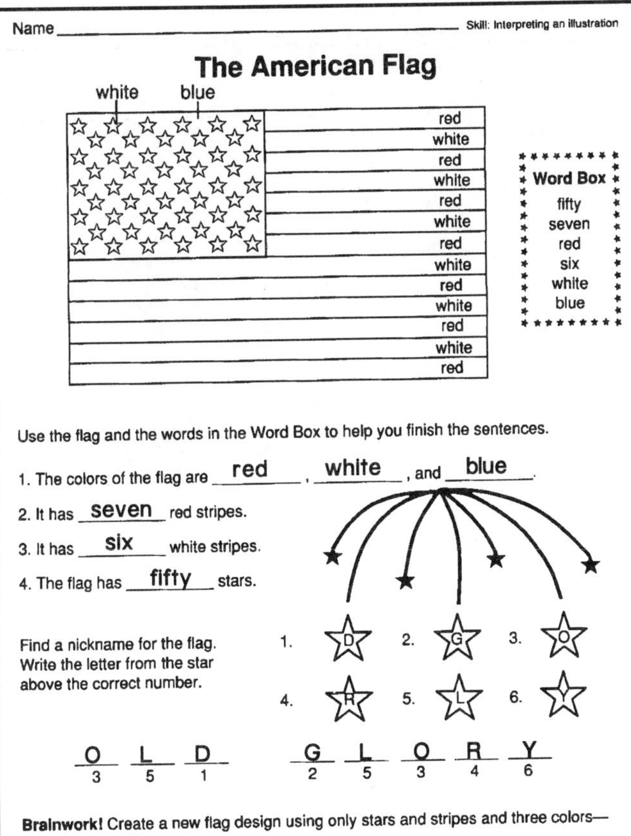

Name ______________________ Skill: Interpreting an illustration

The American Flag

white, blue

red, white, red, white, red, white, red, white, red, white, red, white, red

Word Box: fifty, seven, red, six, white, blue

Use the flag and the words in the Word Box to help you finish the sentences.

1. The colors of the flag are red, white, and blue.
2. It has seven red stripes.
3. It has six white stripes.
4. The flag has fifty stars.

Find a nickname for the flag. Write the letter from the star above the correct number.

1. D 2. G 3. O 4. R 5. L 6. Y

O L D G L O R Y
3 5 1 2 5 3 4 6

Brainwork! Create a new flag design using only stars and stripes and three colors—red, white, and blue.

Page 3

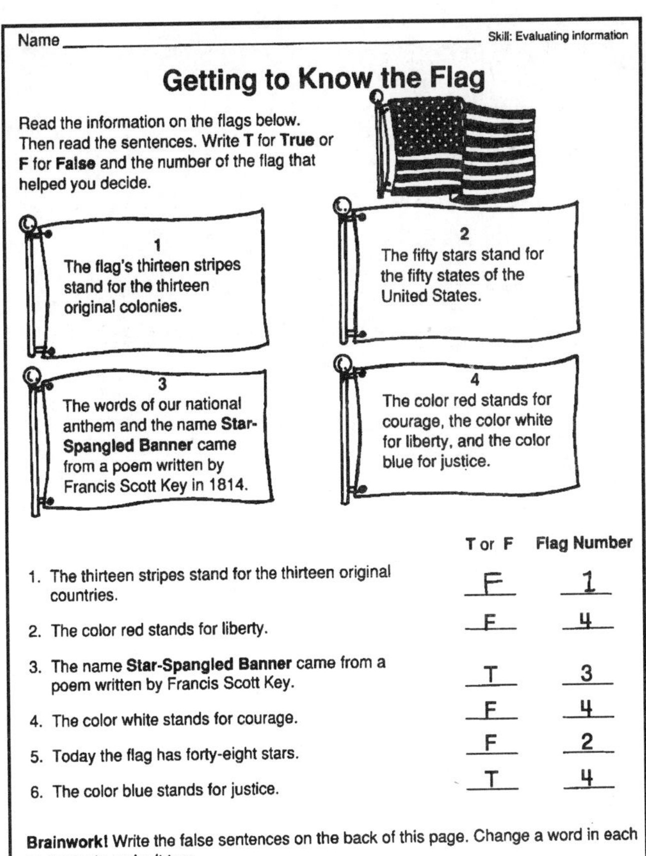

Name ______________________ Skill: Evaluating information

Getting to Know the Flag

Read the information on the flags below. Then read the sentences. Write **T** for **True** or **F** for **False** and the number of the flag that helped you decide.

1. The flag's thirteen stripes stand for the thirteen original colonies.

2. The fifty stars stand for the fifty states of the United States.

3. The words of our national anthem and the name **Star-Spangled Banner** came from a poem written by Francis Scott Key in 1814.

4. The color red stands for courage, the color white for liberty, and the color blue for justice.

	T or F	Flag Number
1. The thirteen stripes stand for the thirteen original countries.	F	1
2. The color red stands for liberty.	F	4
3. The name **Star-Spangled Banner** came from a poem written by Francis Scott Key.	T	3
4. The color white stands for courage.	F	4
5. Today the flag has forty-eight stars.	F	2
6. The color blue stands for justice.	T	4

Brainwork! Write the false sentences on the back of this page. Change a word in each sentence to make it true.

Page 4

© Frank Schaffer Publications, Inc.

Answer Key

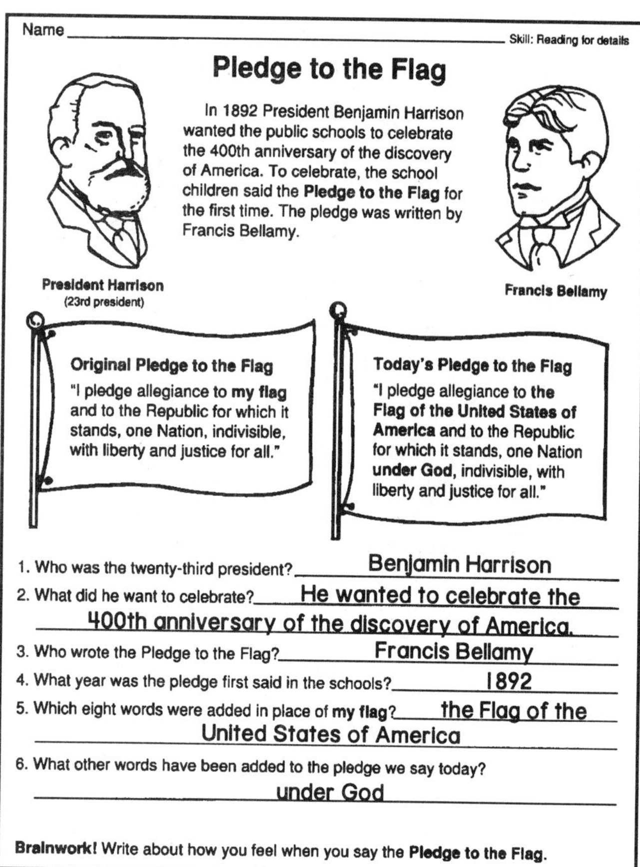

Name ____________________ Skill: Reading for details

Pledge to the Flag

In 1892 President Benjamin Harrison wanted the public schools to celebrate the 400th anniversary of the discovery of America. To celebrate, the school children said the **Pledge to the Flag** for the first time. The pledge was written by Francis Bellamy.

Original Pledge to the Flag
"I pledge allegiance to **my flag** and to the Republic for which it stands, one Nation, indivisible, with liberty and justice for all."

Today's Pledge to the Flag
"I pledge allegiance to the **Flag of the United States of America** and to the Republic for which it stands, one Nation **under God**, indivisible, with liberty and justice for all."

1. Who was the twenty-third president? Benjamin Harrison
2. What did he want to celebrate? He wanted to celebrate the 400th anniversary of the discovery of America.
3. Who wrote the Pledge to the Flag? Francis Bellamy
4. What year was the pledge first said in the schools? 1892
5. Which eight words were added in place of **my flag**? the Flag of the United States of America
6. What other words have been added to the pledge we say today? under God

Brainwork! Write about how you feel when you say the **Pledge to the Flag.**

Page 5

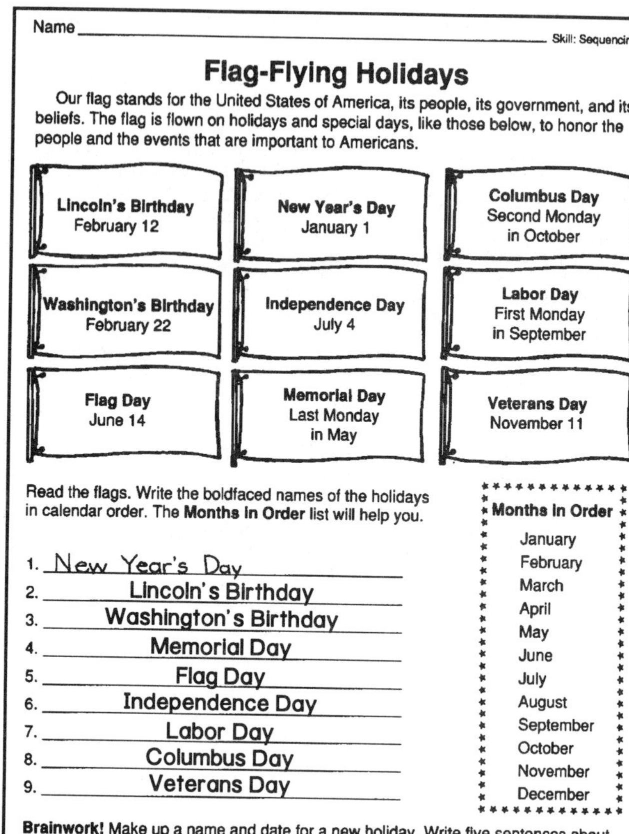

Name ____________________ Skill: Sequencing

Flag-Flying Holidays

Our flag stands for the United States of America, its people, its government, and its beliefs. The flag is flown on holidays and special days, like those below, to honor the people and the events that are important to Americans.

Lincoln's Birthday February 12
New Year's Day January 1
Columbus Day Second Monday in October
Washington's Birthday February 22
Independence Day July 4
Labor Day First Monday in September
Flag Day June 14
Memorial Day Last Monday in May
Veterans Day November 11

Read the flags. Write the boldfaced names of the holidays in calendar order. The **Months in Order** list will help you.

1. New Year's Day
2. Lincoln's Birthday
3. Washington's Birthday
4. Memorial Day
5. Flag Day
6. Independence Day
7. Labor Day
8. Columbus Day
9. Veterans Day

Months in Order
January
February
March
April
May
June
July
August
September
October
November
December

Brainwork! Make up a name and date for a new holiday. Write five sentences about the holiday. Tell why the flag should be flown on the day.

Page 6

Our Capital

This page may be used as a book cover.

Our Capital
Our great capital city,
Long may it stand
As the seat of government
For all our land.

Name ____________________

Page 7

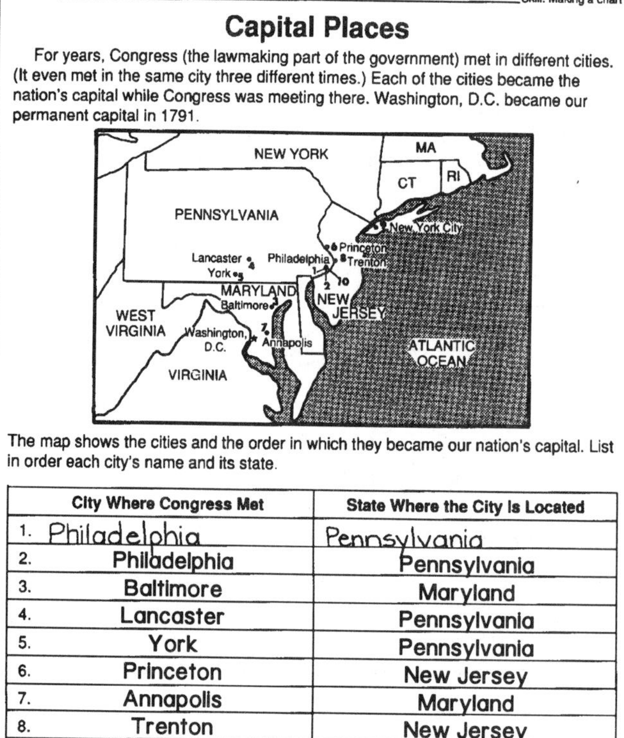

Name ____________________ Skill: Making a chart

Capital Places

For years, Congress (the lawmaking part of the government) met in different cities. (It even met in the same city three different times.) Each of the cities became the nation's capital while Congress was meeting there. Washington, D.C. became our permanent capital in 1791.

The map shows the cities and the order in which they became our nation's capital. List in order each city's name and its state.

	City Where Congress Met	State Where the City Is Located
1.	Philadelphia	Pennsylvania
2.	Philadelphia	Pennsylvania
3.	Baltimore	Maryland
4.	Lancaster	Pennsylvania
5.	York	Pennsylvania
6.	Princeton	New Jersey
7.	Annapolis	Maryland
8.	Trenton	New Jersey
9.	New York City	New York
10.	Philadelphia	Pennsylvania

Brainwork! Write the name of a city you'd choose as the capital and tell why.

Page 8

© Frank Schaffer Publications, Inc.

Answer Key

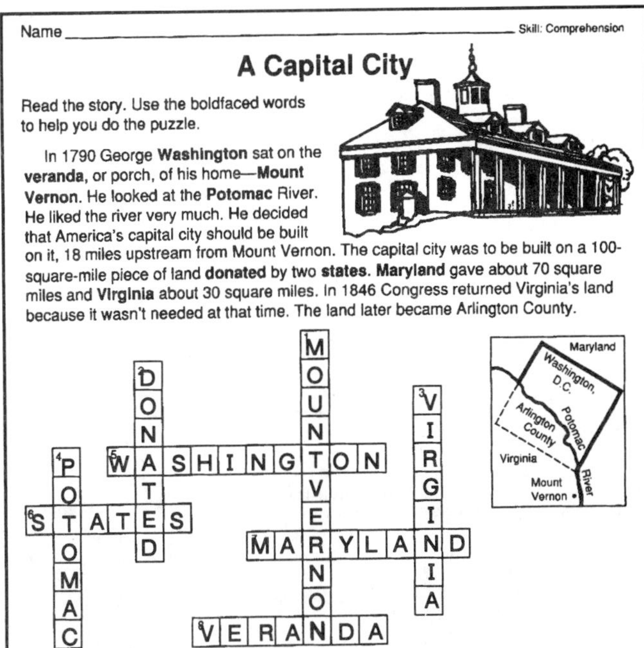

Name________________ Skill: Comprehension

A Capital City

Read the story. Use the boldfaced words to help you do the puzzle.

In 1790 George **Washington** sat on the **veranda**, or porch, of his home—**Mount Vernon**. He looked at the **Potomac** River. He liked the river very much. He decided that America's capital city should be built on it, 18 miles upstream from Mount Vernon. The capital city was to be built on a 100-square-mile piece of land **donated** by two **states**. **Maryland** gave about 70 square miles and **Virginia** about 30 square miles. In 1846 Congress returned Virginia's land because it wasn't needed at that time. The land later became Arlington County.

Crossword answers: 1 MOUNT VERNON, 2 DONATED, 3 VIRGINIA, 4 POTOMAC, 5 WASHINGTON, 6 STATES, 7 MARYLAND, 8 VERANDA

Across
5. Person who decided the place for the capital
6. Maryland and Virginia
7. State that gave more land
8. A porch with a roof

Down
1. George Washington's home
2. To have given something
3. State whose land was returned by Congress
4. River by Mount Vernon

Brainwork! Name a make-believe city after yourself. Describe the city, where it's located, and what makes it a nice place to visit.

Page 9

Name________________ Skill: Reading for detail

Washington, District of Columbia

George Washington — Washington, D.C. — Christopher Columbus

Washington, our capital city, is named after **George Washington**. The land around the city is called the **District of Columbia (D.C.)**. This district is a special piece of land that belongs to the United States government. The name **Columbia** honors **Christopher Columbus**.

Over the years, the city of Washington has grown so large that it now fills the District of Columbia. Today the two names mean the same place.

1. Who owns the District of Columbia? The United States government owns the District of Columbia.
2. What does **D.C.** stand for? D. C. stands for District of Columbia.
3. What person does the name **Columbia** honor? Christopher Columbus
4. What person does the the name **Washington** honor? George Washington
5. What is Washington, D.C.? Washington D.C. is our capital city.
6. Why are the city and the district the same place today? The city of Washington grew so large that it filled the district.

Brainwork! Write why you think George Washington and Christopher Columbus deserve to have Washington, D.C. named after them.

Page 10

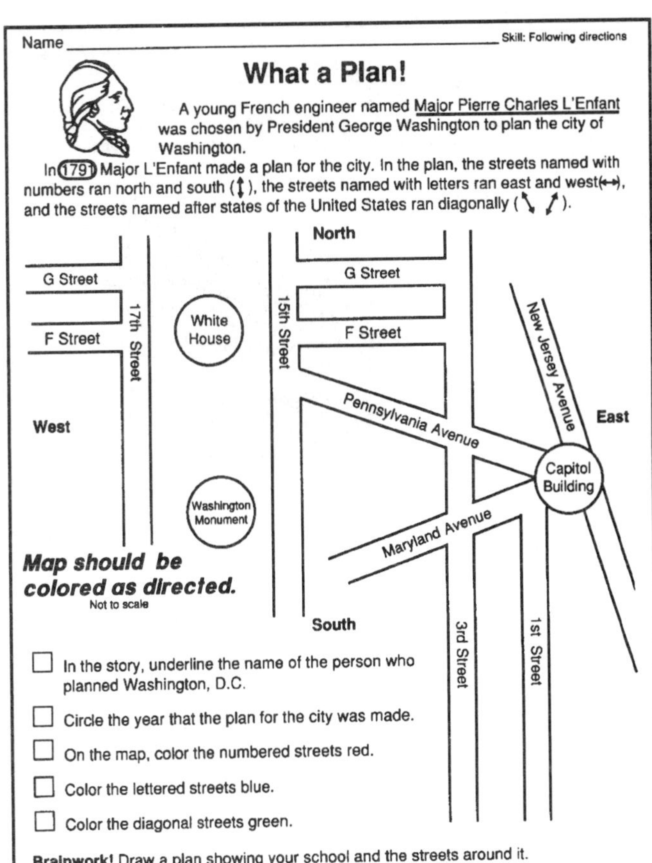

Name________________ Skill: Following directions

What a Plan!

A young French engineer named Major Pierre Charles L'Enfant was chosen by President George Washington to plan the city of Washington.

In (1791) Major L'Enfant made a plan for the city. In the plan, the streets named with numbers ran north and south (↕), the streets named with letters ran east and west(↔), and the streets named after states of the United States ran diagonally (↖ ↗).

Map should be colored as directed.

- ☐ In the story, underline the name of the person who planned Washington, D.C.
- ☐ Circle the year that the plan for the city was made.
- ☐ On the map, color the numbered streets red.
- ☐ Color the lettered streets blue.
- ☐ Color the diagonal streets green.

Brainwork! Draw a plan showing your school and the streets around it.

Page 11

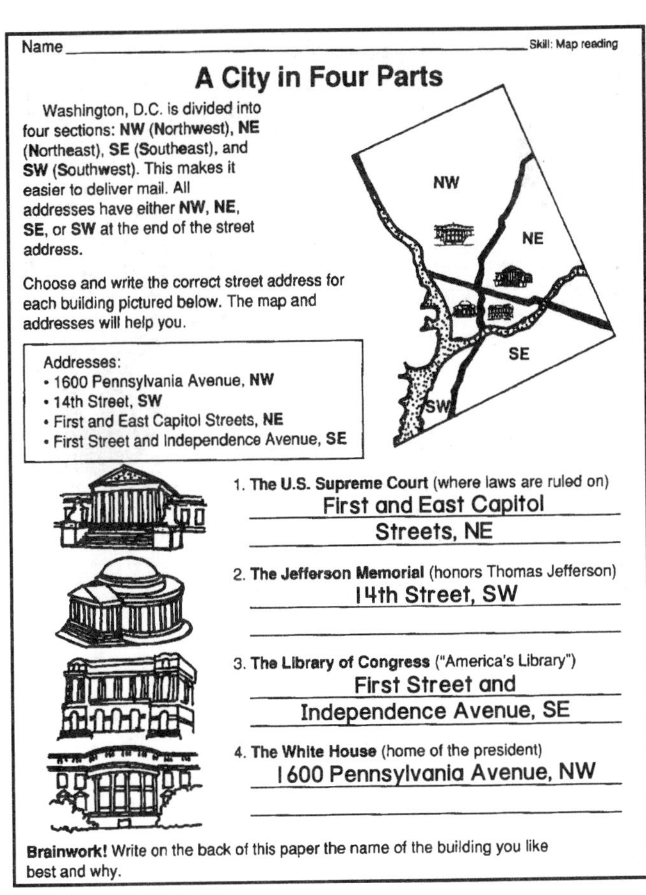

Name________________ Skill: Map reading

A City in Four Parts

Washington, D.C. is divided into four sections: **NW** (**N**orth**w**est), **NE** (**N**orth**e**ast), **SE** (**S**outh**e**ast), and **SW** (**S**outh**w**est). This makes it easier to deliver mail. All addresses have either **NW**, **NE**, **SE**, or **SW** at the end of the street address.

Choose and write the correct street address for each building pictured below. The map and addresses will help you.

Addresses:
- 1600 Pennsylvania Avenue, **NW**
- 14th Street, **SW**
- First and East Capitol Streets, **NE**
- First Street and Independence Avenue, **SE**

1. **The U.S. Supreme Court** (where laws are ruled on) First and East Capitol Streets, NE
2. **The Jefferson Memorial** (honors Thomas Jefferson) 14th Street, SW
3. **The Library of Congress** ("America's Library") First Street and Independence Avenue, SE
4. **The White House** (home of the president) 1600 Pennsylvania Avenue, NW

Brainwork! Write on the back of this paper the name of the building you like best and why.

Page 12

© Frank Schaffer Publications, Inc.

Answer Key

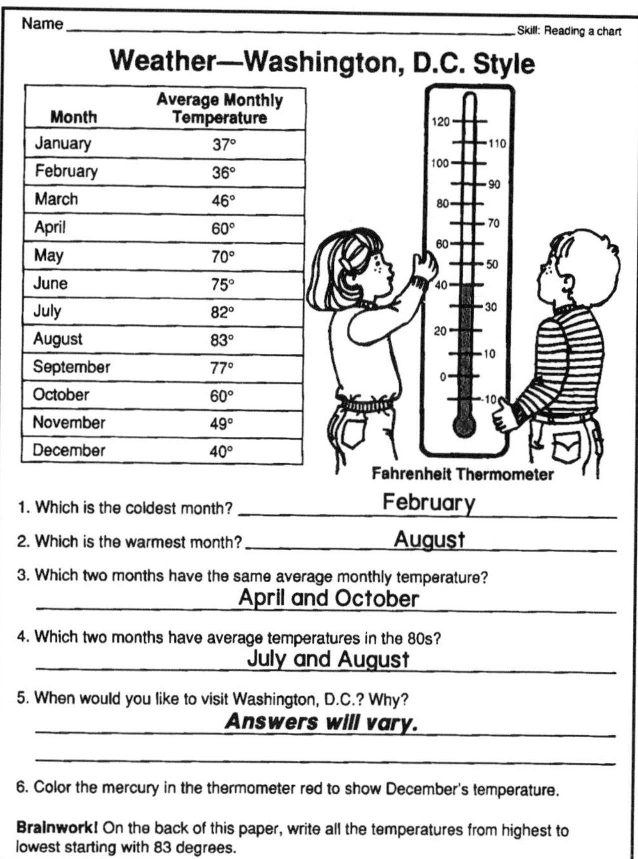
Name ______________________ Skill: Reading a chart

Weather—Washington, D.C. Style

Month	Average Monthly Temperature
January	37°
February	36°
March	46°
April	60°
May	70°
June	75°
July	82°
August	83°
September	77°
October	60°
November	49°
December	40°

1. Which is the coldest month? February
2. Which is the warmest month? August
3. Which two months have the same average monthly temperature? April and October
4. Which two months have average temperatures in the 80s? July and August
5. When would you like to visit Washington, D.C.? Why? ***Answers will vary.***
6. Color the mercury in the thermometer red to show December's temperature.

Brainwork! On the back of this paper, write all the temperatures from highest to lowest starting with 83 degrees.

Page 13

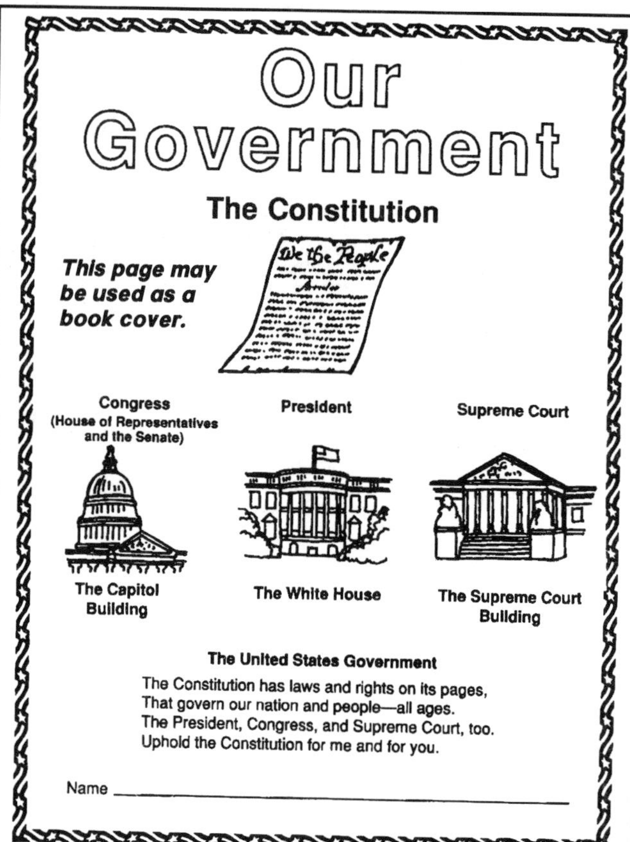
Our Government

The Constitution

This page may be used as a book cover.

Congress (House of Representatives and the Senate) — **The Capitol Building**

President — **The White House**

Supreme Court — **The Supreme Court Building**

The United States Government

The Constitution has laws and rights on its pages,
That govern our nation and people—all ages.
The President, Congress, and Supreme Court, too.
Uphold the Constitution for me and for you.

Name ______________________

Page 14

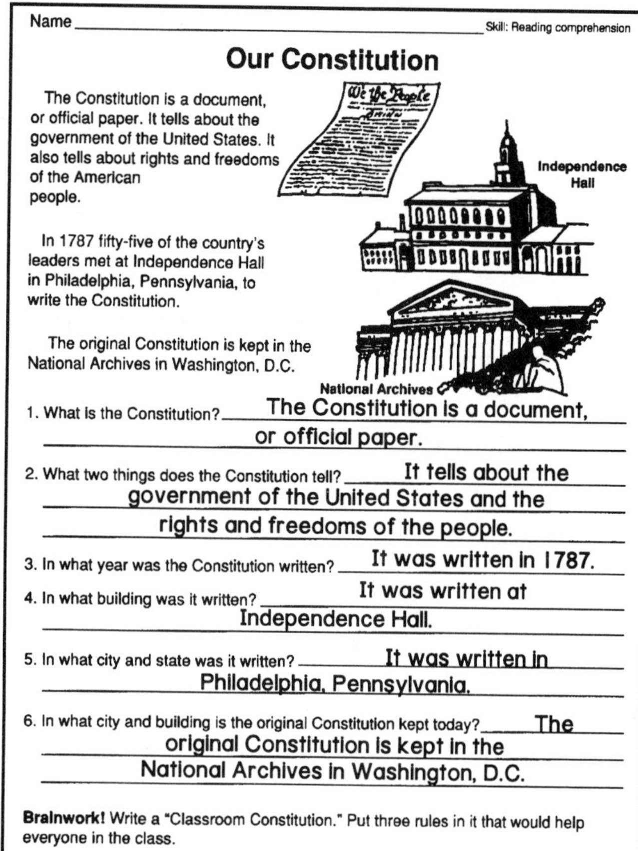
Name ______________________ Skill: Reading comprehension

Our Constitution

The Constitution is a document, or official paper. It tells about the government of the United States. It also tells about rights and freedoms of the American people.

In 1787 fifty-five of the country's leaders met at Independence Hall in Philadelphia, Pennsylvania, to write the Constitution.

The original Constitution is kept in the National Archives in Washington, D.C.

1. What is the Constitution? The Constitution is a document, or official paper.
2. What two things does the Constitution tell? It tells about the government of the United States and the rights and freedoms of the people.
3. In what year was the Constitution written? It was written in 1787.
4. In what building was it written? It was written at Independence Hall.
5. In what city and state was it written? It was written in Philadelphia, Pennsylvania.
6. In what city and building is the original Constitution kept today? The original Constitution is kept in the National Archives in Washington, D.C.

Brainwork! Write a "Classroom Constitution." Put three rules in it that would help everyone in the class.

Page 15

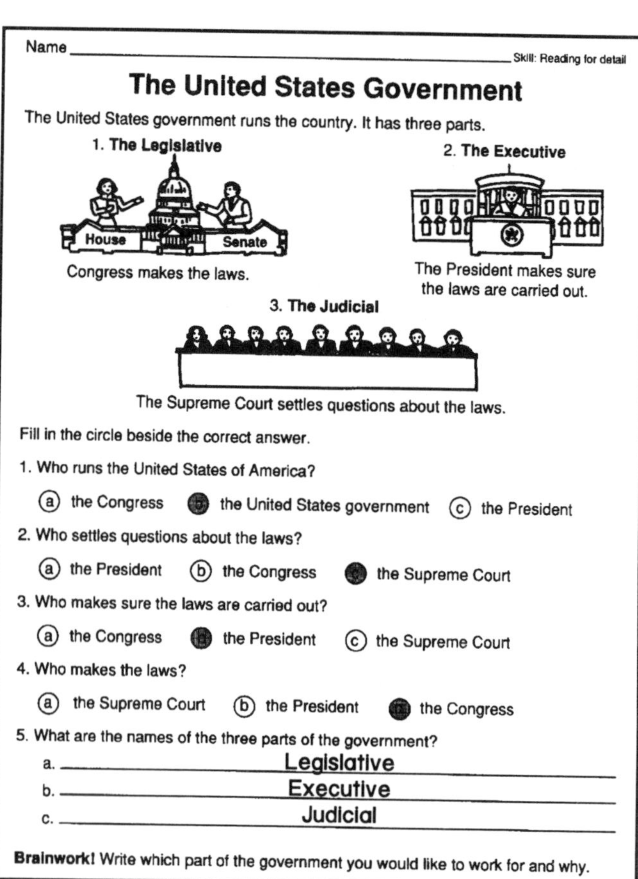
Name ______________________ Skill: Reading for detail

The United States Government

The United States government runs the country. It has three parts.

1. The Legislative

Congress makes the laws.

2. The Executive

The President makes sure the laws are carried out.

3. The Judicial

The Supreme Court settles questions about the laws.

Fill in the circle beside the correct answer.

1. Who runs the United States of America?
   ⓐ the Congress ● the United States government ⓒ the President
2. Who settles questions about the laws?
   ⓐ the President ⓑ the Congress ● the Supreme Court
3. Who makes sure the laws are carried out?
   ⓐ the Congress ● the President ⓒ the Supreme Court
4. Who makes the laws?
   ⓐ the Supreme Court ⓑ the President ● the Congress
5. What are the names of the three parts of the government?
   a. Legislative
   b. Executive
   c. Judicial

Brainwork! Write which part of the government you would like to work for and why.

Page 16

Answer Key

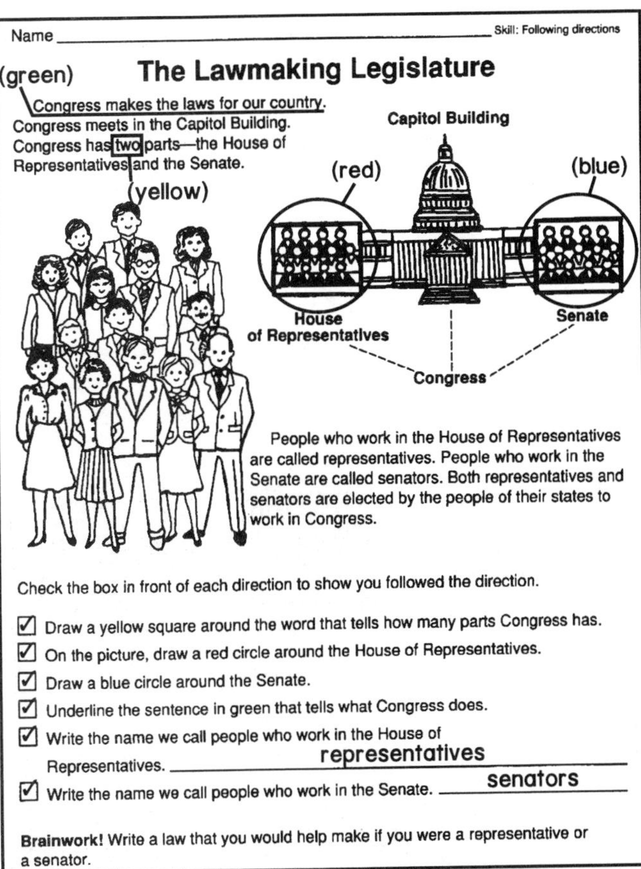

Name ______ Skill: Following directions

The Lawmaking Legislature

(green) Congress makes the laws for our country. Congress meets in the Capitol Building. Congress has two parts—the House of Representatives and the Senate.

People who work in the House of Representatives are called representatives. People who work in the Senate are called senators. Both representatives and senators are elected by the people of their states to work in Congress.

Check the box in front of each direction to show you followed the direction.

☑ Draw a yellow square around the word that tells how many parts Congress has.

☑ On the picture, draw a red circle around the House of Representatives.

☑ Draw a blue circle around the Senate.

☑ Underline the sentence in green that tells what Congress does.

☑ Write the name we call people who work in the House of Representatives. representatives

☑ Write the name we call people who work in the Senate. senators

Brainwork! Write a law that you would help make if you were a representative or a senator.

Page 17

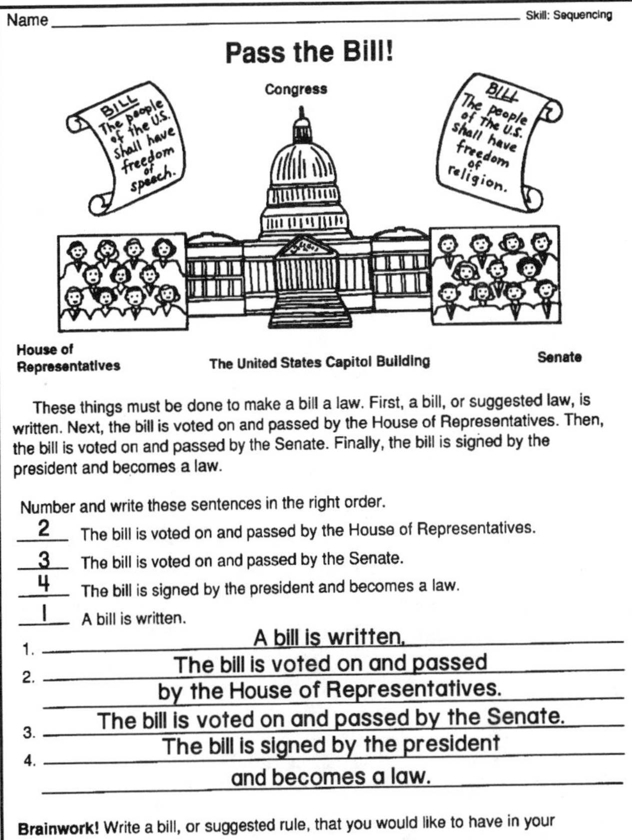

Name ______ Skill: Sequencing

Pass the Bill!

These things must be done to make a bill a law. First, a bill, or suggested law, is written. Next, the bill is voted on and passed by the House of Representatives. Then, the bill is voted on and passed by the Senate. Finally, the bill is signed by the president and becomes a law.

Number and write these sentences in the right order.

2 The bill is voted on and passed by the House of Representatives.
3 The bill is voted on and passed by the Senate.
4 The bill is signed by the president and becomes a law.
1 A bill is written.

1. A bill is written.
2. The bill is voted on and passed by the House of Representatives.
3. The bill is voted on and passed by the Senate.
4. The bill is signed by the president and becomes a law.

Brainwork! Write a bill, or suggested rule, that you would like to have in your classroom.

Page 18

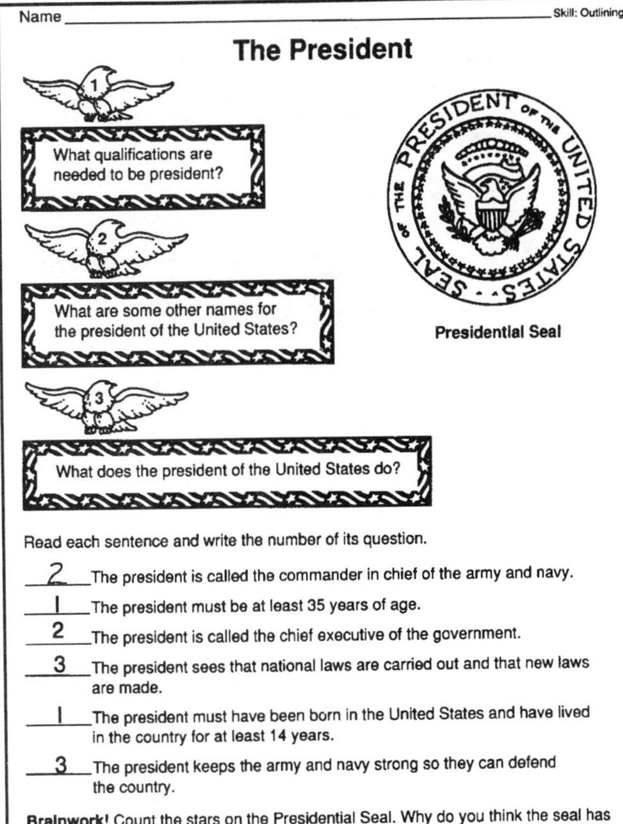

Name ______ Skill: Outlining

The President

1 What qualifications are needed to be president?

2 What are some other names for the president of the United States?

3 What does the president of the United States do?

Presidential Seal

Read each sentence and write the number of its question.

2 The president is called the commander in chief of the army and navy.
1 The president must be at least 35 years of age.
2 The president is called the chief executive of the government.
3 The president sees that national laws are carried out and that new laws are made.
1 The president must have been born in the United States and have lived in the country for at least 14 years.
3 The president keeps the army and navy strong so they can defend the country.

Brainwork! Count the stars on the Presidential Seal. Why do you think the seal has that number of stars?

Page 19

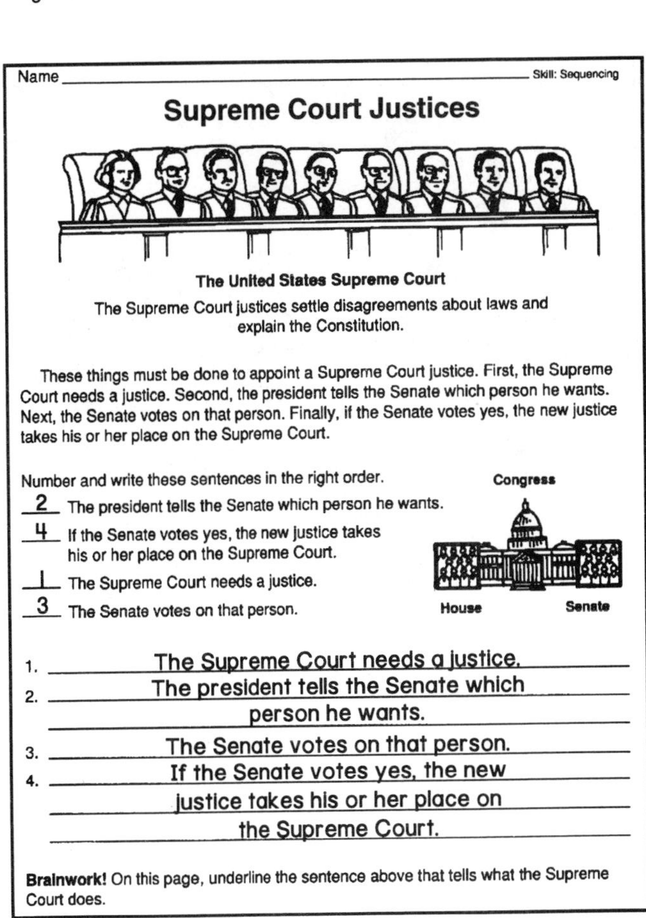

Name ______ Skill: Sequencing

Supreme Court Justices

The United States Supreme Court

The Supreme Court justices settle disagreements about laws and explain the Constitution.

These things must be done to appoint a Supreme Court justice. First, the Supreme Court needs a justice. Second, the president tells the Senate which person he wants. Next, the Senate votes on that person. Finally, if the Senate votes yes, the new justice takes his or her place on the Supreme Court.

Number and write these sentences in the right order.

2 The president tells the Senate which person he wants.
4 If the Senate votes yes, the new justice takes his or her place on the Supreme Court.
1 The Supreme Court needs a justice.
3 The Senate votes on that person.

1. The Supreme Court needs a justice.
2. The president tells the Senate which person he wants.
3. The Senate votes on that person.
4. If the Senate votes yes, the new justice takes his or her place on the Supreme Court.

Brainwork! On this page, underline the sentence above that tells what the Supreme Court does.

Page 20

Answer Key

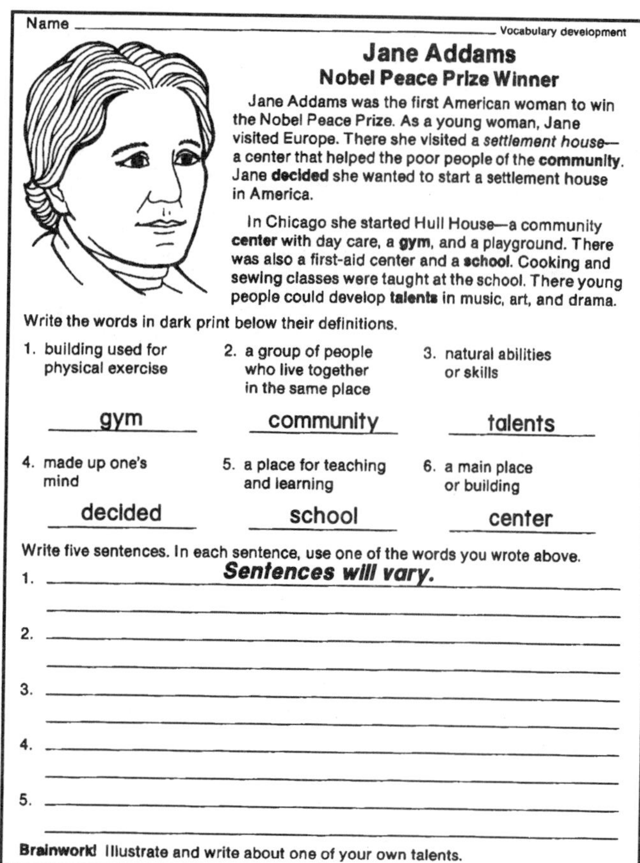

Name ______________________ Vocabulary development

Jane Addams
Nobel Peace Prize Winner

Jane Addams was the first American woman to win the Nobel Peace Prize. As a young woman, Jane visited Europe. There she visited a *settlement house*—a center that helped the poor people of the **community**. Jane **decided** she wanted to start a settlement house in America.

In Chicago she started Hull House—a community **center** with day care, a **gym**, and a playground. There was also a first-aid center and a **school**. Cooking and sewing classes were taught at the school. There young people could develop **talents** in music, art, and drama.

Write the words in dark print below their definitions.

1. building used for physical exercise	2. a group of people who live together in the same place	3. natural abilities or skills
gym	community	talents
4. made up one's mind	5. a place for teaching and learning	6. a main place or building
decided	school	center

Write five sentences. In each sentence, use one of the words you wrote above.

1. ***Sentences will vary.***
2. ______
3. ______
4. ______
5. ______

Brainwork! Illustrate and write about one of your own talents.

Page 21

Name ______________________ Skill: Vocabulary development

Marian Anderson
Singer

Marian Anderson was the first black singer to **appear** at New York City's Metropolitan Opera. She began singing as a child in her church choir. Church members paid for her singing **lessons**. Then her teacher gave her a **scholarship** for more lessons.

Her first **solo** performance was very successful. Marian studied and gave many **concerts** in Europe. Back in the United States, Marian Anderson sang for 75,000 people at the Lincoln Memorial. She had a rich and **beautiful** voice. People all over the world enjoyed her singing. She was given many awards and honors.

Write the words in dark print below their definitions.

1. music for one person to sing	2. pleasing to hear	3. performances of music
solo	beautiful	concerts
4. come before the public	5. a money gift to help a student	6. classes or courses of study
appear	scholarship	lessons

Write four sentences about Marian Anderson. In each sentence, use one of the words you wrote above.

1. ***Sentences will vary.***
2. ______
3. ______
4. ______

Brainwork! List as many music words as you can. Begin with these words from the story: *choir, solo, concerts, voice.*

Page 22

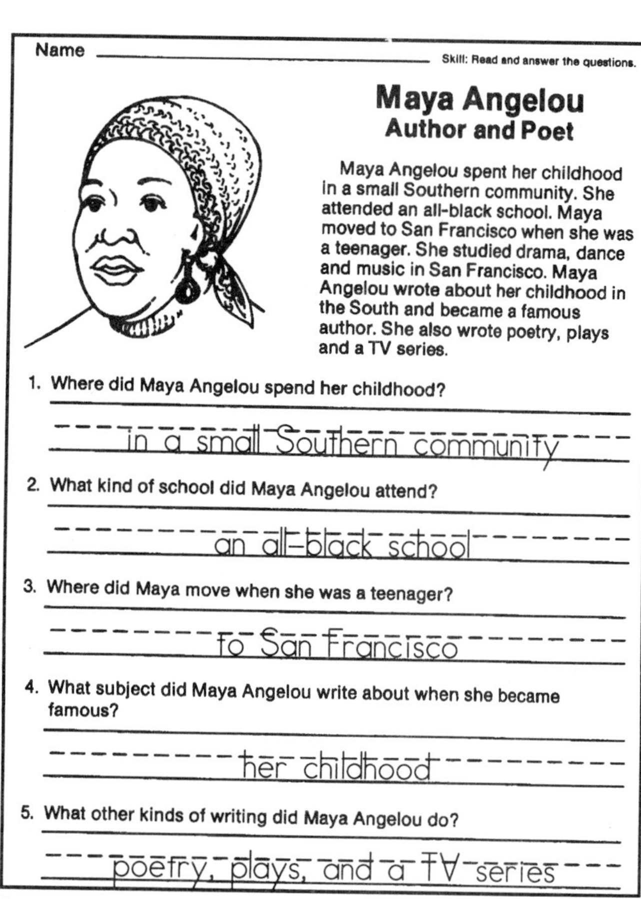

Name ______________________ Skill: Read and answer the questions.

Maya Angelou
Author and Poet

Maya Angelou spent her childhood in a small Southern community. She attended an all-black school. Maya moved to San Francisco when she was a teenager. She studied drama, dance and music in San Francisco. Maya Angelou wrote about her childhood in the South and became a famous author. She also wrote poetry, plays and a TV series.

1. Where did Maya Angelou spend her childhood?
   in a small Southern community
2. What kind of school did Maya Angelou attend?
   an all-black school
3. Where did Maya move when she was a teenager?
   to San Francisco
4. What subject did Maya Angelou write about when she became famous?
   her childhood
5. What other kinds of writing did Maya Angelou do?
   poetry, plays, and a TV series

Page 23

Name ______________________ Skill: Vocabulary development

Susan B. Anthony
Women's Rights Leader

Susan B. Anthony worked her **entire** life so that women could **vote**. She lived over one-hundred years ago. Once she tried to vote but was fined. Susan B. Anthony refused to pay the **fine** but worked even harder to win women the **right** to vote.

She became an **effective** writer and speaker. She wrote for a journal called *The Revolution* that called for the **emancipation** of women. With some other women, she started the National American Woman Suffrage Association. Fourteen years after she died, the "Susan B. Anthony Amendment" to the U.S. Constitution gave women the right to vote.

Write the words in dark print below their definitions.

1. to decide by ballot	2. freedom	3. whole, complete
vote	emancipation	entire
4. lawful claim, privilege	5. making a strong impression	6. money paid as a penalty
right	effective	fine

Write four sentences. In each sentence, use one of the words you wrote above.

1. ***Sentences will vary.***
2. ______
3. ______
4. ______

Brainwork! Make a word search puzzle using the six words above.

Page 24

© Frank Schaffer Publications, Inc.

Answer Key

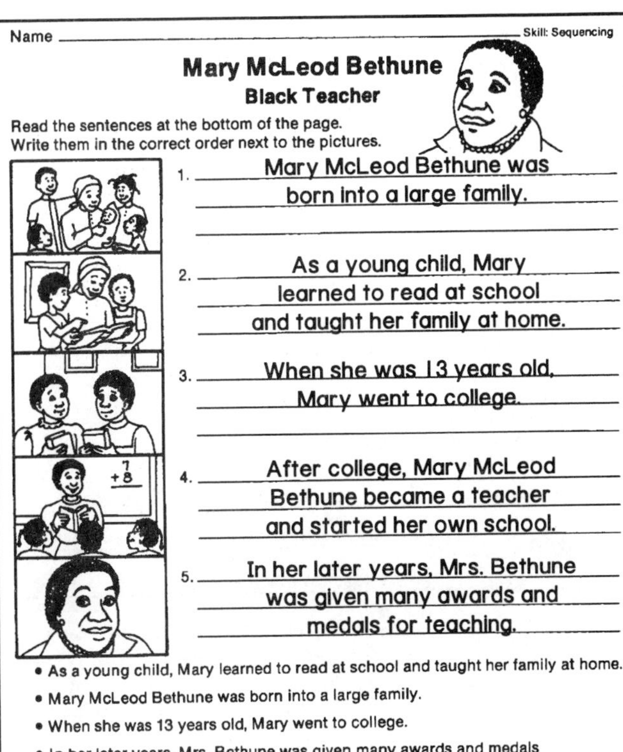

Name ______ Skill: Sequencing

Mary McLeod Bethune
Black Teacher

Read the sentences at the bottom of the page.
Write them in the correct order next to the pictures.

1. Mary McLeod Bethune was born into a large family.
2. As a young child, Mary learned to read at school and taught her family at home.
3. When she was 13 years old, Mary went to college.
4. After college, Mary McLeod Bethune became a teacher and started her own school.
5. In her later years, Mrs. Bethune was given many awards and medals for teaching.

- As a young child, Mary learned to read at school and taught her family at home.
- Mary McLeod Bethune was born into a large family.
- When she was 13 years old, Mary went to college.
- In her later years, Mrs. Bethune was given many awards and medals for teaching.
- After college, Mary McLeod Bethune became a teacher and started her own school.

Brainwork! Young Mary wanted to learn to read more than anything else. Write three sentences about something you want to learn more than anything else.

Page 25

Name ______ Skill: Read and find the answers.

Guion Bluford
Astronaut

Guion Bluford was the first black American in space. He was a mission specialist on the third flight of the space shuttle **Challenger**. He did experiments to study space sickness. He also did tests for new treatments for diabetes and other diseases.

Word Box		
Challenger	space	sickness
diseases	third	specialist

1. Guion Bluford was the first black American astronaut in space.
2. His job was mission specialist.
3. He was on the third flight of the space shuttle Challenger.
4. He studied space sickness and a new treatment for diseases.

Page 26

Name ______ Skill: Read and find the answers.

Ralph Bunche
Winner of Nobel Peace Prize

Ralph Bunche was the first black American to win the Nobel Peace Prize. He studied other governments, helped start the United Nations and helped countries to be peaceful. He said that peace is more than not fighting; he said peace is when children have enough food, homes, schools and happiness.

Word Box		
United Nations	peaceful	Peace
happiness	fighting	first

1. Ralph Bunche was the first black American to win the Nobel Peace Prize.
2. Ralph Bunche helped start the United Nations.
3. He also helped countries to be peaceful.
4. Ralph Bunche said that peace is more than not fighting.
5. He said that peace is when children have enough food, homes, schools and happiness.

Page 27

Name ______ Skill: Read and answer the questions.

George Washington Carver
Scientist

George Washington Carver made scientific discoveries that helped farmers in the South. He taught farmers to grow peanuts, soybeans and sweet potatoes. He also taught them to rotate crops in order to renew the soil.

1. Who was helped by the discoveries of George Washington Carver?
   farmers in the South
2. What kind of discoveries did he make?
   scientific discoveries
3. What three crops did Carver teach farmers to grow?
   peanuts, soybeans, and sweet potatoes
4. What else did George Washington Carver teach farmers?
   to rotate crops
5. Why did Carver teach farmers to rotate crops?
   to renew the soil

Page 28

© Frank Schaffer Publications, Inc.

Answer Key

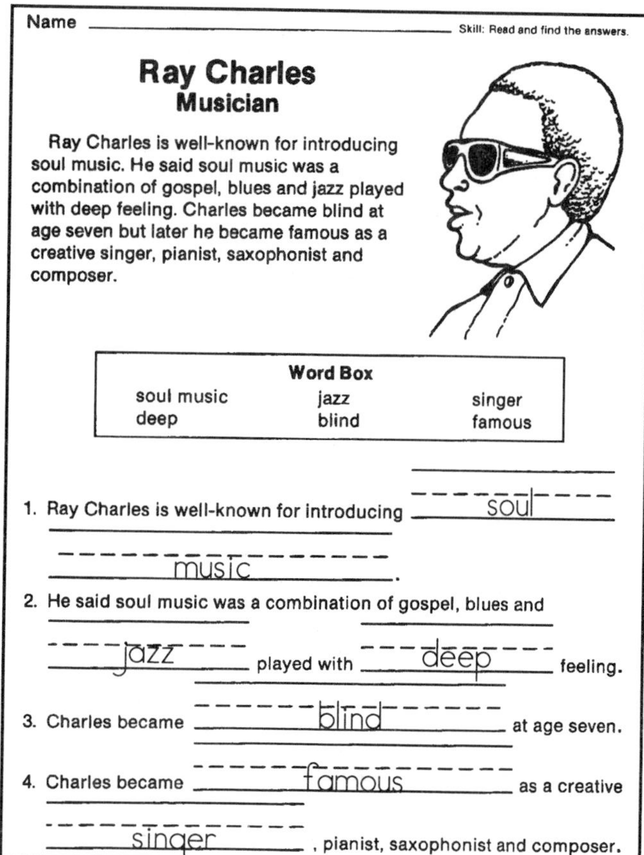

Name ______ Skill: Read and find the answers.

Ray Charles
Musician

Ray Charles is well-known for introducing soul music. He said soul music was a combination of gospel, blues and jazz played with deep feeling. Charles became blind at age seven but later he became famous as a creative singer, pianist, saxophonist and composer.

Word Box

soul music	jazz	singer
deep	blind	famous

1. Ray Charles is well-known for introducing soul music.
2. He said soul music was a combination of gospel, blues and jazz played with deep feeling.
3. Charles became blind at age seven.
4. Charles became famous as a creative singer, pianist, saxophonist and composer.

Page 29

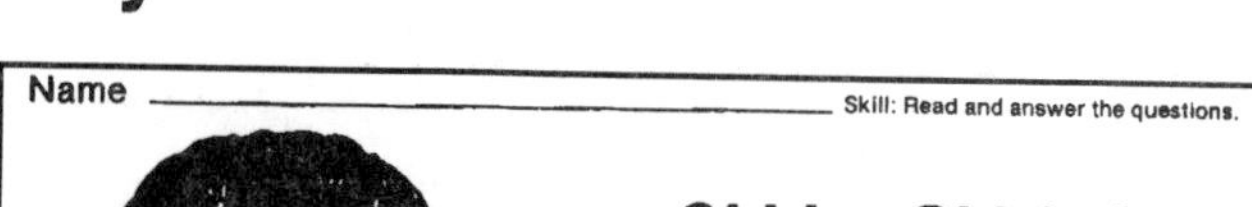

Name ______ Skill: Read and answer the questions.

Shirley Chisholm
Member of Congress

Shirley Chisholm was the first black woman to be a member of the United States Congress. Before becoming a member of Congress, she was a teacher and director of a child-care center. In 1972 she ran for the nomination of United States President.

1. Shirley Chisholm was the first black woman to be a member of what group?
   the United States Congress
2. What are the two jobs she had before becoming a member of Congress?
   teacher and director of a child-care center
3. What did she run for in 1972?
   the presidential nomination
4. When did Shirley Chisholm run for the presidential nomination?
   1972

Page 30

Name ______ Skill: Read and find the answers.

Duke Ellington
Jazz Musician

Duke Ellington was a composer and a musician. He pioneered modern jazz. His band was the first to give jazz concerts regularly. He composed nearly 1,000 songs.

Word Box

jazz	composer	musician
1,000	concerts	band

1. Duke Ellington was a composer and a musician.
2. He pioneered modern jazz.
3. His band was the first to give jazz concerts regularly.
4. He wrote nearly 1,000 songs.

Page 31

Name ______ Skill: Read, color, cut and staple to make a book.

Book is colored, cut, and stapled in order.

Dr. Martin Luther King, Jr.
Civil Rights Leader

As a child Martin Luther King loved to play games and read.
2

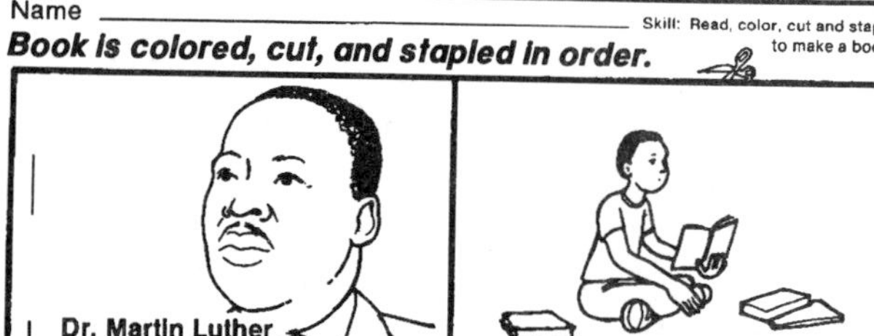

Martin felt uncomfortable when white people were unfriendly to him.
3

In high school Martin decided to be a minister like his father.
4

Dr. King made many speeches. He wanted equality for all people.
5

In 1964 Dr. King won the Nobel Peace Prize for working to change unfair laws in non-violent ways.
6

Page 32

© Frank Schaffer Publications, Inc.

Name ____________ Skill: Sequencing

Emma Lazarus
Poet

Read the sentences at the bottom of the page.
Write them in the correct order next to the pictures.

1. As a young child, Emma Lazarus liked to write poems and stories.
2. When she was eighteen, Emma's poems were printed in a book.
3. As a young woman, she wrote about making America a land of "liberty and justice for all."
4. Emma Lazarus wrote a poem "The New Colossus," to help raise money for the base of the Statue of Liberty.
5. After Emma died, words of her famous poem were placed on the base of the statue.

- When she was eighteen, Emma's poems were printed in a book.
- As a young child, Emma Lazarus liked to write poems and stories.
- After Emma died, words of her famous poem were placed on the base of the statue.
- As a young woman, she wrote about making America a land of "liberty and justice for all."
- Emma Lazarus wrote a poem, "The New Colossus," to help raise money for the base of the Statue of Liberty.

Brainwork! Emma's famous poem "The New Colossus" was written as if the statue were talking to new immigrants. Learn part of the famous poem: "Give me your tired, your poor, your huddled masses yearning to breathe free ..."

Page 33

Name ____________ Skill: Read and answer the questions.

Thurgood Marshall
United States Supreme Court Justice

Thurgood Marshall was the first black American to be a justice of the Supreme Court. Before he became a justice, he had been a lawyer. Thurgood Marshall had worked for integrating public schools. Integrating meant the end of separate schools for blacks and whites.

1. Who was the first black American to be a Supreme Court justice?
   Thurgood Marshall
2. What was Thurgood Marshall before he became a justice of the Supreme Court?
   a lawyer
3. What did Thurgood Marshall work to accomplish?
   integration of the public schools
4. What did integrating mean?
   the end of separate schools for blacks and white

Page 34

Name ____________ Skill: Sequencing

María Martínez
Native American Potter

Read the sentences at the bottom of the page.
Write them in the correct order next to the pictures.

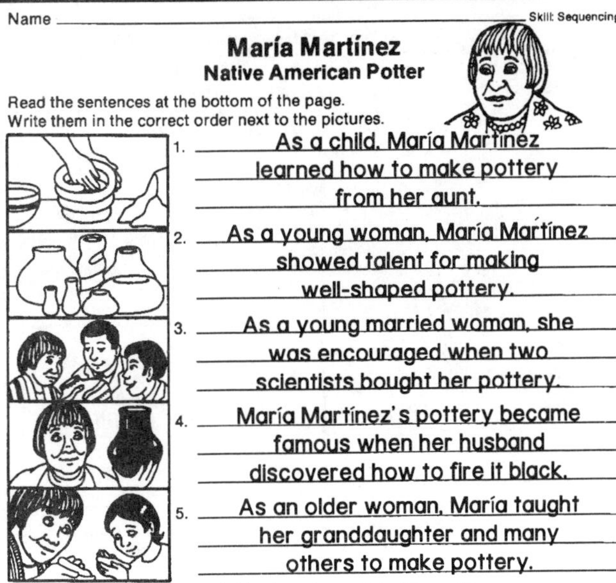

1. As a child, María Martínez learned how to make pottery from her aunt.
2. As a young woman, María Martínez showed talent for making well-shaped pottery.
3. As a young married woman, she was encouraged when two scientists bought her pottery.
4. María Martínez's pottery became famous when her husband discovered how to fire it black.
5. As an older woman, María taught her granddaughter and many others to make pottery.

- As a young woman, María Martínez showed talent for making well-shaped pottery.
- As an older woman, María taught her granddaughter and many others to make pottery.
- As a child, María Martínez learned how to make pottery from her aunt.
- As a young married woman, she was encouraged when two scientists bought her pottery.
- María Martínez's pottery became famous when her husband discovered how to fire it black.

Brainwork! Write five sentences about events in your own life. Put them in the order they happened.

Page 35

Name ____________ Skill: Reasoning, Decoding

Liliuokalani
Queen of Hawaii

Queen Liliuokalani was the last member of the royal family to rule Hawaii. Her father and brother had been kings before her. As a child she learned to read and speak English. She also studied music. When the United States took over Hawaii, she worked hard to save Hawaiian ways of life. She wrote songs about the native Hawaiian ways of life.

a	b	c	d	e	f	g	h	i	j	k	l	m
2	4	6	8	10	12	14	16	18	20	22	24	26
n	o	p	q	r	s	t	u	v	w	x	y	z
28	30	32	34	36	38	40	42	44	46	48	50	52

Use the code above to write the answer to each clue.

Queen Liliuokalani's English name was Lydia. As a child Lydia enjoyed special feasts called l u a u s (24 42 2 42 38). At luaus food was served in big bowls made from gourds called c a l a b a s h e s (6 2 24 2 4 2 38 16 10 38). Luaus included a storyteller, or k a h u n a (22 2 16 42 28 2). The kahuna chanted as h u l a (16 42 24 2) dancers swayed to the music of drums. Lydia wore a flower necklace called a l e i (24 10 18). She greeted her friends with the word a l o h a (2 24 30 16 2) which meant both "hello" and "good-bye." Lydia usually remembered to say "thank you," or m a h a l o (26 2 16 2 24 30).

Brainwork! Write and illustrate the seven Hawaiian words you decoded above.

Page 36

Answer Key

Name ______ Skill: Sequencing

Julia Morgan
Architect

Read the sentences at the bottom of the page.
Write them in the correct order next to the pictures.

1. As a girl in the early 1900's, Julia Morgan wanted to be an architect.
2. At college there were no architecture classes, so she became a civil engineer.
3. After college she became the first woman graduate of a famous architecture school in Paris.
4. As an architect, she designed both simple, inexpensive homes and elaborate, expensive homes.
5. When she died, she had designed 800 buildings including the famous Hearst Castle.

- At college there were no architecture classes, so she became a civil engineer.
- After college she became the first woman graduate of a famous architecture school in Paris.
- As a girl in the early 1900s, Julia Morgan wanted to be an architect.
- When she died, she had designed nearly 800 buildings including the famous Hearst Castle.
- As an architect, she designed both simple, inexpensive homes and elaborate, expensive homes.

Brainwork! Hearst Castle had its own zoo, library, art collection, and outdoor pool. Draw your own castle on the back of this paper.

Page 37

Name ______ Skill: Reasoning, Decoding

Justice Sandra Day O'Connor
First Woman on the Supreme Court

Sandra Day O'Connor is the first woman member of the United States Supreme Court. She became an associate justice of the Supreme Court in 1981. President Reagan chose her for this important job. Before she became an associate justice, Sandra Day O'Connor was a lawyer and a judge. She works extremely hard to know the laws and how they've been used before.

a	b	c	d	e	f	g	h	i	j	k	l	m
26	25	24	23	22	21	20	19	18	17	16	15	14
n	**o**	**p**	**q**	**r**	**s**	**t**	**u**	**v**	**w**	**x**	**y**	**z**
13	12	11	10	9	8	7	6	5	4	3	2	1

Use the code above to write the answer to each clue.

1. Sandra Day O'Connor is the first woman member of the United States Supreme C o u r t (24 12 6 9 7).
2. She was chosen by President R e a g a n (9 22 26 20 26 13).
3. Associate justice of the Supreme Court is a job that is very i m p o r t a n t (18 14 11 12 9 7 26 13 7).
4. Another word for *chose* is a p p o i n t e d (26 11 11 12 18 13 7 22 23).
5. Sandra Day O'Connor has been a l a w y e r (15 26 4 2 22 9) and a j u d g e (17 6 23 20 22).
6. She works hard to know the l a w s (15 26 4 8).

Brainwork! Capitalize the two decoded words needing capitals.

Page 38

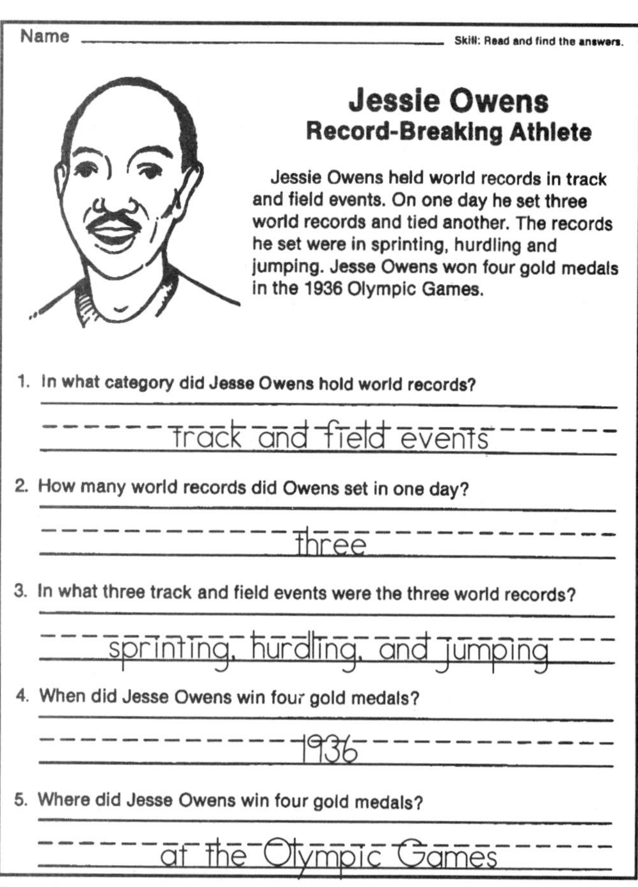

Name ______ Skill: Read and find the answers.

Jessie Owens
Record-Breaking Athlete

Jessie Owens held world records in track and field events. On one day he set three world records and tied another. The records he set were in sprinting, hurdling and jumping. Jesse Owens won four gold medals in the 1936 Olympic Games.

1. In what category did Jesse Owens hold world records?
   track and field events
2. How many world records did Owens set in one day?
   three
3. In what three track and field events were the three world records?
   sprinting, hurdling, and jumping
4. When did Jesse Owens win four gold medals?
   1936
5. Where did Jesse Owens win four gold medals?
   at the Olympic Games

Page 39

Name ______ Vocabulary development

Eleanor Roosevelt
Human Rights Leader

Eleanor Roosevelt worked all her life for human rights—fair treatment for everyone. As the wife of President Franklin D. Roosevelt, she was a very active first lady. She helped her husband who had polio. As his partner, she made many fact-finding trips for him.

She was chosen a **delegate** to the United Nations. As a delegate, she helped **draft** and pass the **Universal** Declaration of Human Rights. The **declaration** states all persons are born **free** and equal in **dignity**. Eleanor Roosevelt worked very hard to get all countries to support the declaration.

Write the words in dark print below their definitions.

1. independent, at liberty — free
2. outline, make a plan — draft
3. concerning everyone — universal
4. public statement or proclamation — declaration
5. representative — delegate
6. pride and self-respect — dignity

Write five sentences. In each sentence, use one of the words you wrote above.

1. ***Sentences will vary.***
2.
3.
4.
5.

Brainwork! Make a crossword puzzle using the six words above and their definitions.

Page 40

© Frank Schaffer Publications, Inc.

Answer Key

Name ________________ Skill: Read, color, cut and staple to make a book.

Book is colored, cut, and stapled in order.

Wilma Rudolph
Record-Breaking Athlete

Wilma Rudolph had a crippling disease and was not able to walk until she was eight years old.
2

After having therapy, she threw away her special shoes. When she was 11, she became active in sports.
3

She was an outstanding basketball player in high school, setting a state record for girls' scoring.
4

In the 1960 Olympics, she became the world's fastest woman runner and won three gold medals.
5

Later Wilma Rudolph broke other world track records.
6

Page 41

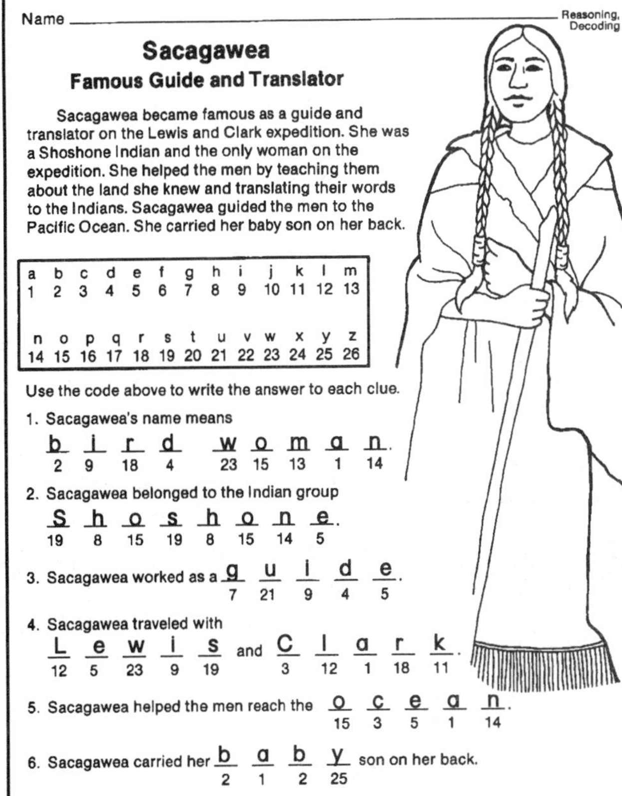

Name ________________ Reasoning, Decoding

Sacagawea
Famous Guide and Translator

Sacagawea became famous as a guide and translator on the Lewis and Clark expedition. She was a Shoshone Indian and the only woman on the expedition. She helped the men by teaching them about the land she knew and translating their words to the Indians. Sacagawea guided the men to the Pacific Ocean. She carried her baby son on her back.

a	b	c	d	e	f	g	h	i	j	k	l	m
1	2	3	4	5	6	7	8	9	10	11	12	13
n	o	p	q	r	s	t	u	v	w	x	y	z
14	15	16	17	18	19	20	21	22	23	24	25	26

Use the code above to write the answer to each clue.

1. Sacagawea's name means b i r d w o m a n. (2 9 18 4 23 15 13 1 14)
2. Sacagawea belonged to the Indian group S h o s h o n e. (19 8 15 19 8 15 14 5)
3. Sacagawea worked as a g u i d e. (7 21 9 4 5)
4. Sacagawea traveled with L e w i s and C l a r k. (12 5 23 9 19 and 3 12 1 18 11)
5. Sacagawea helped the men reach the o c e a n. (15 3 5 1 14)
6. Sacagawea carried her b a b y son on her back. (2 1 2 25)

Brainwork! Three of the decoded words above need capitals. Find them and capitalize them.

Page 42

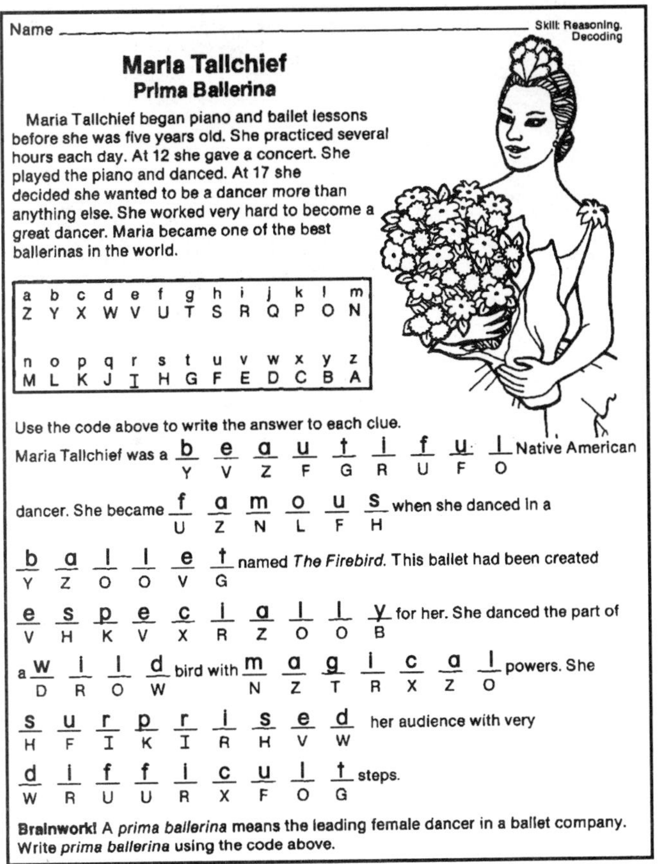

Name ________________ Skill: Reasoning, Decoding

Maria Tallchief
Prima Ballerina

Maria Tallchief began piano and ballet lessons before she was five years old. She practiced several hours each day. At 12 she gave a concert. She played the piano and danced. At 17 she decided she wanted to be a dancer more than anything else. She worked very hard to become a great dancer. Maria became one of the best ballerinas in the world.

a	b	c	d	e	f	g	h	i	j	k	l	m
Z	Y	X	W	V	U	T	S	R	Q	P	O	N
n	o	p	q	r	s	t	u	v	w	x	y	z
M	L	K	J	I	H	G	F	E	D	C	B	A

Use the code above to write the answer to each clue.

Maria Tallchief was a b e a u t i f u l (Y V Z F G R U F O) Native American dancer. She became f a m o u s (U Z N L F H) when she danced in a b a l l e t (Y Z O O V G) named *The Firebird.* This ballet had been created e s p e c i a l l y (V H K V X R Z O O B) for her. She danced the part of a w i l d (D R O W) bird with m a g i c a l (N Z T R X Z O) powers. She s u r p r i s e d (H F I K I R H V W) her audience with very d i f f i c u l t (W R U U R X F O G) steps.

Brainwork! A *prima ballerina* means the leading female dancer in a ballet company. Write *prima ballerina* using the code above.

Page 43

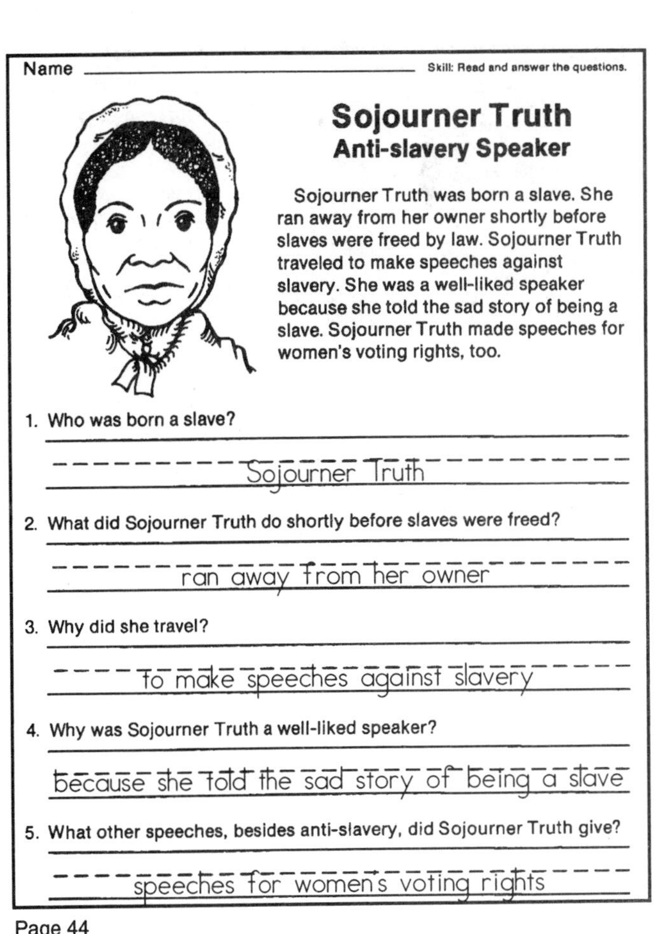

Name ________________ Skill: Read and answer the questions.

Sojourner Truth
Anti-slavery Speaker

Sojourner Truth was born a slave. She ran away from her owner shortly before slaves were freed by law. Sojourner Truth traveled to make speeches against slavery. She was a well-liked speaker because she told the sad story of being a slave. Sojourner Truth made speeches for women's voting rights, too.

1. Who was born a slave?
   Sojourner Truth
2. What did Sojourner Truth do shortly before slaves were freed?
   ran away from her owner
3. Why did she travel?
   to make speeches against slavery
4. Why was Sojourner Truth a well-liked speaker?
   because she told the sad story of being a slave
5. What other speeches, besides anti-slavery, did Sojourner Truth give?
   speeches for women's voting rights

Page 44

© Frank Schaffer Publications, Inc.

Answer Key

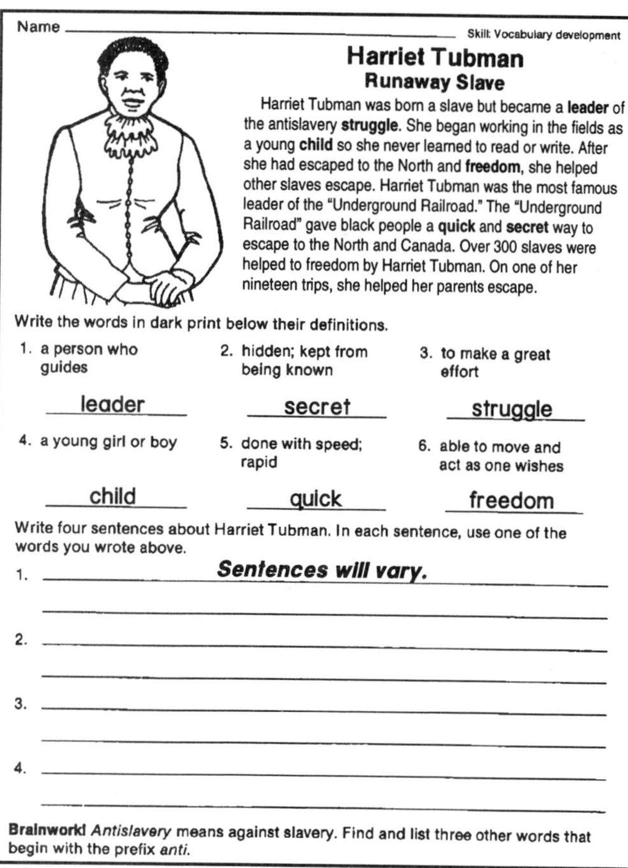

Name ______________________ Skill: Vocabulary development

Harriet Tubman
Runaway Slave

Harriet Tubman was born a slave but became a **leader** of the antislavery **struggle**. She began working in the fields as a young **child** so she never learned to read or write. After she had escaped to the North and **freedom**, she helped other slaves escape. Harriet Tubman was the most famous leader of the "Underground Railroad." The "Underground Railroad" gave black people a **quick** and **secret** way to escape to the North and Canada. Over 300 slaves were helped to freedom by Harriet Tubman. On one of her nineteen trips, she helped her parents escape.

Write the words in dark print below their definitions.

1. a person who guides	2. hidden; kept from being known	3. to make a great effort
leader	secret	struggle
4. a young girl or boy	5. done with speed; rapid	6. able to move and act as one wishes
child	quick	freedom

Write four sentences about Harriet Tubman. In each sentence, use one of the words you wrote above.

1. ***Sentences will vary.***
2. ______________________
3. ______________________
4. ______________________

Brainwork! *Antislavery* means against slavery. Find and list three other words that begin with the prefix *anti*.

Page 45

Name ______________________ Skill: Read and find the answers.

Booker T. Washington
Educator for Black Americans

Booker T. Washington helped improve the lives of black Americans. He believed education, more jobs and better income would help to improve their lives the most. He started a school to train black teachers, farmers, brick makers and carpenters. His ways of teaching by doing were later used by other Americans.

Word Box		
education	improve	jobs
doing	school	income

1. Booker T. Washington helped improve the lives of black Americans.
2. He believed education, more jobs and better income would help black Americans the most.
3. He started a school.
4. His way of teaching by doing was used in other American schools.

Page 46

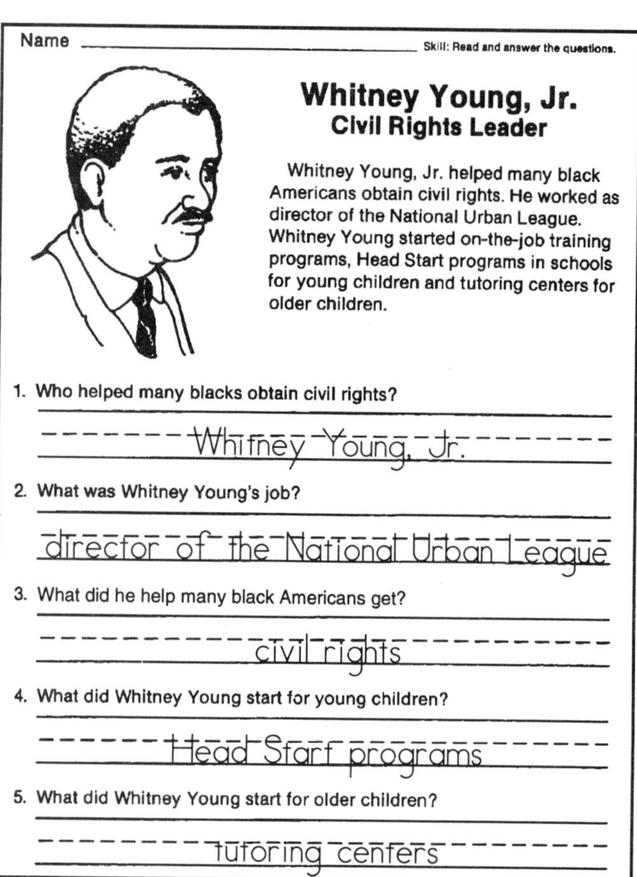

Name ______________________ Skill: Read and answer the questions.

Whitney Young, Jr.
Civil Rights Leader

Whitney Young, Jr. helped many black Americans obtain civil rights. He worked as director of the National Urban League. Whitney Young started on-the-job training programs, Head Start programs in schools for young children and tutoring centers for older children.

1. Who helped many blacks obtain civil rights?
   Whitney Young, Jr.
2. What was Whitney Young's job?
   director of the National Urban League
3. What did he help many black Americans get?
   civil rights
4. What did Whitney Young start for young children?
   Head Start programs
5. What did Whitney Young start for older children?
   tutoring centers

Page 47

Name ______________________ Skill: Compare and contrast

Two Famous Women of Flight

Amelia Earhart

Sally Ride

Amelia Earhart is remembered as the first lady of the air. She loved to fly, bought her own plane, and was the first woman to fly solo across the Atlantic Ocean. Besides being a pilot, Amelia Earhart was an author, fashion designer, photographer, poet, and painter.

Sally Ride will be remembered as America's first woman in space. She flew on the space shuttle *Challenger* as a mission specialist. Dr. Ride is an astronaut and scientist. While growing up, Sally Ride was a nationally ranked junior tennis player.

Decide which famous woman of flight the statement below describes. Write the correct name.

1. America's first woman in space Sally Ride	5. flew on space shuttle Sally Ride
2. first woman to fly solo across Atlantic Ocean Amelia Earhart	6. tennis player Sally Ride
3. owned her own airplane Amelia Earhart	7. was a fashion designer Amelia Earhart
4. famous woman pilot Amelia Earhart	8. famous woman astronaut Sally Ride

Brainwork! Write three ways Amelia Earhart and Sally Ride are alike.

Page 48

© Frank Schaffer Publications, Inc.

Answer Key

Name ____________________ Skill: Compare and contrast

Two Famous Women Educators

Helen Keller

Helen Keller became deaf and blind very young. Anne Sullivan worked hard to teach Helen. Finally Helen learned the word *water* when Anne spelled it in one of Helen's hands while Helen felt water in the other hand. After that Helen learned quickly. She spent her life showing that people with disabilities could learn.

Anne Sullivan

Anne Sullivan was chosen to teach Helen because she, too, had been blind. She had gone to a special school for the blind and deaf. Before Helen learned the word *water,* Anne had spelled out many other words. Finally Helen learned that words were names for things and actions. Anne was pleased when Helen spelled T-E-A-C-H-E-R.

Decide which famous woman educator the statement below describes. Write the correct name.

1. was deaf and blind very young — Helen Keller
2. worked hard to teach Helen — Anne Sullivan
3. was pleased when Helen spelled T-E-A-C-H-E-R — Anne Sullivan
4. finally learned that words were names for things and actions — Helen Keller
5. went to a special school — Anne Sullivan
6. spelled out many words for Helen — Anne Sullivan
7. learned the word *water* after a long time — Helen Keller
8. learned very quickly once she learned words were names. — Helen Keller

Brainwork! Close your eyes and pretend you are blind. Imagine how you would eat dinner. Write three sentences to tell how you would do it differently than now.

Page 49

Name ____________________ Skill: Compare and contrast

Two Famous Scientists

Rachel Carson

Rachel Carson grew up loving the outdoors, reading, and writing stories. In college she studied to be a writer and a scientist. She became the first woman scientist in the Department of Fisheries in 1936. Carson's books told people to care for the world around them. These books made her famous.

Dixy Lee Ray

Dixy Lee Ray grew up loving the sea, climbing mountains, and earning money by putting on puppet shows. In college she studied to be a scientist. As a TV teacher, she made science exciting. Dixy Lee Ray was the first woman to head the Atomic Energy Commission. In 1976 she was elected governor of Washington State.

Decide which famous woman scientist each statement describes. Write the correct name.

1. first woman to head Atomic Energy Commission — Dixy Lee Ray
2. first woman scientist in Department of Fisheries — Rachel Carson
3. wrote books about caring for world around us — Rachel Carson
4. governor of Washington state — Dixy Lee Ray
5. TV teacher who made science exciting — Dixy Lee Ray
6. writing books made her famous — Rachel Carson
7. loved outdoors, reading, and writing stories — Rachel Carson
8. put on puppet shows — Dixy Lee Ray

Brainwork! Rachel Carson was ten years old when her first story was printed. Dixy Lee Ray was twelve years old when she climbed the highest mountain in America. Write your age now and compare yourself with one of the women above.

Page 50

Name ____________________ Skill: Compare and contrast

Two Famous Women in Medicine

Elizabeth Blackwell

Elizabeth Blackwell was born in England and later became the first woman medical student in the United States. She became the first U.S. woman doctor. She started a hospital staffed only by women and a women's medical college. She is remembered for her ideas on cleanliness and ways to prevent illness.

Clara Barton

Clara Barton and some friends started the Red Cross in the United States. She was its first president. During wars the Red Cross helped wounded soldiers. Later the Red Cross began to help victims of floods, tornadoes, earthquakes, and disease. The Red Cross gave materials to rebuild homes and plant crops.

Decide which woman in medicine the statement below describes. Write the correct name.

1. first woman medical student — Elizabeth Blackwell
2. first president of Red Cross — Clara Barton
3. helped start Red Cross — Clara Barton
4. first woman doctor in U.S. — Elizabeth Blackwell
5. worked to expand Red Cross — Clara Barton
6. started hospital staffed only by women — Elizabeth Blackwell
7. started women's medical college — Elizabeth Blackwell
8. remembered for ideas on cleanliness — Elizabeth Blackwell

Brainwork! Write three sentences telling how these two women in medicine were alike.

Page 51

Name ____________________ Skill: Compare and contrast

Two Famous American Artists

Mary Cassatt

Mary Cassatt was the first great American woman artist. As a child she visited museums and galleries in France. It was then she decided to be a painter. People all over the world liked her paintings with their short brush strokes and rich, bright colors. She often painted mothers and children.

Georgia O'Keeffe

Georgia O'Keeffe was a well-known American woman artist. She created an original style of painting by enlarging one object. Often the object filled an entire canvas. The design was clear and exact. She painted single flowers or the skulls of animals. Many of her paintings showed the beauty of the desert.

Decide which famous woman artist the statement below describes. Write the correct name.

1. first great American woman artist — Mary Cassatt
2. created original style of painting — Georgia O'Keeffe
3. decided to be painter when a child — Mary Cassatt
4. painted mothers and children — Mary Cassatt
5. paintings showed beauty of the desert — Georgia O'Keeffe
6. enlarged one object to fill canvas — Georgia O'Keeffe
7. painted with bright colors — Mary Cassatt
8. painted flowers and skulls — Georgia O'Keeffe

Brainwork! Would you rather have a painting in your room by Mary Cassatt or Georgia O'Keeffe? Why? Write your answers.

Page 52

© Frank Schaffer Publications, Inc.

Answer Key

Name ______________________ Skill: Compare and contrast

Two Famous Women Authors

Laura Ingalls Wilder

Laura Ingalls Wilder became famous when she wrote a series of children's books. The nine "Little House" books told of her family's pioneer life. Laura didn't begin writing until she was 65 years old. In 1954 she won the first Laura Ingalls Wilder Award given for outstanding written or artistic work.

Harriet Beecher Stowe

Harriet Beecher Stowe became famous for her book, *Uncle Tom's Cabin*. She was the first American author to write about black people and slavery. Her book told of the horrible lives of slaves. This story caused many people to work to free the slaves. It also hurried the beginning of Civil War.

Decide which famous woman author the statement below describes. Write the correct name.

1. wrote *Uncle Tom's Cabin* — Harriet Beecher Stowe
2. wrote "Little House" series — Laura Ingalls Wilder
3. first to write about black people — Harriet Beecher Stowe
4. first to win Laura Ingalls Wilder Award — Laura Ingalls Wilder
5. wrote about slavery — Harriet Beecher Stowe
6. wrote about pioneer life — Laura Ingalls Wilder
7. began writing at 65 — Laura Ingalls Wilder
8. caused people to work to free the slaves — Harriet Beecher Stowe

Brainwork! Make a list of how these two famous American authors are alike.

Page 53

Name ______________________ Date ____________

First Americans: The Indians

The first people in America were the Indians. No one is sure when they first came, or from where they came. We think they came from Asia. Long ago there may have been a land "bridge" between Russia and Alaska. They could have walked across. Some stayed in Alaska. Others traveled to all parts of North and South America.

There were many tribes of Indians. Each tribe wanted to be left alone. They lived simple lives. They did not build towns with schools. They did not have books. They learned from older people in the tribe.

The Indians had many good ways. They loved the land. They only took whatever they needed from it. They shared with each other. They were free.

1. Who were the first Americans?
the Indians

2. From where could they have come?
Asia

3. How could they have come over here?
They could have walked.

4. What did they not have?
towns, schools, books

5. Write one good thing about Indian ways.
Answers will vary.

TO DO: Begin a book on America. Find out more about the Indians. Draw Indian pictures. How do you think the Indians felt when the white men came? Pretend you were an Indian then. Write how you felt. Find Asia, Russia and Alaska on a map. See how the Indians might have come.

Page 54

Name ______________________ Date ____________

Columbus Finds America

Christopher Columbus lived in Italy. He liked ships. He wanted to sail when he grew up. Some people still thought the world was flat. Columbus wanted to sail around the world. Then he could prove it was round.

One day he went to the King and Queen of Spain. They wanted to find a shorter way to sail to India. They wanted Columbus to find gold. Columbus asked for ships to sail. He was given three. He got a crew together. They sailed many weeks. It was long and hard. Some of the men wanted to go back. Columbus said, "No! We must sail on!" Then, on October 12, 1492, Columbus landed near South America. He had found the Americas!

1. How did Columbus think the world was shaped?
round

2. Who gave ships to Columbus?
the King and Queen of Spain

3. What did Columbus say to his men?
"We must sail on!"

4. What was Columbus sent to find?
a shorter way to India and gold

5. When did he find the Americas?
October 12, 1492

TO DO: Look at a world map. Find Italy and Spain. See how far Columbus sailed. He was brave. Have you ever been brave? Write a story about it. Save it for your book.

Page 55

Name ______________________ Date ____________

Many Explorers

Columbus was an explorer. An explorer puts his flag in the ground when he lands. This means that the land is discovered and claimed by his country. Columbus sailed for Spain. He planted the Spanish flag on the shore.

After Columbus, other Spanish explorers came. They started little towns in South America. Then they went to the southwestern part of the United States. They put up their flags. They pushed the Indian aside. They forgot that he was there first.

Rulers of other lands heard about the Americas. They sent explorers too. Soon there were flags of France, Holland, and England in the new land.

1. What must explorers do when they find a new land?
They must put their flag in the ground.

2. What does this mean?
The land was discovered and claimed by that country.

3. Columbus was born in Italy. Why did he have a Spanish flag?
He sailed for Spain.

4. What other lands sent explorers?
France, Holland, England

5. What part of the United States was discovered?
the southwestern part

TO DO: Look at a world map. Find these lands: France, Holland, Spain. Draw their flags. Label them. Put them in your book.

Page 56

Answer Key

Name ____________________ Date ____________

Jamestown

When you claim a new land, you need more than just a flag in the ground. Your people must live there too. The King of England wanted English people in this new land. He didn't think the land belonged to the Indians.

In 1607 three ships left England for America. They came here to live. They came to get rich. They chose a place and called it Jamestown. They named it for their king, James.

They began to look for gold. Then they ran out of food. Many people got sick. Some died. These were hard times.

Then they saw that the land was good. So they began farming. The people of Jamestown did not find gold. But they got rich from the fine land.

1. What must the people do to own the land?
They must live there.

2. After whom was Jamestown named?
King James of England

3. Why did these people come?
to get rich or to own land

4. What did they look for?
They looked for gold.

5. What made them rich?
farming and the fine land

TO DO: Draw a picture of Jamestown. Find stories in the library about it. Who were Captain John Smith and Pocahontas? Write a story about them.

Page 57

Name ____________________ Date ____________

Black Americans

Most people came to America because they wanted to come. Some came to be free. Some came to get rich. But some came as slaves.

Many people started farms in what are now the southern states of America. The farms grew very large. More workers were needed. So men from America sailed to Africa. They captured many of the black people who lived in Africa. They brought the slaves to America. The slaves were forced to work on the farms. They were treated very badly. Black people were slaves in America for many years. Slavery in America ended when Abraham Lincoln made it against the law to own slaves.

Today all Americans are free. Free Americans are every color!

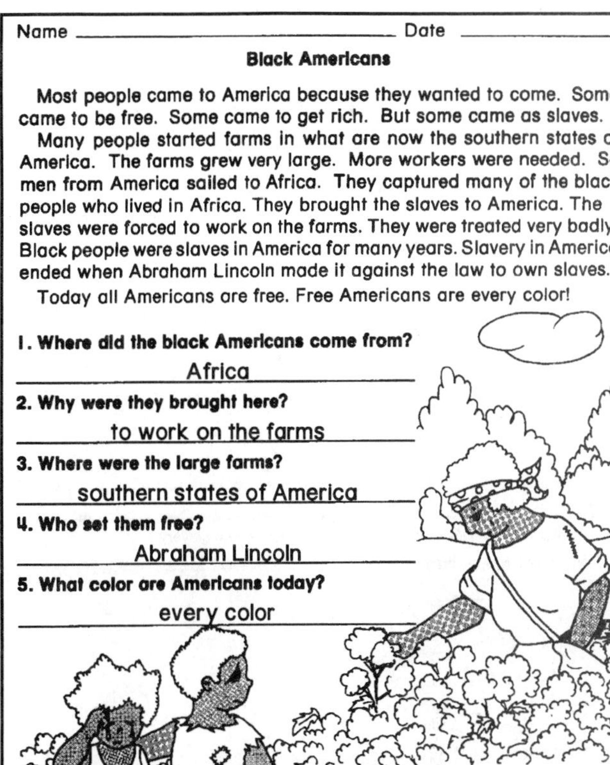

1. Where did the black Americans come from?
Africa

2. Why were they brought here?
to work on the farms

3. Where were the large farms?
southern states of America

4. Who set them free?
Abraham Lincoln

5. What color are Americans today?
every color

TO DO: Find Africa on a world map. Look in the library for books about slavery. Pretend you lived in Africa and were forced to go to America on a ship. How would you feel? Write a story. Talk about freedom. What does it mean to be "free"?

Page 58

Name ____________________ Date ____________

Pilgrims And The Mayflower

There were some unhappy people in England. The King said they had to go to his church. They wanted to go to their own churches. Someone said, "Let's go to America. There we can be free to worship as we wish."

About 100 Pilgrims left England on the Mayflower. It was a small ship. The sea was stormy. People got sick. It was a hard trip.

They were to go to Jamestown. They got to America, but not to Jamestown. The wind blew them farther north. They landed at Plymouth Rock in December of 1620.

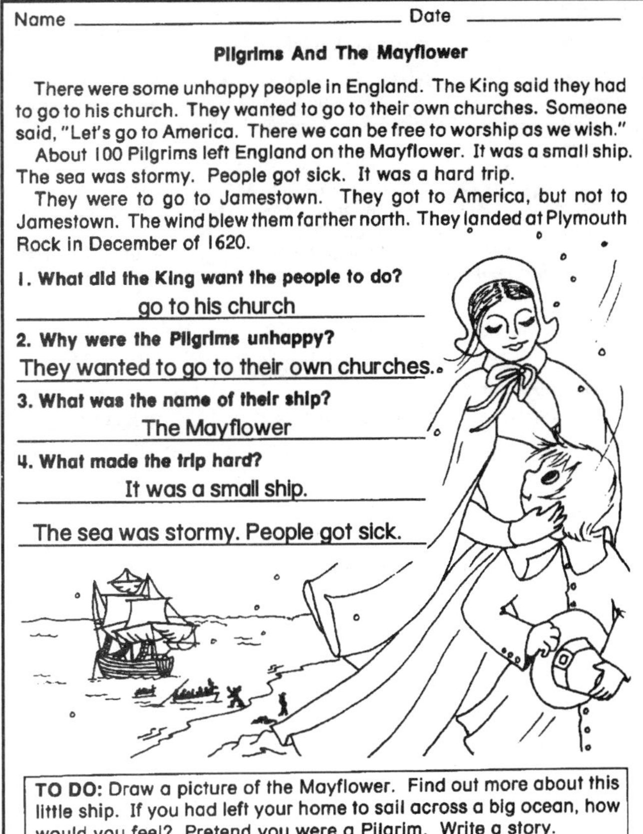

1. What did the King want the people to do?
go to his church

2. Why were the Pilgrims unhappy?
They wanted to go to their own churches.

3. What was the name of their ship?
The Mayflower

4. What made the trip hard?
It was a small ship.
The sea was stormy. People got sick.

TO DO: Draw a picture of the Mayflower. Find out more about this little ship. If you had left your home to sail across a big ocean, how would you feel? Pretend you were a Pilgrim. Write a story.

Page 59

Name ____________________ Date ____________

The First Thanksgiving

It was winter when the Pilgrims landed. They slept on the Mayflower at night. They chopped down trees in the daytime. They made houses and a fort. The Pilgrims made beds and tables. It was a long, hard winter. They ran out of food. Many Pilgrims got sick and died.

In the spring they met a kind Indian named Squanto. He showed them how to plant and grow food.

In the fall the Pilgrims picked lots of food from their gardens. They were very thankful. They asked the Indians to come for a big dinner. This was the first Thanksgiving.

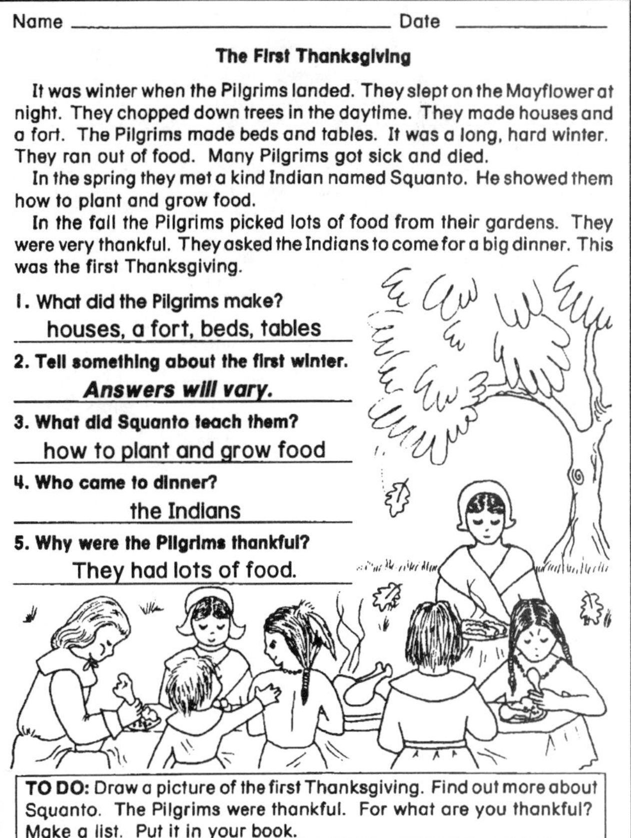

1. What did the Pilgrims make?
houses, a fort, beds, tables

2. Tell something about the first winter.
Answers will vary.

3. What did Squanto teach them?
how to plant and grow food

4. Who came to dinner?
the Indians

5. Why were the Pilgrims thankful?
They had lots of food.

TO DO: Draw a picture of the first Thanksgiving. Find out more about Squanto. The Pilgrims were thankful. For what are you thankful? Make a list. Put it in your book.

Page 60

Answer Key

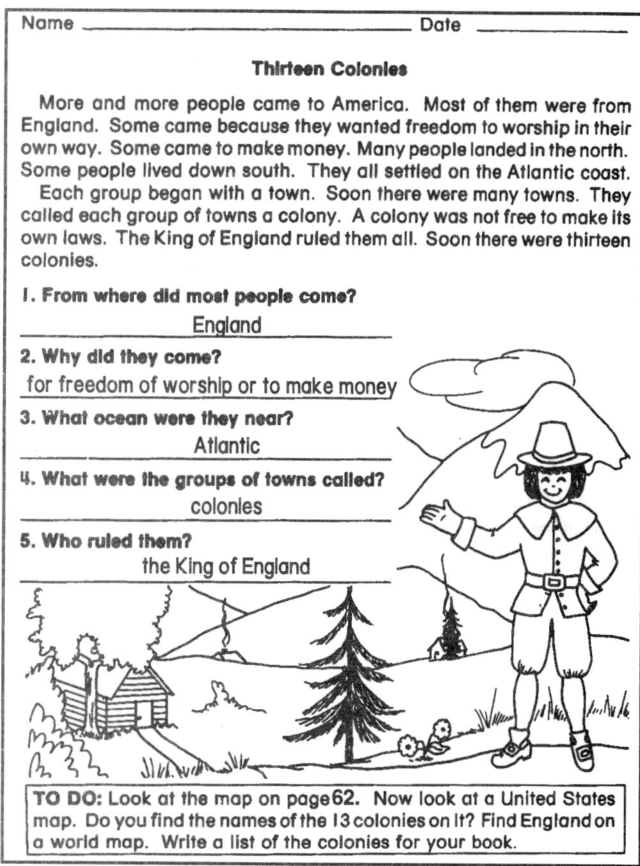

Name ______________________ Date ____________

Thirteen Colonies

More and more people came to America. Most of them were from England. Some came because they wanted freedom to worship in their own way. Some came to make money. Many people landed in the north. Some people lived down south. They all settled on the Atlantic coast.

Each group began with a town. Soon there were many towns. They called each group of towns a colony. A colony was not free to make its own laws. The King of England ruled them all. Soon there were thirteen colonies.

1. From where did most people come?

England

2. Why did they come?

for freedom of worship or to make money

3. What ocean were they near?

Atlantic

4. What were the groups of towns called?

colonies

5. Who ruled them?

the King of England

TO DO: Look at the map on page 62. Now look at a United States map. Do you find the names of the 13 colonies on it? Find England on a world map. Write a list of the colonies for your book.

Page 61

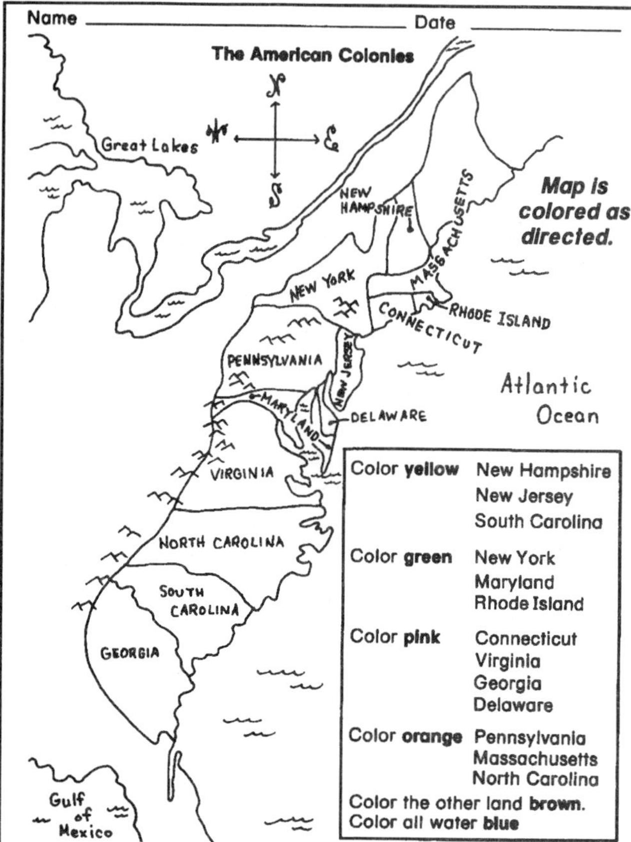

Name ______________________ Date ____________

The American Colonies

Color **yellow**	New Hampshire New Jersey South Carolina
Color **green**	New York Maryland Rhode Island
Color **pink**	Connecticut Virginia Georgia Delaware
Color **orange**	Pennsylvania Massachusetts North Carolina

Color the other land **brown**.
Color all water **blue**

Page 62

Name ______________________ Date ____________

Life in the Colonies

Life in the early colonies was hard. The people had to chop down trees. They had to make everything they needed. They slept on straw mats. They had to grow their own food. Animals were hunted for meat and fur. Many people were sick. Many died.

As years went by, life got better. The colonists built ships. They sailed to England to buy things. They built better homes. Many people slept on soft feather beds. The colonies were growing, happy places.

1. What did the people have to make?

everything they needed

2. Where did they get the wood?

They chopped down trees.

3. Where did they get their food?

They grew their food.

4. How did they get soft beds and better homes?

They sailed to England to buy things and they built homes.

5. Where did they get their ships?

They built them.

TO DO: Pretend you lived in a colony. If you had to make everything you needed, what would you make first? Then what? List six or eight things.

Page 63

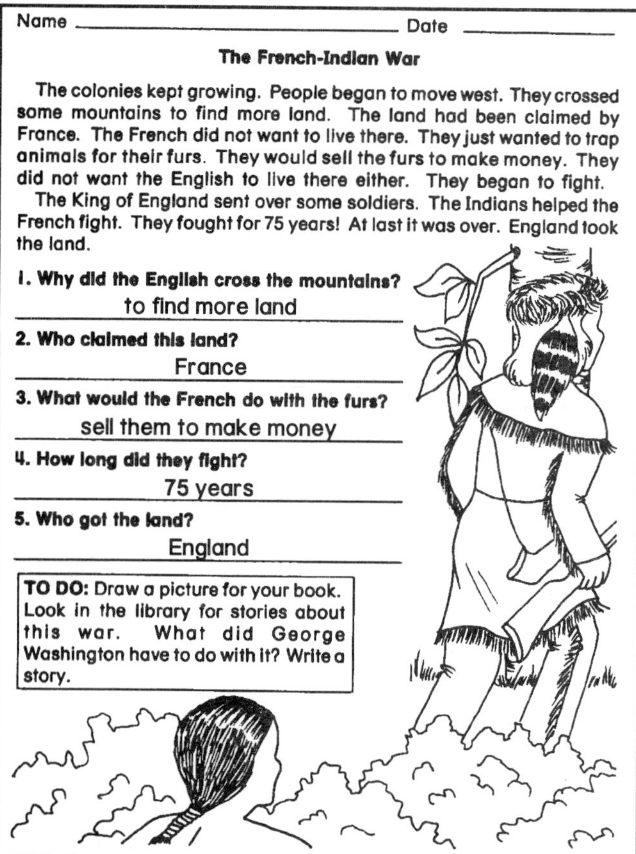

Name ______________________ Date ____________

The French-Indian War

The colonies kept growing. People began to move west. They crossed some mountains to find more land. The land had been claimed by France. The French did not want to live there. They just wanted to trap animals for their furs. They would sell the furs to make money. They did not want the English to live there either. They began to fight.

The King of England sent over some soldiers. The Indians helped the French fight. They fought for 75 years! At last it was over. England took the land.

1. Why did the English cross the mountains?

to find more land

2. Who claimed this land?

France

3. What would the French do with the furs?

sell them to make money

4. How long did they fight?

75 years

5. Who got the land?

England

TO DO: Draw a picture for your book. Look in the library for stories about this war. What did George Washington have to do with it? Write a story.

Page 64

Answer Key

Name ______________________ Date ____________

The Boston Tea Party

The French-Indian War cost England a lot of money. The King thought the colonists should help pay for the war. He put a tax on tea and other goods from England that the colonists would buy. This tax would help pay for the war.

The colonists were angry. They said, "It is not fair! We did not vote for this. We will not pay a tax we did not vote for!" The King said, "You will!" The colonists said, "We won't!"

One night some colonists dressed up like Indians. They went to the harbor. They got on an English ship. They threw all the boxes of tea into the water. They called it "The Boston Tea Party."

1. Why did the King put a tax on things?
He thought the colonists should help pay for the war.
2. Why were the colonists angry?
They did not vote for the tax.
3. How did the colonists dress up?
like Indians
4. Was "Boston Tea Party" a good name? Why?
Answers will vary.

TO DO: Draw a picture of this "party." The English and the colonists did not agree. Set up chairs facing each other. Some students be colonists, some be English. Tell why you feel you are right.

Page 65

Name ______________________ Date ____________

The Colonists Want To Be Free!

The colonists tried and tried to talk to the King. They asked him to let them help make their laws. The King would not hear of it!

Near Boston there was a battle between some colonists and some English soldiers. Men were killed on both sides.

Then the King hired some German soldiers to come fight the colonists. There was going to be a war.

Leaders from the colonies met. Thomas Jefferson wrote an important paper. It told the world that the colonies were going to become one free country. The date was July 4, 1776, which is now called the birthday of our country.

1. What did the colonists want?
to help make their laws

2. Who did the King hire to fight the colonists?
German soldiers

3. Who wrote an important paper?
Thomas Jefferson

4. What did the paper say?
The colonies were going to become one free country.

5. When is our country's birthday?
July, 4 1776

TO DO: Do you think the colonists had the right to help make their laws? If you had been Thomas Jefferson, what would you have said? Think carefully, then write it down.

Page 66

Name ______________________ Date ____________

A New Flag

Each colony had its own flag. But now they would be fighting as a team. They wanted one flag for all!

George Washington was made the leader of the colonial army. They needed a flag to follow. They needed a flag to fly over their camps and to carry into battle.

It is said that Betsy Ross made our first flag. Washington wanted 13 stripes for the 13 colonies. He wanted them to be red and white. Betsy Ross put a square of blue in the corner. On the blue was a circle of 13 stars.

The leaders of the colonies liked the new flag. They voted for it on June 14, 1777. Now June 14 is called Flag Day.

1. Who was the leader of the colonial army?
George Washington

2. Why did they want a new flag?
They wanted one flag for all!

3. How many stripes and stars were on the first flag?
13 stripes and 13 stars

4. What colors did Washington want?
red and white

5. When is Flag Day?
June 14

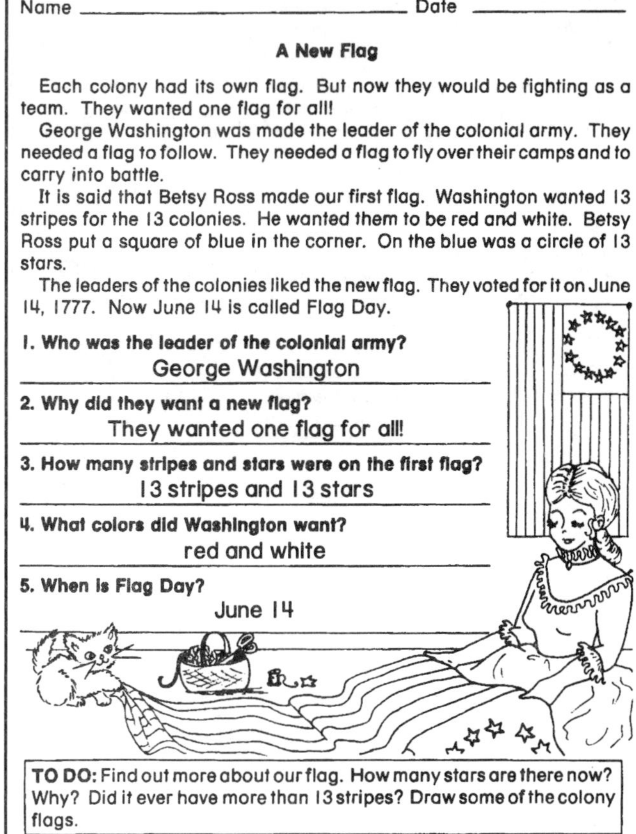

TO DO: Find out more about our flag. How many stars are there now? Why? Did it ever have more than 13 stripes? Draw some of the colony flags.

Page 67

Name ______________________ Date ____________

Flag is made as directed.

How To Make A Star

Here is how to make a star. Make 13 white ones. Now get some red, white, and blue paper. Make the first American flag.

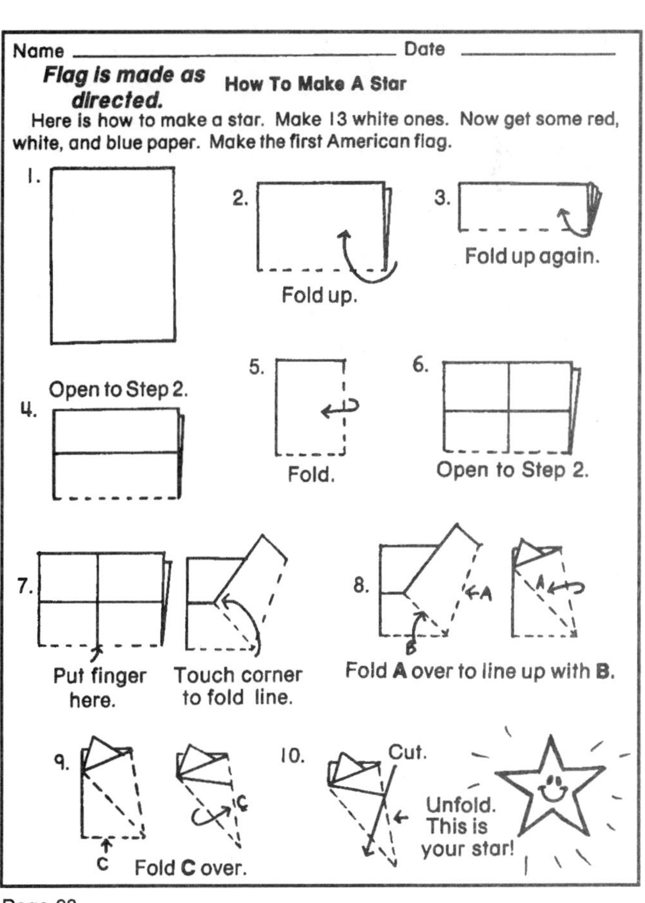

Page 68

© Frank Schaffer Publications, Inc.

Answer Key

Name ______________________ Date __________

The Fight For Freedom

The Revolutionary War began. For a long time it looked like the colonists would never win. The English soldiers were stronger. They had better guns and training.

One winter was very bad. The colonial army was out of food. They were sick. They were cold. Snow was on the ground and some soldiers had no shoes.

George Washington was a good leader. He bought food with his own money. He tried to cheer up the men.

Then the people of France decided to help the colonists. With the help of the French soldiers, the colonists won the war. There was now a new free country: the United States of America!

1. Why were the English winning?
   The soldiers were stronger.
   They had better guns and training.
2. What made Washington a good leader?
   He bought food for the men and cheered them up.
3. What country helped the colonists?
   France
4. What was the new country's name?
   the United States of America

TO DO: Use your library. Find books about this war. Who were some of the leaders besides Washington? Make a list or write a story.

Page 69

Name ______________________ Date __________

A New Government

A new country had been born. Now the colonies were called states. George Washington and others were wise. They knew the states needed a new kind of government. They called together leaders from all the states.

For many days the men worked. They wrote a wonderful plan. This plan has helped our country grow faster than any other country in the world! They made sure there would be no king giving orders. They made sure the people had the right to vote. They made sure there were many freedoms.

The people all agreed on the plan. Then they chose George Washington to be their president.

1. What did the colonies become?
   States
2. What did the states need?
   a new kind of government
3. Who wrote this plan?
   leaders from all the states
4. Name something good about the plan.
   Answers will vary.
5. Who became the first president?
   George Washington

TO DO: The new government gave us many freedoms. Look in the library. Talk to others. Then write down a list of our freedoms. What would it be like without them? Think about it.

Page 70

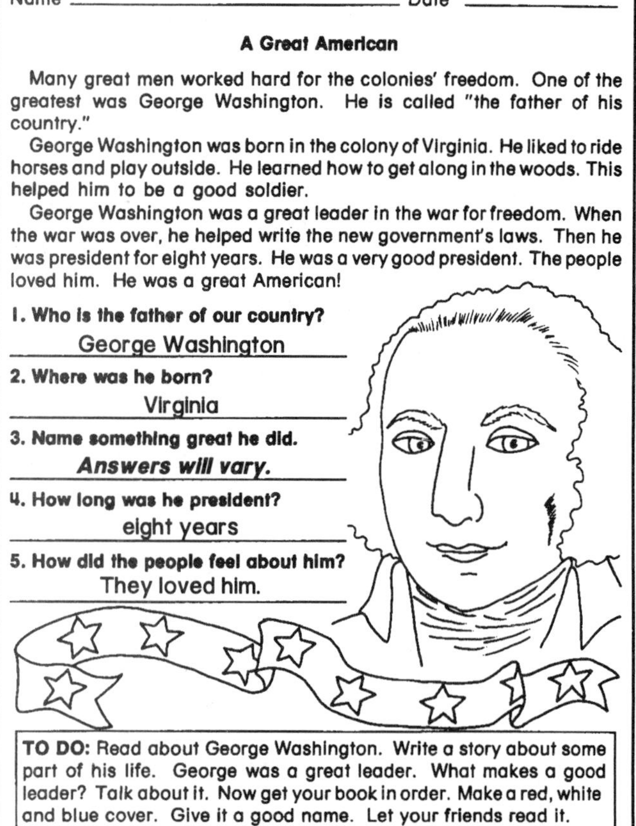

Name ______________________ Date __________

A Great American

Many great men worked hard for the colonies' freedom. One of the greatest was George Washington. He is called "the father of his country."

George Washington was born in the colony of Virginia. He liked to ride horses and play outside. He learned how to get along in the woods. This helped him to be a good soldier.

George Washington was a great leader in the war for freedom. When the war was over, he helped write the new government's laws. Then he was president for eight years. He was a very good president. The people loved him. He was a great American!

1. Who is the father of our country?
   George Washington
2. Where was he born?
   Virginia
3. Name something great he did.
   Answers will vary.
4. How long was he president?
   eight years
5. How did the people feel about him?
   They loved him.

TO DO: Read about George Washington. Write a story about some part of his life. George was a great leader. What makes a good leader? Talk about it. Now get your book in order. Make a red, white and blue cover. Give it a good name. Let your friends read it.

Page 71

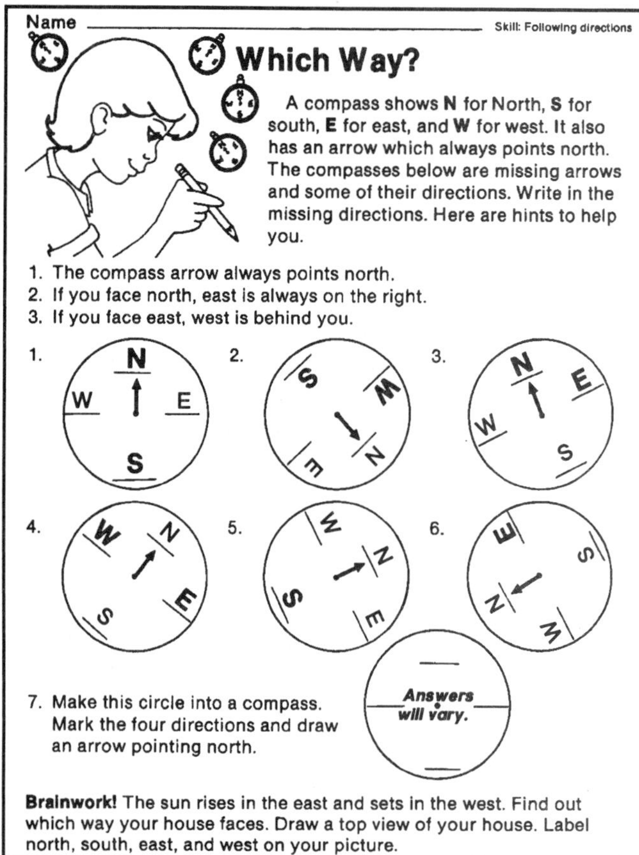

Name ______________________ Skill: Following directions

Which Way?

A compass shows **N** for North, **S** for south, **E** for east, and **W** for west. It also has an arrow which always points north. The compasses below are missing arrows and some of their directions. Write in the missing directions. Here are hints to help you.

1. The compass arrow always points north.
2. If you face north, east is always on the right.
3. If you face east, west is behind you.

7. Make this circle into a compass. Mark the four directions and draw an arrow pointing north.

Answers will vary.

Brainwork! The sun rises in the east and sets in the west. Find out which way your house faces. Draw a top view of your house. Label north, south, east, and west on your picture.

Page 72

© Frank Schaffer Publications, Inc.

Answer Key

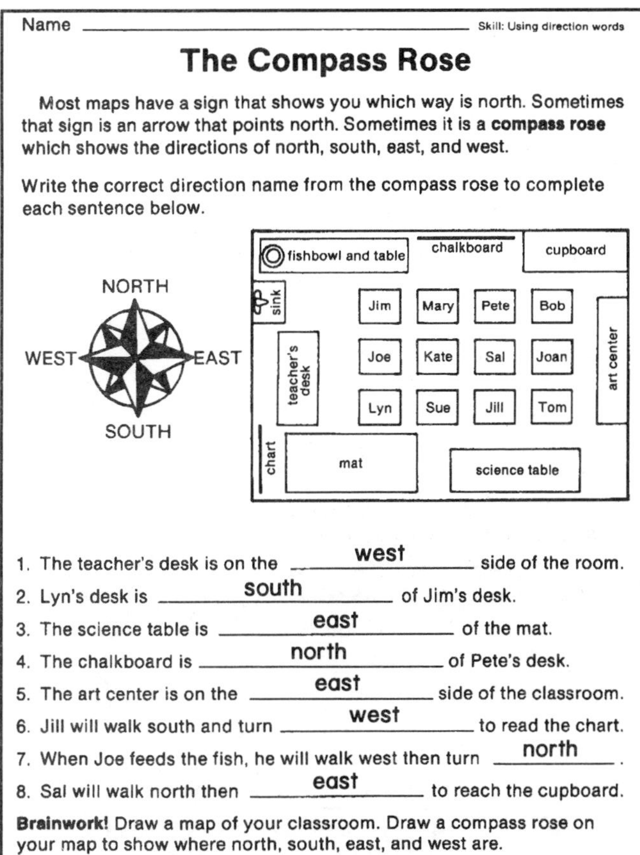

Name ______________________ Skill: Using direction words

The Compass Rose

Most maps have a sign that shows you which way is north. Sometimes that sign is an arrow that points north. Sometimes it is a **compass rose** which shows the directions of north, south, east, and west.

Write the correct direction name from the compass rose to complete each sentence below.

1. The teacher's desk is on the ___west___ side of the room.
2. Lyn's desk is ___south___ of Jim's desk.
3. The science table is ___east___ of the mat.
4. The chalkboard is ___north___ of Pete's desk.
5. The art center is on the ___east___ side of the classroom.
6. Jill will walk south and turn ___west___ to read the chart.
7. When Joe feeds the fish, he will walk west then turn ___north___.
8. Sal will walk north then ___east___ to reach the cupboard.

Brainwork! Draw a map of your classroom. Draw a compass rose on your map to show where north, south, east, and west are.

Page 73

Name ______________________ Skill: Using map symbols

Important Places in the City

Symbols are drawings which stand for important things on a map. Here are some symbols you might find on a map.

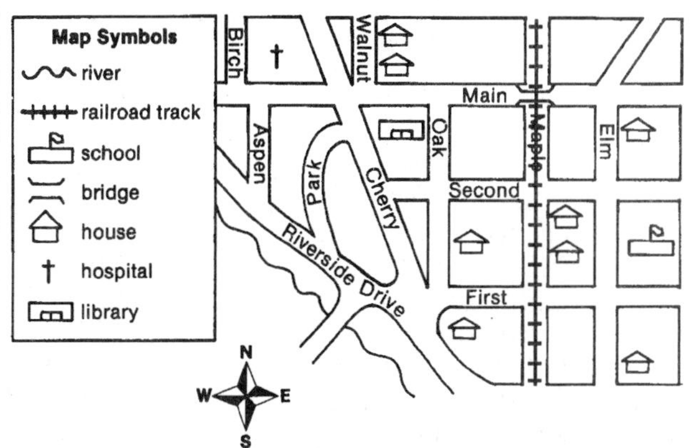

Follow the directions below to draw the correct symbols where they belong on this map.

1. Draw the school symbol on the east side of Elm between First and Second.
2. Draw the hospital symbol on Main between Birch and Cherry.
3. Draw the railroad track symbol down the middle of Maple.
4. Draw the bridge symbol on Main where it crosses over the railroad tracks.
5. Draw the library symbol on Cherry between Second and Main.

Brainwork! Make up symbols for the important things around your school. Show these symbols on a map of your school.

Page 74

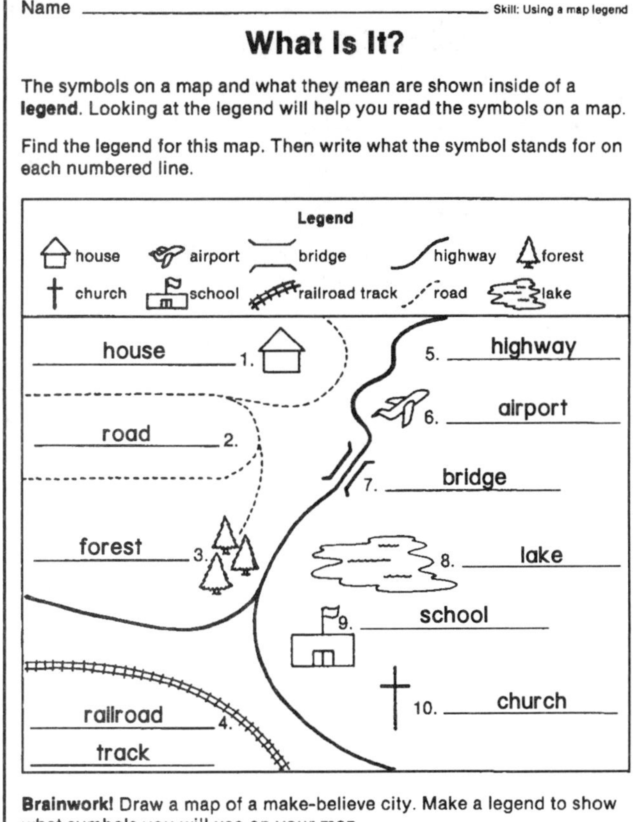

Name ______________________ Skill: Using a map legend

What Is It?

The symbols on a map and what they mean are shown inside of a **legend**. Looking at the legend will help you read the symbols on a map.

Find the legend for this map. Then write what the symbol stands for on each numbered line.

1. house
2. road
3. forest
4. railroad track
5. highway
6. airport
7. bridge
8. lake
9. school
10. church

Brainwork! Draw a map of a make-believe city. Make a legend to show what symbols you will use on your map.

Page 75

Name ______________________ Skill: Following directions

How Do We Get There?

Jim and Jenny are invited to a party at Clara's house. They have planned a route to walk to the party. Read their directions. Draw a line on the map below to show where Jim and Jenny will walk.

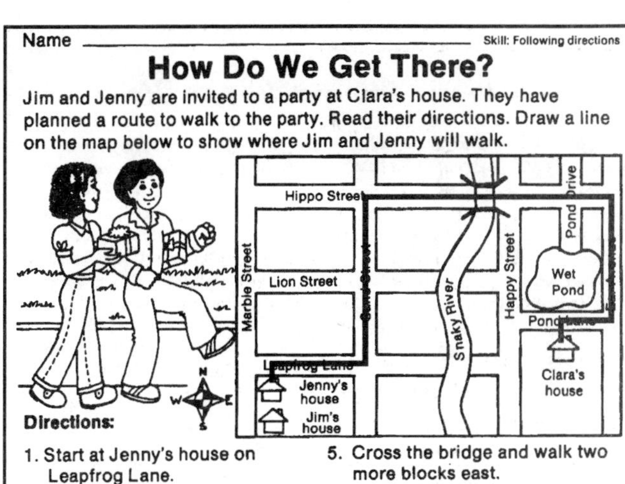

Directions:

1. Start at Jenny's house on Leapfrog Lane.
2. Go east one block.
3. Turn north on Sand Street and walk two blocks.
4. Turn east on Hippo Street and walk to the bridge.
5. Cross the bridge and walk two more blocks east.
6. Turn south on Ear Avenue and go to Pond Lane.
7. Go west on Pond Lane to Clara's house.
8. There is a shorter way to Clara's house **after** Jim and Jenny go across the bridge. Write the steps here. Go south on Happy Street to Pond Lane. Turn east on Pond Lane.

Brainwork! Imagine you live on the corner of Hippo and Marble. Draw your house and your route to Clara's house.

Page 76

© Frank Schaffer Publications, Inc.

Answer Key

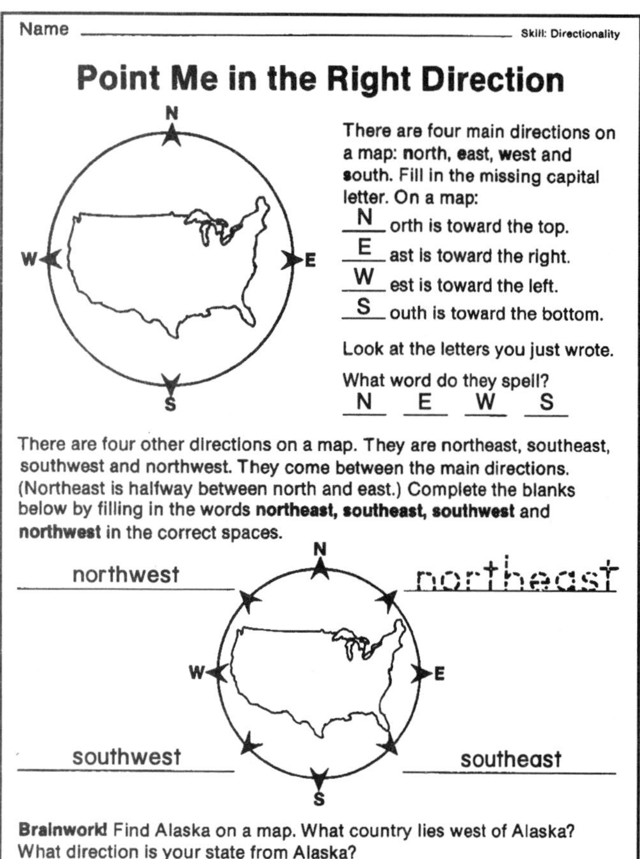

Name ______________________ Skill: Directionality

Point Me in the Right Direction

There are four main directions on a map: **north**, **east**, **west** and **south**. Fill in the missing capital letter. On a map:

N orth is toward the top.
E ast is toward the right.
W est is toward the left.
S outh is toward the bottom.

Look at the letters you just wrote.
What word do they spell?
N E W S

There are four other directions on a map. They are northeast, southeast, southwest and northwest. They come between the main directions. (Northeast is halfway between north and east.) Complete the blanks below by filling in the words **northeast, southeast, southwest** and **northwest** in the correct spaces.

northwest — northeast
southwest — southeast

Brainwork! Find Alaska on a map. What country lies west of Alaska? What direction is your state from Alaska?

Page 77

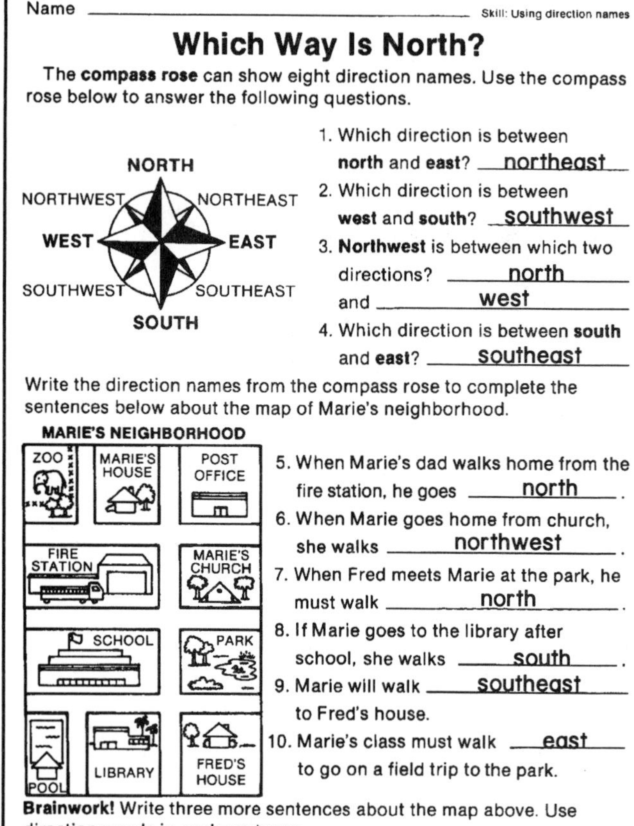

Name ______________________ Skill: Using direction names

Which Way Is North?

The **compass rose** can show eight direction names. Use the compass rose below to answer the following questions.

1. Which direction is between **north** and **east**? northeast
2. Which direction is between **west** and **south**? southwest
3. **Northwest** is between which two directions? north and west
4. Which direction is between **south** and **east**? southeast

Write the direction names from the compass rose to complete the sentences below about the map of Marie's neighborhood.

MARIE'S NEIGHBORHOOD

5. When Marie's dad walks home from the fire station, he goes north.
6. When Marie goes home from church, she walks northwest.
7. When Fred meets Marie at the park, he must walk north.
8. If Marie goes to the library after school, she walks south.
9. Marie will walk southeast to Fred's house.
10. Marie's class must walk east to go on a field trip to the park.

Brainwork! Write three more sentences about the map above. Use direction words in each sentence.

Page 78

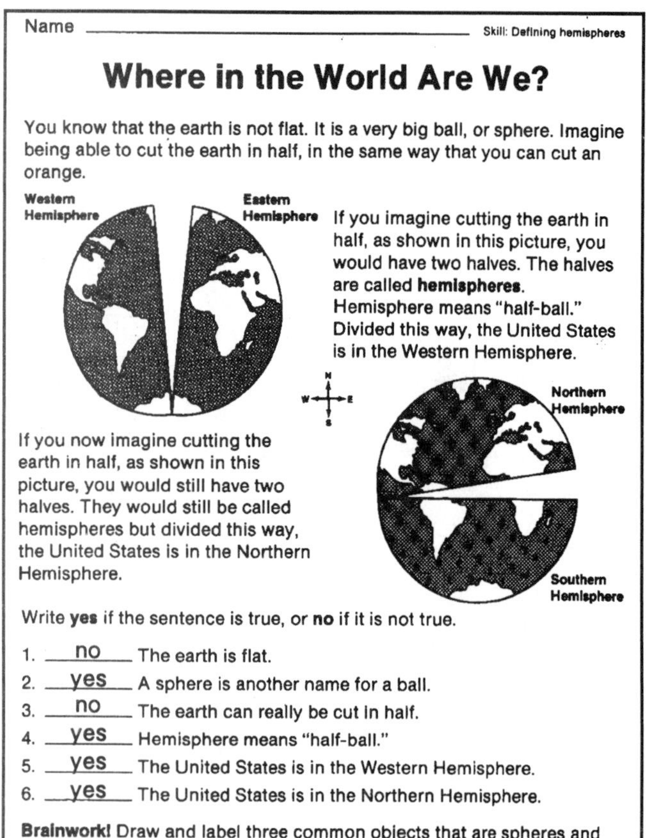

Name ______________________ Skill: Defining hemispheres

Where in the World Are We?

You know that the earth is not flat. It is a very big ball, or sphere. Imagine being able to cut the earth in half, in the same way that you can cut an orange.

If you imagine cutting the earth in half, as shown in this picture, you would have two halves. The halves are called **hemispheres**. Hemisphere means "half-ball." Divided this way, the United States is in the Western Hemisphere.

If you now imagine cutting the earth in half, as shown in this picture, you would still have two halves. They would still be called hemispheres but divided this way, the United States is in the Northern Hemisphere.

Write **yes** if the sentence is true, or **no** if it is not true.

1. no The earth is flat.
2. yes A sphere is another name for a ball.
3. no The earth can really be cut in half.
4. yes Hemisphere means "half-ball."
5. yes The United States is in the Western Hemisphere.
6. yes The United States is in the Northern Hemisphere.

Brainwork! Draw and label three common objects that are spheres and three that are hemispheres.

Page 79

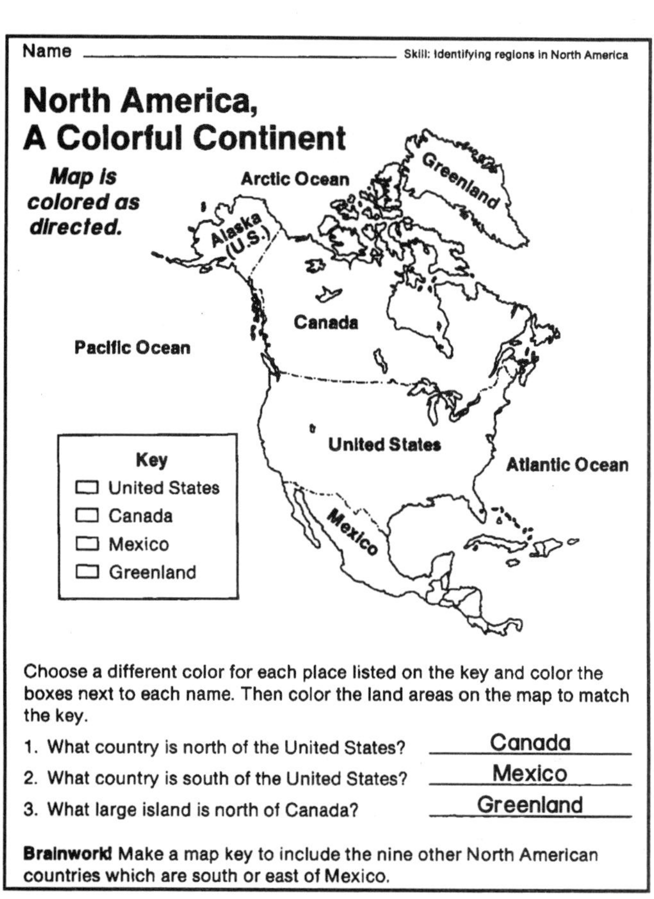

Name ______________________ Skill: Identifying regions in North America

North America, A Colorful Continent

Map is colored as directed.

Choose a different color for each place listed on the key and color the boxes next to each name. Then color the land areas on the map to match the key.

1. What country is north of the United States? Canada
2. What country is south of the United States? Mexico
3. What large island is north of Canada? Greenland

Brainwork! Make a map key to include the nine other North American countries which are south or east of Mexico.

Page 80

© Frank Schaffer Publications, Inc.

Answer Key

Around the Globe

Name ______________________ Skill: Continents

The world is divided into seven large land masses. These big areas are called **continents**. Their names are Asia, Africa, Europe, North America, South America, Australia, and Antarctica. Asia is the largest continent. More than half of the world's people live there. No one lives on Antarctica because it's too cold!

The map shows where some students were born. Fill in the table below with the correct continent names.

Names	Continents Where They Were Born
Carlos	South America
Ivan	Asia
Tanya	Africa
Mike	North America
Kim	Asia
Marco	Europe
Maria	North America
Joyce	Australia

Brainwork! Draw a picture of the continent where you were born.

Page 81

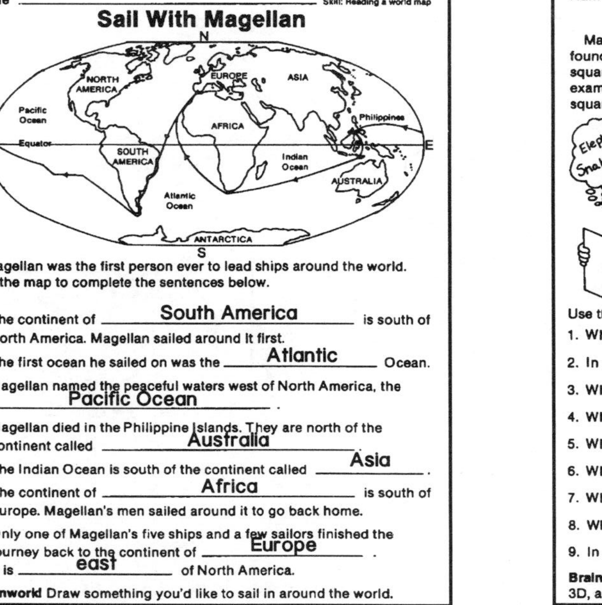

Sail With Magellan

Name ______________________ Skill: Reading a world map

Magellan was the first person ever to lead ships around the world. Use the map to complete the sentences below.

1. The continent of South America is south of North America. Magellan sailed around it first.
2. The first ocean he sailed on was the Atlantic Ocean.
3. Magellan named the peaceful waters west of North America, the Pacific Ocean.
4. Magellan died in the Philippine Islands. They are north of the continent called Australia.
5. The Indian Ocean is south of the continent called Asia.
6. The continent of Africa is south of Europe. Magellan's men sailed around it to go back home.
7. Only one of Magellan's five ships and a few sailors finished the journey back to the continent of Europe. It is east of North America.

Brainwork! Draw something you'd like to sail in around the world.

Page 82

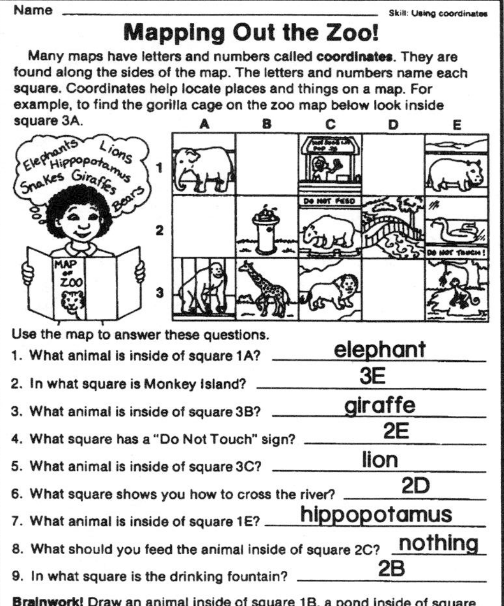

Mapping Out the Zoo!

Name ______________________ Skill: Using coordinates

Many maps have letters and numbers called **coordinates**. They are found along the sides of the map. The letters and numbers name each square. Coordinates help locate places and things on a map. For example, to find the gorilla cage on the zoo map below look inside square 3A.

Use the map to answer these questions.

1. What animal is inside of square 1A? elephant
2. In what square is Monkey Island? 3E
3. What animal is inside of square 3B? giraffe
4. What square has a "Do Not Touch" sign? 2E
5. What animal is inside of square 3C? lion
6. What square shows you how to cross the river? 2D
7. What animal is inside of square 1E? hippopotamus
8. What should you feed the animal inside of square 2C? nothing
9. In what square is the drinking fountain? 2B

Brainwork! Draw an animal inside of square 1B, a pond inside of square 3D, and a picnic table inside of square 2A.

Page 83

Find the Treasure

Name ______________________ Skill: Using a map grid, Following directions

A treasure is hidden on this map **grid**. A grid is a set of lines. Along the margins of this grid are letters and numbers called **coordinates**. These letters and numbers name each square. (The horse is inside square B4.)

Follow these directions. Draw a line to show your path.

1. Start at the **X** in A1.
2. Go to the haystack in B2.
3. Walk around the hay and you will see an old house in A4. Go there.
4. Don't go in. That house is haunted. Run to the car in E5.
5. Whoops! There are no car keys. Cross over the bridge in E4.
6. Jump over the pond in D3.
7. Go north to C3. Walk over the log between C3 and C2.
8. Go to B1. Peek in the barn.
9. Now go straight south to the next square.
10. You have found the treasure! It is in the school.

Brainwork! Draw a map with a grid and pictures like the one above. Write directions to a treasure. Let a friend try to find your treasure!

Page 84

What Can You Tell From a Map?

Name ______________________ Skill: Recognizing types of maps

Different maps of the same place tell different things about it.

This map shows cities. **Political Map**

This map shows mountains and rivers. **Physical Map**

This map shows rainfall. **Climate Map**

This map shows things that are grown or made. **Product Map**

Write the name of the map that you could use to:

1. Find out where two major rivers cross. Physical Map
2. Find the capital city of a state. Political Map
3. See how much it rains in a certain place. Climate Map
4. Find out where forests are grown. Product Map
5. Learn where mountains are located. Physical Map

Brainwork! Write five questions that can be answered with the maps above.

Page 85

Let's Take a Field Trip!

Name ______________________ Skill: Understanding scale

Each map has a **scale** that tells you the distance on the map that is equal to the real distance on earth. This map shows where some important buildings in a city are found. This is the scale for this map.

A class in Mulberry School would like to go to a place near the school for a field trip. The school's principal said the students cannot go more than one mile from school. Using the scale of miles, measure to find out which places are one mile or less from the school. Then complete the table below.

Places the Class Can Go	Places the Class Cannot Go
post office	museum
library	police station
swimming pool	zoo
fire station	bakery
park	train station
city hall	store

Brainwork! Find a map. Use its scale to write the distance between two places.

Page 86

© Frank Schaffer Publications, Inc.

Answer Key

Name ________________ Skill: Using a scale

How Far Is It?

Use the scale on the map to answer the questions below. The entrance for each ride is shown by the ⌂.

For example: How far is it from the park's main entrance to the entrance for the Double Ferris Wheel ride? 50 yards

Whoops Amusement Park — Main Entrance, Double Ferris Wheel, Thrill Ride, Wild West Track, Space Twister, Loopy Roller Coaster, Refreshments, Roll Ride, Swimming Pool, Speedy Bumper Cars, Merry-Go-Round. Scale: 0 50 100 150 200; 1 inch = 100 yards

1. I want to go on the Loopy Roller Coaster first. How far is it from the park's main entrance? 150 yards
2. I'm thirsty. How far do I have to go from the Loopy Roller Coaster to buy something to drink? 100 yards
3. The Roll Ride looks like fun! How far is the ride from the refreshment stand? 200 yards
4. How far is the swimming pool from the Roll Ride? 50 yards
5. After a swim, I want to ride the Speedy Bumper Cars and the Space Twister. How far will I have to walk to ride both? 300 yards

Brainwork! Which three rides would you like to go on? How far is each of them from the main entrance of the park?

Page 87

Name ________________ Skill: Recognition of areas by configuration

Regions of the United States

Midwestern States; Western States; Northeastern States; Southern States

The map shows one way the states can be divided into areas. Study the shapes. Then write the name of the dark area shaded on each map below.

Southern States	Western States
Northeastern States	Midwestern States

Brainwork! Write the area your state is in. List your state and all the other states in that area.

Page 88

Name ________________ Skill: Visual discrimination

States in Sets

Use the large map to find and color the sets of states below.

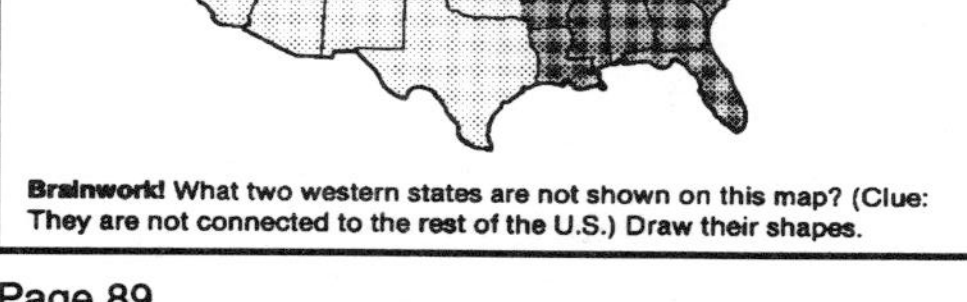

1. Color the southern states green.
2. Color the midwestern states orange.
3. Color the western states yellow.
4. Color the northeastern states blue.

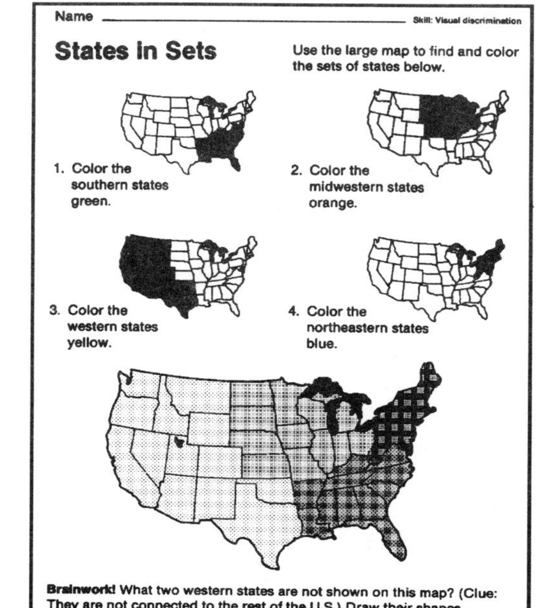

Brainwork! What two western states are not shown on this map? (Clue: They are not connected to the rest of the U.S.) Draw their shapes.

Page 89

Name ________________ Skill: Recognizing configuration

United States Assembly

Cut out the puzzle pieces. Fit them together to make a map of the United States. Then glue them onto paper.

Brainwork! Color your state red.

Page 90

Name ________________ Skill: Map reading

The Northeastern States

Use this map of the northeastern United States to help you do the activities below.

Canada; Maine; Vermont; New Hampshire; Massachusetts; Rhode Island; Connecticut; New York; L. Ontario; L. Erie; Pennsylvania; New Jersey; Delaware; Maryland; West Virginia; Atlantic Ocean

1. How many states are part of the northeastern United States? 12
2. Which state is farthest north and east? Maine
3. Which state do you think has a name that means "Penn's woods?" Pennsylvania
4. The **L.** in **L. Ontario** stands for **Lake.** What state touches Lake Ontario? New York
5. Color all the northeastern states that do not touch the Atlantic Ocean **green.**
6. Color the smallest state, Rhode Island, **red.**

Brainwork! Write the names of the northeastern states in ABC order.

Page 91

Name ________________ Skill: Map reading

The Southern States

Use this map of the southern United States to help you do the activities below.

1. How many states are part of the southern United States? 11
2. Which state is spelled with four s's and four i's? Mississippi
3. What ocean is east of South Carolina? Atlantic Ocean
4. What state reaches farther south than all others? Florida
5. Some states sound like people's names. Write the name of the state that sounds like each of these names:

George Georgia Carol North or South Carolina
Louise Louisiana Ken Kentucky

Brainwork! Georgia is known for its peanut crop. Find out what president came from Georgia and raised peanuts! Write three facts about him.

Page 92

© Frank Schaffer Publications, Inc.

Answer Key

Name ______ Skill: Map reading

The Midwestern States

Use this map of the midwestern United States to help you do the activities below.

1. How many states are part of the midwestern United States? 12
2. The L. in **L. Michigan** stands for **Lake**. How many states touch Lake Michigan? 4
3. Two rivers are shown on the map. What are their names? Missouri River, Mississippi River
4. Name a state that touches both rivers. Iowa or Missouri
5. What state has two parts separated by a lake? Michigan
6. What state is south of Minnesota? Iowa
7. Color the four lakes shown on the map **blue**.
8. Color the states whose names begin with vowels **orange**.

Brainwork! Find out what these midwestern cities have to do with cars: Indianapolis, Indiana and Detroit, Michigan. Write your findings.

Page 93

Name ______ Skill: Map reading

The Western States

Use this map of the western United States to help you do the activities below.

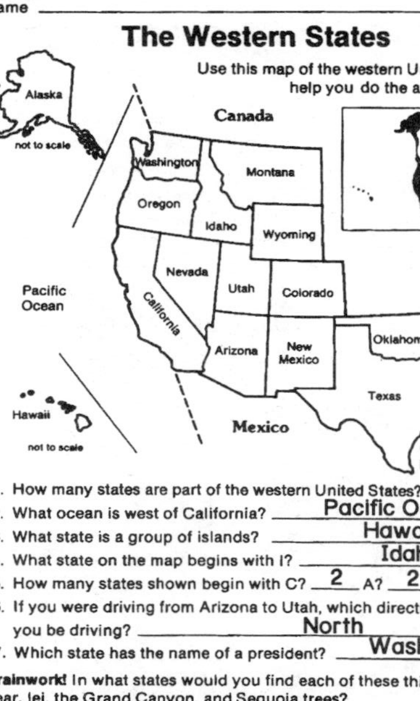

1. How many states are part of the western United States? 15
2. What ocean is west of California? Pacific Ocean
3. What state is a group of islands? Hawaii
4. What state on the map begins with I? Idaho
5. How many states shown begin with C? 2 A? 2 O? 2
6. If you were driving from Arizona to Utah, which direction would you be driving? North
7. Which state has the name of a president? Washington

Brainwork! In what states would you find each of these things: polar bear, lei, the Grand Canyon, and Sequoia trees?

Page 94

Name ______ Skill: State abbreviations—western U.S.

USA for Short

Each state is numbered. Find it on the map. Write the state's two-letter abbreviation next to its name.

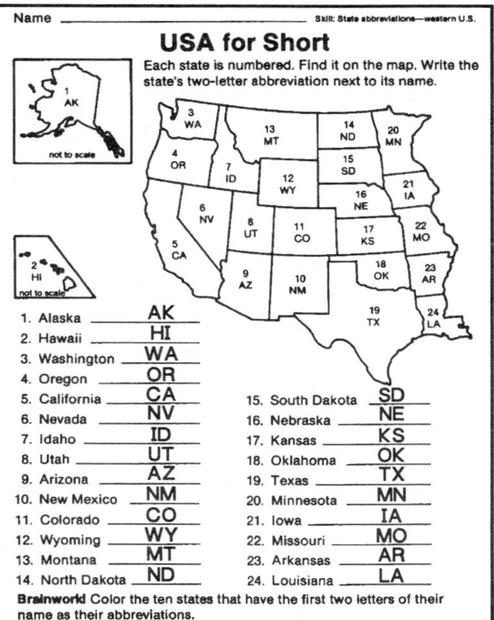

1. Alaska AK	15. South Dakota SD
2. Hawaii HI	16. Nebraska NE
3. Washington WA	17. Kansas KS
4. Oregon OR	18. Oklahoma OK
5. California CA	19. Texas TX
6. Nevada NV	20. Minnesota MN
7. Idaho ID	21. Iowa IA
8. Utah UT	22. Missouri MO
9. Arizona AZ	23. Arkansas AR
10. New Mexico NM	24. Louisiana LA
11. Colorado CO	
12. Wyoming WY	
13. Montana MT	
14. North Dakota ND	

Brainwork! Color the ten states that have the first two letters of their name as their abbreviations.

Page 95

Name ______ Skill: State abbreviations—eastern U.S.

USA for Short

Each state is numbered. Find it on the map. Write the state's two-letter abbreviation next to its name.

1. Michigan MI	19. Maine ME
2. Wisconsin WI	20. New Hampshire NH
3. Illinois IL	21. Massachusetts MA
4. Indiana IN	22. Rhode Island RI
5. Ohio OH	23. Connecticut CT
6. Kentucky KY	24. New Jersey NJ
7. Tennessee TN	25. Delaware DE
8. Mississippi MS	26. Maryland MD
9. Alabama AL	
10. Georgia GA	
11. Florida FL	
12. South Carolina SC	
13. North Carolina NC	
14. Virginia VA	
15. West Virginia WV	
16. Pennsylvania PA	
17. New York NY	
18. Vermont VT	

Brainwork! Color the eight states whose abbreviations are the first and last letters of their names.

Page 96

Name ______ Skill: Applying map skills

Major City Hunt

Each • on the map stands for a city. Read the clues below. Write the clue number in the box by the city it tells about.

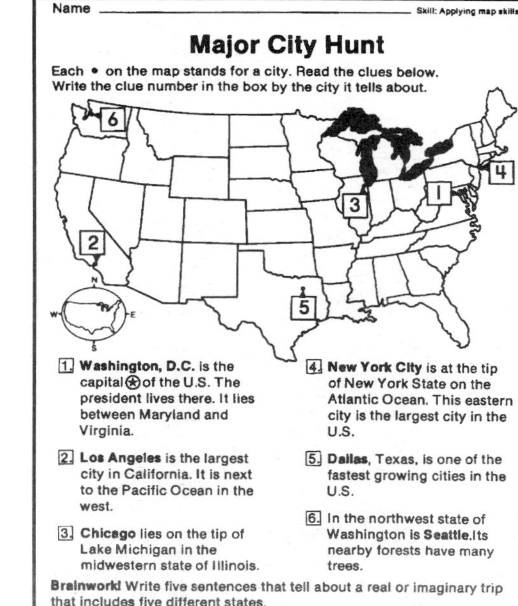

1. **Washington, D.C.** is the capital ⊛ of the U.S. The president lives there. It lies between Maryland and Virginia.
2. **Los Angeles** is the largest city in California. It is next to the Pacific Ocean in the west.
3. **Chicago** lies on the tip of Lake Michigan in the midwestern state of Illinois.
4. **New York City** is at the tip of New York State on the Atlantic Ocean. This eastern city is the largest city in the U.S.
5. **Dallas**, Texas, is one of the fastest growing cities in the U.S.
6. In the northwest state of Washington is **Seattle.** Its nearby forests have many trees.

Brainwork! Write five sentences that tell about a real or imaginary trip that includes five different states.

Page 97

Name ______ Skill: Drawing conclusions

What State Am I?

Read the clues. Write the name of the state.

States
Hawaii, Rhode Island
Florida, Texas
California, Alaska

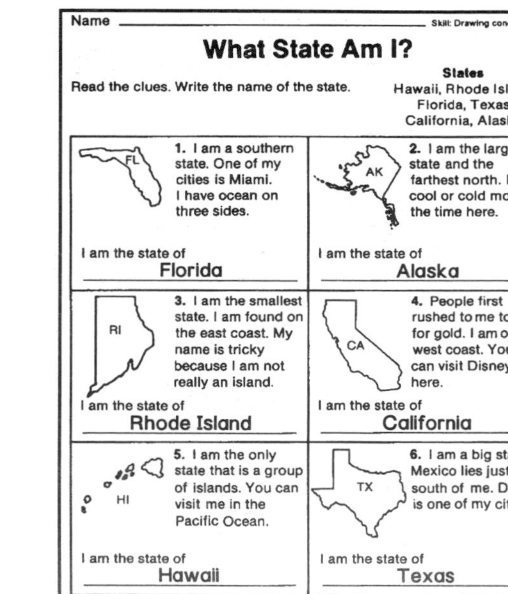

1. I am a southern state. One of my cities is Miami. I have ocean on three sides.
I am the state of Florida

2. I am the largest state and the farthest north. It is cool or cold most of the time here.
I am the state of Alaska

3. I am the smallest state. I am found on the east coast. My name is tricky because I am not really an island.
I am the state of Rhode Island

4. People first rushed to me to look for gold. I am on the west coast. You can visit Disneyland here.
I am the state of California

5. I am the only state that is a group of islands. You can visit me in the Pacific Ocean.
I am the state of Hawaii

6. I am a big state. Mexico lies just south of me. Dallas is one of my cities.
I am the state of Texas

Brainwork! Write a riddle about another state.

Page 98

© Frank Schaffer Publications, Inc.

Answer Key

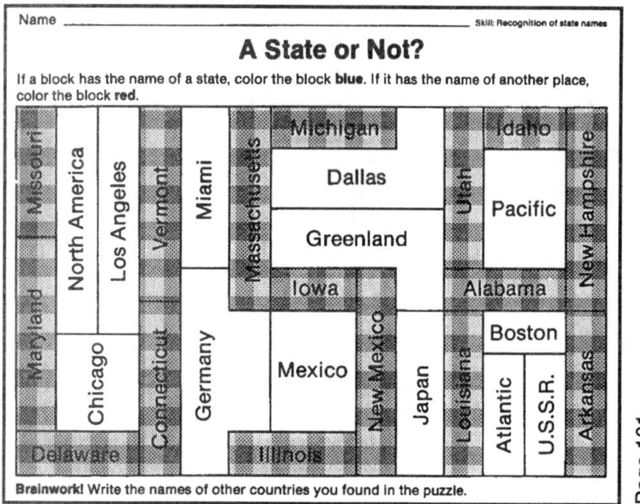

Name ______ Skill: Recognition of state names

A State or Not?

If a block has the name of a state, color the block **blue**. If it has the name of another place, color the block **red**.

Brainwork! Write the names of other countries you found in the puzzle.

Page 101

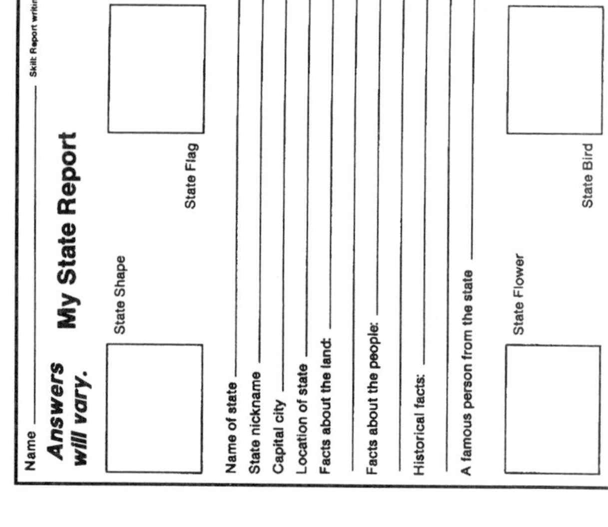

Name ______ Skill: Report writing

Answers will vary.

My State Report

State Shape

State Flag

Name of state ______

State nickname ______

Capital city ______

Location of state ______

Facts about the land: ______

Facts about the people: ______

Historical facts: ______

A famous person from the state ______

State Flower

State Bird

Brainwork! Make a travel poster advertising your state.

Page 104

Name ______ Skill: Unscramble state names

Scrambled States

The names of twelve states are spelled correctly on the map. Unscramble the mixed-up words below to spell the names of these states.

1. hioO — O h i o
2. zonaAri — A r i z o n a
3. giaGeor — G e o r g i a
4. weN seyJer — N e w J e r s e y
5. tanaMon — M o n t a n a
6. esseeTenn — T e n n e s s e e
7. neMai — M a i n e
8. gonOre — O r e g o n
9. sinWiscon — W i s c o n s i n
10. adeNev — N e v a d a
11. adoColor — C o l o r a d o
12. homaOkla — O k l a h o m a

Brainwork! Scramble the names of five other states. Give them to a friend to unscramble.

Page 100

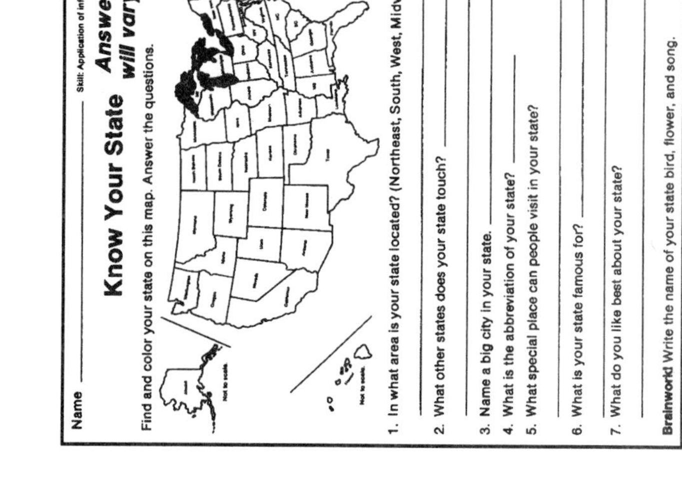

Name ______ Skill: Application of information

Know Your State

Answers will vary.

Find and color your state on this map. Answer the questions.

1. In what area is your state located? (Northeast, South, West, Midwest) ______
2. What other states does your state touch? ______
3. Name a big city in your state. ______
4. What is the abbreviation of your state? ______
5. What special place can people visit in your state? ______
6. What is your state famous for? ______
7. What do you like best about your state? ______

Brainwork! Write the name of your state bird, flower, and song.

Page 103

Name ______ Skill: Using a map index

Know Your State Capitals!

1 2 3 4 5 6 7 8 9 10 11 12 13

A B C D E F G H

Carson City, Sacramento, Salt Lake City, Santa Fe, Topeka, Austin, Nashville, Columbus, Atlanta, Boston

The **map index** below lists certain states. The letter and number after each state tell you in which square you'll find its capital city. The letter and number pairs are called **coordinates**. Write the name of the capital city before its state name on the map index below.

1. Salt Lake City (Utah) D4
2. Sacramento (California) D1
3. Boston (Massachusetts) B13
4. Atlanta (Georgia) F10
5. Carson City (Nevada) D2
6. Santa Fe (New Mexico) E5
7. Nashville (Tennessee) E10
8. Columbus (Ohio) D10
9. Topeka (Kansas) D7
10. Austin (Texas) G7

Brainwork! Use a United States map to locate and write the names of three other state capitals on the map above.

Page 99

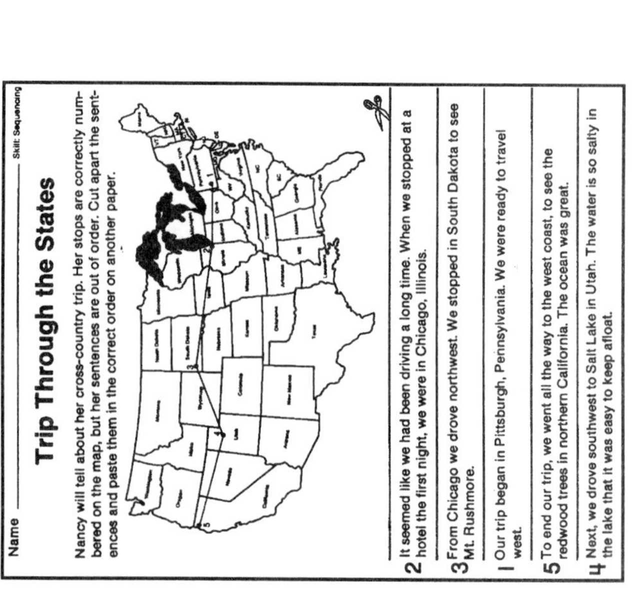

Name ______ Skill: Sequencing

Trip Through the States

Nancy will tell about her cross-country trip. Her stops are correctly numbered on the map, but her sentences are out of order. Cut apart the sentences and paste them in the correct order on another paper.

2 It seemed like we had been driving a long time. When we stopped at a hotel the first night, we were in Chicago, Illinois.

3 From Chicago we drove northwest. We stopped in South Dakota to see Mt. Rushmore.

1 Our trip began in Pittsburgh, Pennsylvania. We were ready to travel west.

5 To end our trip, we went all the way to the west coast, to see the redwood trees in northern California. The ocean was great.

4 Next, we drove southwest to Salt Lake in Utah. The water is so salty in the lake that it was easy to keep afloat.

Page 102

© Frank Schaffer Publications, Inc.